not from Out of Town

Honey Cove Book 1

Natalie Jess & Evy Aster

Greenstone Publishing

Copyright © 2025 by Greenstone Publishing

All rights reserved.

No portion of this book may be reproduced in any form without written permission from the publisher or author, except as permitted by U.S. copyright law. Without in any way limiting the author's and publisher's exclusive rights under copyright, any use of this publication to "train" generative artificial intelligence (AI) technologies to generate text is expressly prohibited.

The story, all names, characters, and incidents portrayed in this production are fictitious. No identification with actual persons (living or deceased), places, buildings, and products is intended or should be inferred.

No generative artificial intelligence (AI) was used in the writing of this work.

Cover Design by Lily Bear Design Co.

Interior Format by Luna Blooms PA

Edits by Kristen Hamilton

Proofread by Andra Prewett

dedication

To all women. May you feel your strength and power.

contents

Prologue: Poppy	1
Prologue: Owen	7
Chapter 1: Poppy	13
Chapter 2: Owen	19
Chapter 3: Poppy	25
Chapter 4: Owen	31
Chapter 5: Poppy	37
Chapter 6: Owen	43
Chapter 7: Poppy	49
Chapter 8: Owen	55
Chapter 9: Poppy	61
Chapter 10: Owen	65
Chapter 11: Poppy	69
Chapter 12: Owen	75

Chapter 13: Poppy	81
Chapter 14: Owen	85
Chapter 15: Poppy	91
Chapter 16: Owen	95
Chapter 17: Poppy	101
Chapter 18: Owen	105
Chapter 19: Poppy	111
Chapter 20: Owen	115
Chapter 21: Poppy	121
Chapter 22: Owen	127
Chapter 23: Poppy	133
Chapter 24: Owen	139
Chapter 25: Poppy	145
Chapter 26: Owen	149
Chapter 27: Poppy	155
Chapter 28: Owen	159
Chapter 29: Poppy	167
Chapter 30: Owen	173
Chapter 31: Poppy	179
Chapter 32: Owen	185
Chapter 33: Poppy	191
Chapter 34: Owen	195
Chapter 35: Poppy	201
Chapter 36: Owen	207

Chapter 37: Poppy	213
Chapter 38: Owen	217
Chapter 39: Poppy	223
Chapter 40: Owen	227
Chapter 41: Poppy	233
Chapter 42: Owen	237
Chapter 43: Poppy	243
Chapter 44: Owen	249
Chapter 45: Poppy	255
Chapter 46: Owen	259
Chapter 47: Poppy	263
Chapter 48: Owen	269
Chapter 49: Poppy	275
Chapter 50: Owen	279
Chapter 51: Poppy	285
Chapter 52: Owen	289
Chapter 53: Poppy	293
Chapter 54: Owen	297
Chapter 55: Poppy	303
Chapter 56: Owen	309
Chapter 57: Poppy	315
Chapter 58: Owen	319
Chapter 59: Poppy	325
Chapter 60: Owen	329

Chapter 61: Poppy	335
Chapter 62: Owen	339
Chapter 63: Poppy	345
Chapter 64: Owen	349
Chapter 65: Poppy	355
Chapter 66: Owen	359
Chapter 67: Poppy	365
Chapter 68: Owen	369
Chapter 69: Poppy	375
Chapter 70: Owen	379
Chapter 71: Poppy	385
Chapter 72: Owen	389
Chapter 73: Poppy	395
Chapter 74: Owen	399
Chapter 75: Poppy	403
Chapter 76: Owen	407
Chapter 77: Poppy	413
Acknowledgements	416
About the Authors	417

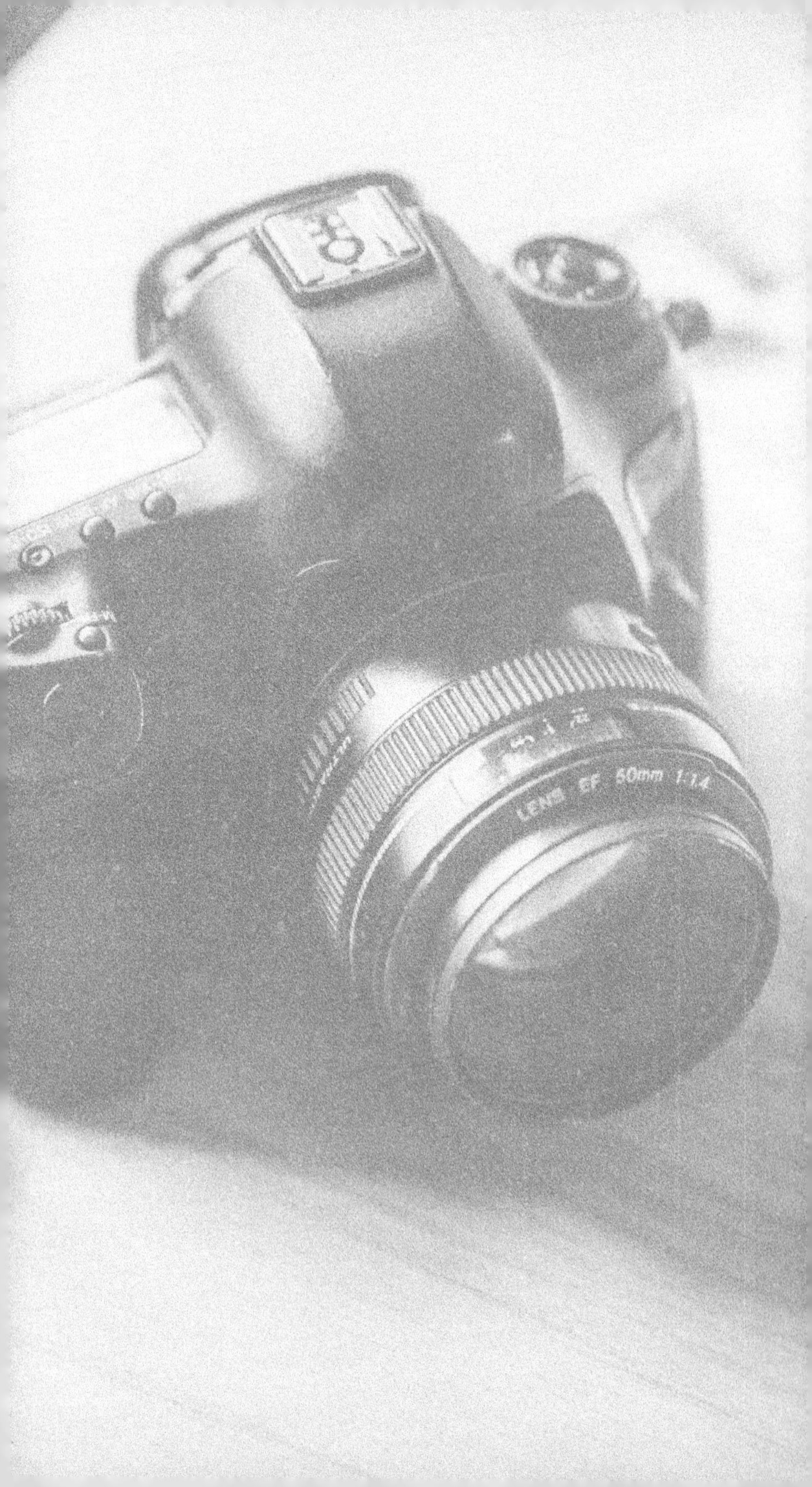
LENS EF 50mm 1:1.4

PROLOGUE

Poppy

"I don't think I can do this anymore."

His words slice through the air like a knife, driving what little air I had in my lungs out. Gasping, I turn and see the eyes of every single one of his family members boring into me. *He must be talking about trimming the tree or setting out the plates for dinner.*

"What?" I ask tentatively, the light from the fireplace gives Steven's face an ethereal glow. *He's always been so handsome.* Forcing a smile, I wrap my arms around myself, sinking deeper into his family's overstuffed chair.

"I can't do this anymore. Us. I thought that I could, that we were endgame, but I can't. We aren't." He looks away, into the fire. Doesn't even have the decency to look me in the eye as he's breaking up with me.

Blinking my eyes slowly, I glance again around the room and see his sister stifling a giggle. His mom is busying herself with adding more tinsel to the tree and his dad is nose-deep in his glass of whiskey. No words come to mind, everything blank with the incredible shock of what is happening. I nod, sliding my body slowly from the chair and look to grab my things and head towards the door. Tripping over the plush entryway rug in my haste, I see it's started snowing outside again. *Merry. Fucking. Christmas.*

He doesn't follow me, just lets me glide out of his life with the click of a door and an empty wineglass on his end table. His sister's muted voice carries from the living room, "It was about time." A giggle added to the end.

Once I'm finally outside, I breathe deeply and close my eyes, letting the snowflakes fall onto my face. *Shit, he drove me here.* Pulling my coat and hat on, I sink down onto the step and grab my phone to call Andi. I'm sure she'll come pick me up, but even so, it's an hour or so drive from Honey Cove. *I could be here a while.*

How did this happen?

"Andi?" My voice sounds small.

"Poppy! Did he do it? Oh my god, how big is the ring?" Her excitement at what we thought tonight was going to be brings me back to the present moment and I blink back tears, but it's no use.

"No. I need you to come get me." My voice cracks with every other word.

"Are you hurt? What happened?"

"Please, can you just come out here and pick me up? I'll text you the address. I need to leave, *now*." The sound of her grabbing things and whispering to her boyfriend Brandon on the other end lets me know she's coming and understands the gravity of what's happened.

"Of course, I'm on my way."

The sound of crunching snow tells me Andi is pulling up the driveway. Shaking the snow that's fallen on me, I walk towards her car but before I can get there, she's out and moving for the door.

"They made you sit out here?" There's fire in her eyes as she barrels through the snow.

"Please, don't. Just let's go."

She looks back at me and sees the tears streaming down my face that I haven't been able to stop no matter how many times I've tried over the course of the last hour. Rushing towards me, she envelopes me into a tight hug.

"I'm so sorry," she whispers into my hair before ushering me into the car. "I really want to yell something, but I want it noted that I'm restraining myself here."

Despite the situation, a snicker makes its way past my lips. She pulls out of the driveway and away from the house without incident. Watching it blink out of view in the mirror, I replay the entire weekend, searching for anything that could have given me a sign of what was to come, but find nothing.

My brain starts to function again slowly, my initial fight or flight response fading. What was numbness now is being replaced with anger, doubt, sadness. I was *so* sure he was proposing this weekend. *Who breaks up with someone on Christmas day at their parents' house?*

We're silent for a while. I think she knows that I need a little space. My sniffles and occasional nose blowing are the only sounds echoing through the car. Once we hit the little town nearby, she pulls through a drive thru to grab us both some coffee. I'm thankful for the steaming, warm cup she hands me, breathing in the roasted scent deeply.

"What do you need?" She whispers it and for the first time I look over at her. My eyes spill over with a fresh round of tears.

"I just don't know how I'm going to face everyone. Everywhere there are reminders of him. Five years. I can't believe he did it like that after five years. I just can't imagine telling everyone, I don't think I can take the stares and pity."

"He's a jerk and he was never good enough for you." She shakes her head and my jaw drops. She's never said anything like that before. I open my mouth to say something, but she holds up a hand to stop me. "You don't need to keep defending him, not any more. Everyone knows it. *You* were the catch in this situation and if he didn't figure that out, well screw him."

She pauses before continuing, "I will tell people. You don't need to handle this. We can have Noah spread the word too so no one will bother you about it. But I'm not sure I can fix the pity looks, especially at work."

"Oh my god, school. The kids. One of them made me a wedding invitation before break. I can't do this." I bury my face in my hands. Living in a small town is wonderful for the support and love we all have for one another, but when you go through a crisis or you'd prefer not to share something with its thousand residents, it can be a bit suffocating.

"Maybe you can take a break. A longer break. Do you have days saved up?"

"Not enough."

"We'll think of something. I got you." She reaches into the back seat and produces one of the largest water bottles I've ever seen. "Drink, you're going to dehydrate from all those tears and I will *not* let him take one more thing from you."

PROLOGUE

Owen

"Just get in here; we already called him from my phone," Brandon yells to his brother who keeps trying to enter the video chat from their parents' computer in the other room.

"How is it that the person in I.T. is the worst at this?" Graham, our youngest cousin, mumbles.

"I am not the worst at this," James says, entering the room while frowning at Graham and Brandon. "We could have all been in the den where we could see him on the computer screen instead of crowding around a phone."

I'm just sitting in my apartment in New York as these guys figure things out and continue their argument over whether cell reception or the internet is the best choice for a video call. I don't want to crush James's argument and say that the internet at that house is atrocious so I let them continue.

They're all wearing our standard Christmas sweaters so it looks like they're sitting down for a "cousins photo," just without me. The jealousy I usually feel when I see them together with me off in the Big Apple doesn't hit quite as strong today though.

"The video hasn't cut out on you, right?" Brandon asks me, effectively shifting the conversation to why we're here.

"Nope, I caught all of that," I say, chuckling.

"Why aren't you wearing your sweater?" James asks, squinting at the phone.

"My dad is working until six for last-minute orders that came in, so I'm not leaving to help my mom get dinner ready until five, which still gives me an hour." The sweaters were given to us by my mom and her siblings a couple of years ago when Graham turned nineteen, thinking he'd be mostly done growing so we could all match. Unfortunately, my family didn't get to head to the coast of Maine this year for Christmas to see everyone, but we agreed to wear the slightly scratchy sweaters for our parents.

"Who cares about what he's wearing right now? What's the big news?" Brandon asks, leaning forward in his excitement.

"It's not that big of a deal," I start, trying to keep my emotions tempered. There were a few things that needed to be in place before things really felt official, so I've been sitting on this news for a few days.

"We'll be the judge of that."

"Okay, so a few weeks ago, I found a temporary position posted for a high school English teaching job in Maine."

All three of them raise their eyebrows almost in unison and for some reason I'm nervous. God, what if they only like seeing me a little each summer and one major holiday each year?

"I interviewed a few rounds and then right before break started, I did a sample lesson where I recorded myself teaching and sent that in for them to see my style and how I interact with my students."

Why aren't they saying anything? Brandon looks like he's about ready to interrupt, but stays quiet. Maybe I should have sent this over our group chat so I don't have to watch them process this. I rub my hand on the back of my neck and give a little laugh so I don't start rambling.

"Apparently, they liked it and I was offered the position."

I wait for them to respond.

And wait.

The silence is only broken by Samson meowing at a bird from his cat tree, pulling my attention to the bustling neighborhood outside the window.

Finally, Brandon, whose eyes are huge, says, "And?"

"What do you mean?"

"Did you accept?" He sounds intense, which I hope is a good sign because he's usually so easy to read.

"Yeah."

"Which school?" Graham asks.

Something feels so strange right now. I thought they'd be happy for me.

"The high school in Honey Cove."

"So you'll be moving to Honey Cove, right?" James is always the one who wants the more practical details, so I'm not surprised with his question.

I nod in response.

"You'll be five to fifteen minutes away then. When does it start?"

"The first Monday in March."

Brandon makes a choked sound and slams a hand down on Graham's knee.

"When do you move?" James seems to be the only one speaking now and Graham peeks at Brandon who looks slightly crazed.

"Late-February. It'll give my school time to find my replacement and, in theory, I'll find something else in Maine for next school year." I pause, feeling a little unsure of what to think. "To stay."

Suddenly, everything turns into utter chaos as Brandon leaps from the couch cheering, pulling Graham up with him. James tries to ask me more questions, but the coffee table gets bumped and the phone falls over only to be picked up by Brandon who is still jumping.

Relief washes over me. They want this as much as I do.

"Wait, did you know something already?"

"Aunt Mae dropped a hint a few days ago that we might see more of you soon, so we've been dying for details and if it was really happening. But she wouldn't say anything else," Graham admits with a huge smile on his face, setting the phone back on the coffee table. "Your mom must have said something to her."

That makes sense. They do talk regularly and I've been open with my parents about this prospect.

"How are your folks feeling?" he asks, his shaggy hair falling in his face.

My heart gives a little squeeze. They're the hardest to leave. I have buddies here, for sure, but I've always felt it was hard to connect with people here. "They're supportive of the move and know I've been, well, not unhappy or anything like that, but not grounded here, I suppose. My mom is excited that it's near you all and not a random small town and I think my dad has officially given up any hope that I'll take over the floral shop one day. But he already wrote up a tentative schedule for the shop so he can drive the U-Haul to Maine with me."

"Give us the official dates and we can take off work to help you move in." I'm half-surprised that James hasn't whipped out his phone to check his calendar. "Do you have a place in mind?"

"I'll let you know, but it'll likely be the first for moving in. There are a few apartments I already inquired about right on the boardwalk." If I'm lucky enough to get into one of those, I'll have a killer view of the cove itself, which I'm hoping for.

"Oh my god, we're going to have so many cousins' nights," Brandon almost yells, barely keeping his excitement in check.

A huge smile spreads across my face. These guys, who have always been there for me, will finally be in my life more than a couple times each year.

"I can't wait."

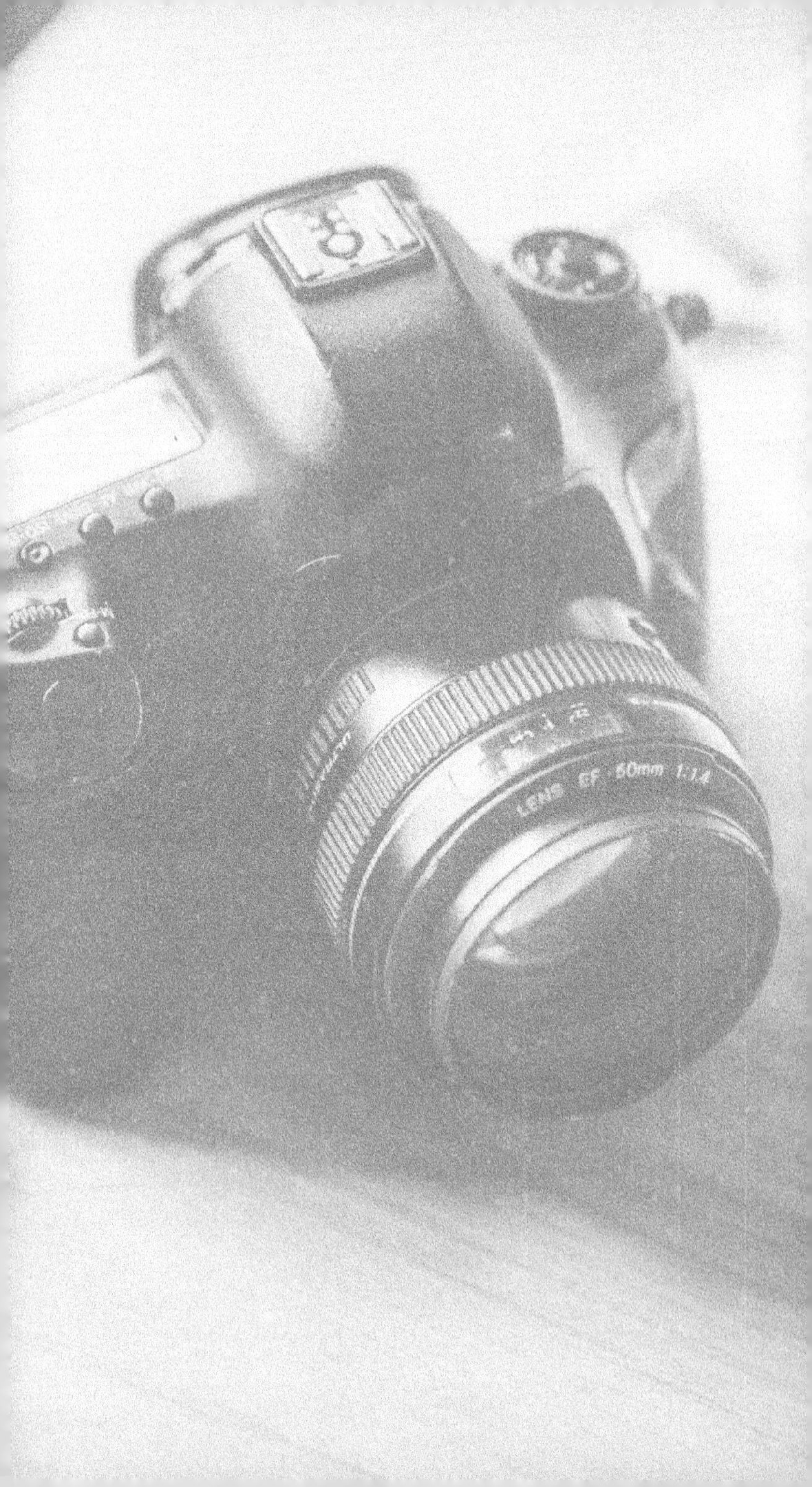
LENS EF 50mm 1:1.4

CHAPTER ONE

Poppy

Late-July

My breath comes out in sharp exhales as beads of sweat drip down my chest and my hotel door clicks shut behind me. Dropping down to the floor, I stretch my neck out and take a much needed rest. That was the longest I've gone in a long time. Must be something about this Toronto air or maybe I just feel lighter after shedding Steven from my life. Get it together. I can't keep thinking about him.

Unlacing my running shoes I start to stretch my already tightening muscles while turning on the TV in my room. Before I get sucked into the thralls of a rerun of *Big Bang Theory*, I jump at the sound of my ringing phone and the loud vibrations it makes against the night stand. Andi's name pops up and I feel a smile stretch across my face. She's already called three times this week and there's only so much I can update her on, but it feels good to talk with her just the same. I know she's been worried about me. Between her and my parents, I'm being "checked in on" every day.

"Hi." Despite her heavy-handed affections, I miss my best friend. She knows she's been my best friend since junior high, but I don't think she knows how much I've learned I need her in my life after everything I've been through these past months. The support she's given me over through all this makes her feel more like a sister than anything else.

"Oh honey, how are you? I can't believe I get to see you in just a couple of weeks," she croons over the phone. She is getting married in three weeks and I am heading home to Honey Cove just in time for the nuptials. My stomach tightens at the thought of being home, and at a *wedding. Any* wedding. I am really happy for her. Her husband-to-be, Brandon, is an amazing man and seems to really care about her, which is all I can ask for. *And he actually wants to marry her.*

Shaking my head, I bring my thoughts back to our present conversation. "I'm doing good, I just finished a fifteen mile run. I can't believe the big day is coming up so soon either. How is all the planning coming along?"

She has insisted on doing everything herself to help save money. I get it, but some things just seem better left to the professionals in my opinion. Although I lack a bit of the "DIY" sense that she seems to excel at.

"Things are going pretty well. I had my last fitting today for my dress and we placed the final order with the floral shop yesterday. Brandon is still working on the song list for dancing, but it's coming together I think..." she trails off.

"What is it?" Something is up. It isn't like her to not share something. *Although,* I have asked her to keep me out of Honey Cove news. Just seemed better to have a clean break for a while, but this seems different.

"Nothing, well, I'm so sorry, but I just wanted to check about your plus one. I know I'm the worst for asking and I'll make it up to you when you get here, but I have to put in the order for the food and of course you get a plus one, but I know you probably won't use it and it's awkward but I just wanted to ask." She spits it all out as quickly as possible. *Take a breath, you are not your plus one status. You are not your plus one status.*

"I'm sorry I didn't respond about it." *I didn't even think about it.* "No, no plus one for me. Just me." My inadvertent sigh sounds more pathetic than I'd hoped.

"No, you don't need to apologize. The timing is horrible and again, I'm the worst. So you can hate me for it, but not for too long because you'll be home so soon." I can hear her smiling through the phone and wish we could go out tonight for drinks, catch up and just be us again.

"I could never hate you. I'm so happy for you, truly. I hope you know that."

"I do sweetie, thank you. Soooo, did you pick out your dress yet?"

"Actually, I bought it yesterday. It's long, red as requested, and flowy. I think you'll like it." She squeals with happiness. Besides all the talk of how I'm doing, our conversations have revolved around my maid of honor dress for her wedding and what asset of mine it will show off. She means well, but I have no intention of showing anything off with intent. I've been really happy on my own and am hoping I'll be at home too.

She's also respected my "no Honey Cove" talk while I've been away. It's been hard to adhere to with the wedding planning, but she's been able to stick to it mostly, breaking it only once to tell me a story of how a seagull got stuck in the screened window of Bobbi's coffee shop on the boardwalk.

"But does it show off your boobs? I requested that too. Send me a picture immediately. Oh, and your plane gets in at 9:00 a.m. the morning of, right?"

"Yes, I'll be there in the morning and Uber over to the house straight away so I can help with whatever is needed and make my hair slot time with no stress. I'll be there and have my dancing shoes on for all those songs Brandon is choosing. And, no comment on the boobs part."

"Oh yes, your epic dance moves. I can't wait. For the wedding of course, but also to see you. I've missed you." She grows quiet on the other end of the line and things take a more serious tone.

"I'm excited too," I say slowly and before it's even left my lips I realize that it's not the full truth. I'm excited to see her, especially on her wedding day. But, I'm not excited to go home. I think she knows it, too, but we won't talk about that. Not right now, anyways.

My heart feels heavy thinking about all the questions and everything that comes with going home. I'm a little bit nervous and uneasy about what will come next. Steven won't be at the wedding and I won't see him right away, but can't avoid the inevitable run-in when the town is so small. I also don't want to deal with all the stares and the questions. After being gone for so long, I totally get it, people are wondering.

We've been silent for a minute before she adds. "I'll call you again in a few days? What are your plans like?"

I talk through the new places I'll sightsee, the photo-op spots I'll be driving to. That's been my focus here in Toronto, getting back into my photography, taking time for myself and leaning into whatever is going on with my future. *I will not let this break me.*

Eventually the conversation slows and I finish with, "Well I hope you have a good night, say hi to Brandon for me."

"Will do, his groomsmen are in town right now for their fittings and the bachelor party, so he's a little busy," she giggles. All of them were planning on staying at her and Brandon's house, which means she has a house full of men right now. In any other life I would be jealous, but right now, with that many men under one roof, I wouldn't stay there if she paid me. A slight pang of guilt washes over me as I remember phoning into Andi's bachelorette party last week with a promise to take her out once we're all back together.

Hanging up, I turn the volume back up on my show, but can't seem to focus on it. I felt so good after my run, but now I just feel spent. I still can't talk about anything to do with Steven without getting this way. It's been six months. *Six months* since he dumped me at his parents' on Christmas. I was so sure he'd propose. Hell, the whole town was sure he'd propose.

Afterwards I just left. I couldn't stand to face everyone after it had been built up as this big moment in our relationship and everyone was expecting it. I put in for an extended leave at work, which was surprisingly approved, and got on a plane.

I haven't talked to him since the breakup and don't even know what I would say if I did. He and even his family were so uncaring. I would have thought they'd at least respect me enough to do more than let me sit on their front step in the snow while waiting to be picked up, but they didn't. The reality of the amount of time I wasted on him has sunk in while I've been away and I made a promise to myself to not let that happen again.

I love Honey Cove more than I can put into words, and my life there, but I needed space to process through everything that happened and what is next for me. *Andi's wedding will be a good opportunity to see everyone and get it all out in the open. Rip that Band-Aid off.*

I try not to think about how Band-Aids can also hurt like hell.

CHAPTER TWO

Owen

I silently prepare for one of the most awkward parts imaginable during a suit fitting: measuring the inseam.

The man handling all of us inherited the shop from his father who inherited it from his father, which is why Brandon loved the place. If something had family history, he was in.

Which is also how I got here even though I only recently moved to Honey Cove. The cousin who previously could only visit him a few times each year was automatically a groomsman.

"Thank you, sir," the owner says as I widen my stance.

Clive? Clyde? I wasn't paying close attention and now feel like a prick for not remembering his name. Especially considering the fact that he's now running a hand up the inside of my leg.

"All done, sir," he says.

Damn, he's fast and I didn't feel a thing, thank god.

"Is there anything else you need from me?" I ask as he stands and motions for me to step down from the pedestal.

"I have everything I need." He nods and waves Brandon up for his turn.

"I told you this place was incredible," Brandon says, slapping me on the back.

"You definitely did," I say, smiling at his unbridled enthusiasm.

I purposefully sit with the others instead of pretending to look at more suits. If the hiring committee members were impressed earlier today, I'll be in Maine for good and everyone here, with the exception of the nice man who took my measurements, will be more than just casual acquaintances and relatives who I see on special occasions. They might become my *real* family.

"Owen, Andi mentioned something about you staying?" asks James.

So much for getting my mind off of that.

"I just had an interview for a full-time position with the school in Honey Cove today, actually. So maybe."

"Is it for the same position you're teaching now?"

"A little different, but still English. But instead of being temporary, I'd be on track to qualify for tenure in a few years."

"That's awesome, man. When do you hear?" Graham, the youngest of the cousins, asks.

I shrug. "They said they'll be in touch."

"What's it for?"

"High school English again, but I'd be teaching juniors and seniors." I try to sound casual, but the reality is I'm half a heartbeat away from breaking out in a full-body sweat. For some reason, even after being a teacher for five years, a damn good one at that, every single time I have to do a sample lesson or an observation, I'm a hot mess until I hear the results.

"I remember high school English; I hated it," Graham laughs.

"So did I," I reply. "But I had a great professor in college freshman year who changed how I looked at it and I wanted to help kids, well, not hate it."

"Gnarly." Graham holds out his fist and I bump it, holding back a chuckle at him embracing his inner-surfer with his shoulder-length sun-bleached hair.

"Brandon, what should we wear to the rehearsal dinner?" I ask, taking the attention off of me and my upcoming news.

"Business casual," he replies.

"That means nothing and you know it," his brother calls out.

"Fair enough." The groom gives us a smirk. "Button-down shirts, slacks, no sneakers. Ties aren't needed. That better?"

"It's a real answer."

"That's everything, gentleman," Clive/Clyde says. "We have you all scheduled for your final fittings on the seventh at six-thirty. Is that still acceptable?"

This man sounds like a butler in a British period drama, just without the accent.

We all nod and suppress smiles.

"Excellent, I look forward to seeing you all then."

Ten minutes later, we're standing in the parking lot. Brad, Brandon's best friend from school, is on his phone trying to nail down a day when his almost-girlfriend, according to him, is in town at the same time he is.

"Final day to let me know," Brandon's hands clamp down on Graham's and my shoulders as his eyebrows waggle. "Any change in your plus-one status?"

"Nope, I'm good going stag."

"And you?" They both look at me expectantly. I get the feeling that everyone thinks I'm just being tight-lipped about my dating life here, but there's simply nothing to tell.

"No date for me, either," I say with a chuckle. "It looks like Brad is the only groomsman who is bringing one."

"Alright, I promised Andi that I'd check. She was a little worried that no one would be dancing during the reception with several of you not bringing anyone."

"Tell her not to worry, we'll each grab an auntie for a few songs if the dance floor is looking sparsely populated," I reassure him.

"Okay, now that we have that out of the way," says Brandon, rubbing his hands together. "Who has time for some coffee at Bobbi's?"

"I'm in," Graham says as James raises his hand like a student in class would.

"Definitely," I reply, always up for their home-roasted brews. Honestly, it's the best coffee I've ever had and the fact I live a couple of doors away from it is a huge bonus.

"Excellent, we'll continue the mantivities there!" I swear his enthusiasm knows no bounds.

"We're not saying 'mantivities.' We talked about this on the way here," James calls over his shoulder as he gets in the driver's seat.

"You talked about it, yes," Brandon says, walking around his brother's car to get into the passenger seat. "See you all in a few minutes!"

Brad, Graham, and I wave and get into our separate cars. When I'm settled, I take a moment, watching everyone pull out of their spots through my rearview mirror.

I'm not an overly sentimental person, but the whole point in moving here was to connect with these guys who I used to only see once or twice a year. I've only been here a few months, but I can see the future I imagined. That future in this small community, where I can feel rooted and belong rather than being another guy on the subway in the big city. I already recognize more people here on any given day than I did in New York.

I feel as if I'm settling into my forever, even if I haven't found that person just yet.

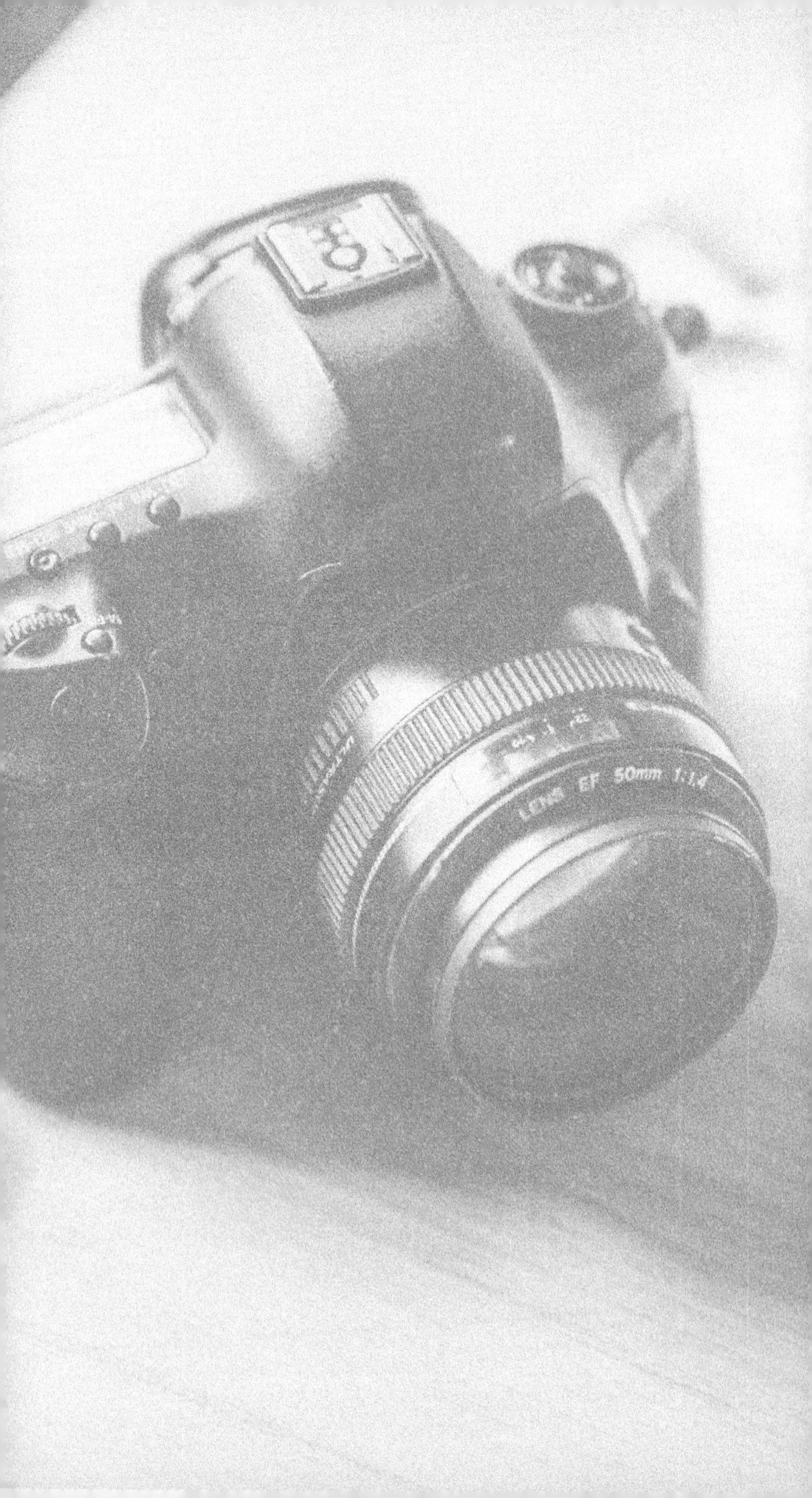
LENS EF 50mm 1:1.4

CHAPTER THREE

Poppy

Late August

I pace back and forth in my room. Two more hours until I need to head out. It's four am and I can't sleep any longer so I have already showered and tidied my small room. I can't believe it's already the day before the wedding. Even though I've been here for a few weeks and on a Florida beach before that, it still hasn't felt like enough space, enough time to process through everything. My mom has always told me that I need my time to think before deciding. My dad is the same way and often drives her crazy, but when he does make a decision, she knows it's exactly what he wants. Fog licks around the downtown skyline outside my window. Despite my best efforts, I can't help imagining seeing everyone at the wedding, then mentally walking through my schedule for today, the flight, my dress, my hair.

I've gone over it in my head a million times. My plan is to talk with Leslie first. Assuming Leslie will be there, *damn my no Honey Cove rule,* Leslie *loves* a good piece of gossip and I'm sure has already heard and shared around *her* version of my story. I'm betting if I clue her in right away, she will spread it to everyone else and then I won't have to talk to them. It's worth a shot at least. Andi has also been talking to people in preparation for my return, so maybe things won't be as bad as I think.

I start to pack up the few belongings I left with. It will be nice to have my closet again at least, my books, my fresh coffee beans from

Bobbi's, the boardwalk to run on, and sunrises over the water. *See this is good, you're thinking of positive things.*

I try to capitalize on my mood and start to make more of a list of the things I'm looking forward to at home. *My space.* Although I haven't cleaned it out yet, I'll have to remove all traces of my previous version of my life when I get back. That won't be fun, but I do love my little home near the ocean. At least that can wait until after the wedding. *My students. My friends.* My typical running routes by the beach. The warm sun on the boardwalk. Game nights with Noah. Smiling, I think about our last one before my impromptu journey and make a note to text him before I get on the plane.

You've got this. I am feigning confidence in my new "me" focused life, even going so far as to write down my list on the hotel notepad to reference when I need to. I have been happy on my own and think I can be at home too. Life will look different, but I feel more ready for that now.

Turning on the TV, I decide to spend my last hour watching some trashy shows before checking out and heading to the airport. *I do love a trashy show.*

I slam my keycard down on the counter significantly harder than I intended, making myself jump. "Oh my, I'm so sorry!" I smile at the worker, Sally, who has become like a friend to me my past couple weeks here in Toronto.

Crumbs bounce off her blue uniform as she smashes a donut into her mouth. Brushing some of her curly gray hairs out of her face, she leans forward and grabs my keycard.

"Oh, that's okay, sweetie. Don't you worry about it." Sally has listened to all my travels, given advice on the best tourist spots, and even brought me soup after a very unfortunate food poisoning incident last week. "Are you finally heading home? You must have an early flight." She smiles at me.

"Yeah, my best friend is getting married and I'm in the wedding. Plus, my leave is up and school will be starting soon." *Time to get used to the questions I suppose. This isn't so bad.*

"That sounds fun. Do you get to wear a fancy dress and have a cute date?" Sally asks. I wince without thinking and she notices, frowning at my sudden change in mood. I know that she doesn't know.

"Yes, there's a fancy dress. But no cute date for me. I'm er—newly single you could say." I was hoping to avoid this talk with her, pay my bill, and be on my way. But I figured it would inevitably come up at some point with all of our chit chats. I'd been successful avoiding it so far by saying I was on a solo trip to explore my photography.

"Newly single? I can't believe a beautiful young woman like you can't find someone." Sally gets a pass for that comment because she's older and is usually so sweet.

"Yup, haven't been able to nail that down yet. I was close…" I trail off and chuckle awkwardly, forcefully willing my inner monologue to stop.

"I'm happy and better on my own." I smile at Sally again. She gives me a smirk that tells me she doesn't believe me. *Hell, I don't know if I believe myself.*

"Well, I'll miss you and getting to see the beautiful photos you've taken." She shuffles around the small counter to give me a hug of sorts, then shuffles back. "Have fun at the wedding and maybe this will be a fresh start for you."

"Thank you Sally, enjoy your visit with your grandson. Don't let him have the cookies from the shop down the street again though, okay?"

"I won't! Have an amazing time at the wedding and make sure to come back to visit sometime." Sally waves frantically at me as I shuffle out of the hotel with my large pack. Would this be a fresh start for me, even with heading back to the same life minus the guy?

I'm still not looking forward to seeing everyone again, but after my list-making this morning, I'm feeling some hints of excitement to be in Honey Cove again. *If I have to face them, at least I get to do it in my fancy dress, right?*

CHAPTER FOUR

Owen

Brandon stands at the head of the table, rehearsal dinner in full swing, and conversations begin to die down. The conversation I was having with Andi's cousin, Ashley, was not creating a life-long bond. She's very clearly in love with her ex, who is invited to the wedding and she hopes to rekindle things. It's obvious from what she's already told me that they're completely wrong for each other and I feel like that should be enough for anyone to move on. I want to tell her that she should count herself lucky that he broke things off when he did because now she knows. Or should know. I've had too many buddies who knew they were with a good person, but it wasn't *their* person. Then, they would end up staying because it was easy and not because it was right.

But I just met Ashley and that seems like a lot to dump on a bridesmaid the night before her cousin's wedding. Weddings are when we're supposed to imagine our special person is right around the corner, even though it feels like mine must be on a different planet at this point.

Maybe I'm just extra cynical today because the phone call came as I was getting dressed for tonight. Erin was completely professional and kind and even complimentary, but it was still a major blow not getting the teaching position. It was nice Noah messaged just before I left for this dinner, asking if I wanted to grab a beer. He's a ridiculously nice guy which is probably why the students at Honey Cove High School love their school counselor. Normally, I'd take him up on hanging out, but I'm not sure how late the rehearsal dinner will go tonight, so I'll make sure I find time to see him before I move back to New York.

"Thank you all so much for being here and being part of our day. I know tomorrow you'll have your fill of me and I promise I'll try to not be insufferable." Brandon winks at Andi who rolls her eyes while laughing. "But tonight is our time to thank you all for being part of our lives and our journey. So with that, I promise I'm not suddenly a huge sap, but I have something to say to each of you. I'll keep it to one sentence so things don't get weird."

"Graham, you're the youngest of the cousins, but you've already shown what kind of man you're going to be and I'm honored to have you here, standing with me. Owen, I know we haven't seen each other nearly enough over the years, but I've always admired you and can't tell you how much our time together has meant since you took the temporary position this spring in Honey Cove. We can't wait to have you here for good."

I nod and can feel my cheeks heating as my gut plummets. I didn't want to rain on Brandon's parade, so I didn't tell anyone I didn't get the job. I'm glad that everyone has been so happy to have me here and wish I hadn't gotten the news until *after* the wedding so I could have held out hope in staying.

"Brad, you've been the peanut butter to my jelly since middle school football and if you hadn't talked me into getting coffee at Bobbi's before that impromptu volleyball game, I don't know when I would have met Andi, so I owe you one. Finally, James, my brother, my best friend, the guy I've looked up to my whole life, you mean the world to me and I wouldn't be here today if it weren't for you." Brandon holds up his beer. "To each of my boys standing with me tomorrow while I get to marry the woman of my dreams."

We all clink our glasses and James wipes his eyes.

Ashley makes eye contact with me as she takes her sip of bubbly and I give her what I hope is a kind smile. Not a smile that says 'I hope you change your mind before the wedding and decide you're better off without your ex because you deserve more.' That smile would be too much.

Honestly, I don't know what my problem has been lately. It's not just tonight, but I didn't even *want* to find a date for the wedding. Maybe it's something with the move possibly being temporary—well, it's officially temporary now—so I didn't want to go out with someone if I knew I might not get to stay here. In New York, I suppose I got used to dates that never went anywhere. Maybe I'm simply done putting time and effort into people who I know right away aren't the one.

A gentle kick under the table gets my attention. Graham tips his head toward Andi who started her speech while I was apparently zoning out, trying to figure out why no one has so much as caught my eye in over a year. Damn, apparently, I've been wanting something *real* for longer than I realized.

"So, I know that she's not here, yet, she's getting in tomorrow morning, I promise. I just talked with her and she's packed, of course. But Poppy. Poppy is the sister I never had and the fact that she's coming back early from her time away means the world to me. Since she's not here, I'm going to ask you all to please just be aware that people are going to have questions for her, especially anyone local. I'm not afraid to go full-on bridezilla on anyone who makes her cry by prying too much. So, if things look tense, jump in and get my girl a drink."

She pauses and looks each of us in the eye.

Jesus, I never knew Andi had this side to her.

"Also, don't you dare tell her I asked y'all to do anything, because she'll be pissed at me, and, once again, I'll have to resort to being bridezilla because my bestie has enough on her plate and so do I, so, just be your lovely selves."

Brandon tugs her down so they're face-to-face and says, "We'll do our best to keep bridezilla at bay, I promise."

He uses his other hand to pull her in for a fierce kiss that has both sets of parents blushing and Andi fanning her face when they break apart.

"Thank you. Alright, I have some thank yous for all my ladies who will be standing there while I officially marry this stud muffin. Mine might be longer, so buckle up buttercups."

She is nothing if not honest. I down the rest of my beer as the server walks around with a pitcher to refill us. I let my thoughts drift to what little I've heard about this mysterious Poppy.

The interim art teacher came in last-minute, a little before my position opened. I know that much, and even though people have talked about Poppy being on leave, it sounds like a bad break up. I've been tempted to ask someone about it because every now and then I'd hear someone reference how hard it must have been for her, but that sounds like a huge invasion of privacy for someone I haven't even met. Plus, if it were me, I wouldn't want people *still* talking about it months later. I resist the urge to find her photo again on the school's website so I know which face to put with her tomorrow, but it should be obvious. It's not like I haven't seen pictures of her and Andi, but so many are when they were teens and maybe early college. I'm just feeling nosy, I guess.

It must just be the mystery that's intriguing me.

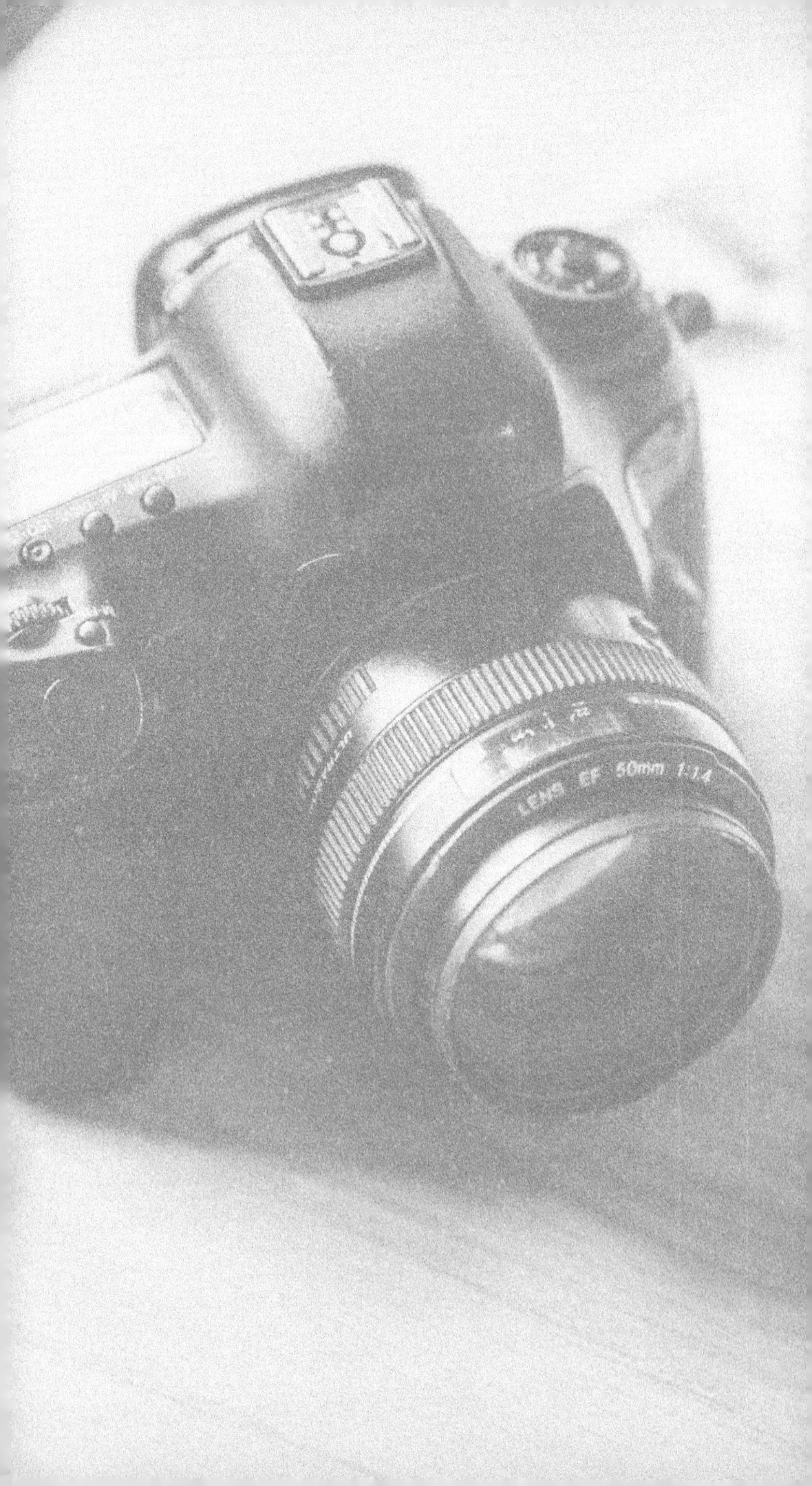
LENS EF 50mm 1:1.4

CHAPTER FIVE

Poppy

For ten in the morning, the airport is crazy. Why did I think this would be the ideal flight over leaving last night? I don't remember now, but I was *definitely* wrong. Between all the business people and the pre-weekend rush for travel, it is jam-packed. Pushing through people, I grab my suitcase and then head over to the car pick up lines. I, at least, had the sense to call for a car as soon as we landed.

I rush over to the car as soon as I see it pull up. *I can't wait to have my own car again.* I smile, mentally adding this to my list of positives to being home again. Another positive? Getting to see my best friend on the happiest day of her life in an hour. I tell my driver where I'm headed, then settle in to not think about what is to come and instead, think about the newest book I picked up.

Suddenly there's a knocking on the window so loudly it makes me squeal. "*What is it?* God," I shriek. I turn and see we have arrived at the house, my book is on the floor of this nice man's car and a line of drool is now at home on his door. *I must have dozed off.* Grinning sheepishly at him as I slowly open the door and get out, I add, "I'm so, so sorry. I didn't realize I'd fallen asleep."

He gives me a slightly annoyed look, but says, "That's alright. I have to clean it in between customers anyways." He moves around to the back and hands me my bag.

Reaching into my purse, I pull out a hefty tip for the inconvenience. His day isn't starting out great with me as his passenger. "Thank you again. I know it was a longer drive!" I try to give him my best "sorry" face one last time before he pulls out of the driveway and down the gravel road.

For the first time, I turn my attention to the house with a big breath. It's a gorgeous old farmhouse that Brandon's grandparents left to his family when they passed. The picturesque front porch is complete with shutters and a swing. It's still quite early, but I'm surprised by the lack of activity outside. Maybe everyone is out back.

After grabbing my things and heading over to the front door, I slowly creak it open, only to find a bustling mess of people, caterers, and flowers. Flowers *everywhere*. I move quietly along, hoping to blend in with the crowd and find Andi so I can see her first without making a scene.

"Oh my goodness, it's Poppy. What in the world? We didn't think you'd show."

I grimace and roll my eyes. The shrieking is coming from Andi's sister Janice who is not my favorite person in the world.

"Thanks, Janice. As you can see, I'm here. So, there's that." I look her up and down. She's already dressed to the nines with her own assets on display. I smile as I see Leslie down a hallway. *Now's my chance.* I slip away from Janice and glance back as she just stares after me.

"Leslie," I shout a little too loudly down the not large hallway. Everyone in the kitchen turns and looks at me. Gawking. I smile and wave to them. "Just going to talk to Leslie over there." *Act natural, this is fine.* I sidestep and catch up to Leslie.

"Hi, Leslie, how's it going?" *What was my plan with talking to her again?*

As predicted, she asks me all about my travels and what happened with Steven. I give her the most basic details. Did he break my heart? *Yes.* Am I okay? *Yes.* Why did I leave? *I was sad.* This one was only a partial truth. Sure, I was sad about being dumped, when I thought we were getting engaged—but I was also ashamed. I thought Steven was it for me, end of story. Married, 2.5 kids, and a garage type for me. When that turned out not to be true, I couldn't face everyone in our small town who had been excited for that future right along with me. I was able to imagine a new story for myself while on my trip though. *Now I just need to show everyone else that too.*

After talking with Leslie for a while and imparting all of the details I rehearsed so many times that I'm hoping she'll share with everyone else so I don't have to, I start my hunt for Andi again. I bump into, who I assume, is a groomsman I don't know heading up the stairs. He clearly had a little too much fun the night before, but also has a cute butt that I may or may not have checked out after he passed me by. We awkwardly talked about the tightness of the stairs and we're on our way. He didn't act like he knew my sob story, which was kind of refreshing. I gathered he was from Brandon's side of the family, which explained why I wasn't sure who he was.

I finally find Andi in her and Brandon's room. She's standing by a window, holding her dress up to the light. The beautiful lace gown has a mermaid cut that will be gorgeous on her. The light is shining through the fabric, bathing it and her in an ethereal glow. *The perfect bride.* "Hey beautiful," I say, smiling at her from the doorway.

"Ah, Poppy!" She throws her dress down on the bed and I'm suddenly mauled to the floor. After an extended time of hugging, jumping up and down and twirling, we end up sitting, facing each other on the bed, hand in hand. "How was the flight? How are you? You're so tan! Did you eat already?" I just laugh.

"So many questions and I should be asking you the most important one on your big day. Are you ready for this?" I'm surprised to see her on the verge of crying. "Oh, honey, are you okay? What is it?"

"Everything is just perfect now that you're here. I'm just so happy, Poppy."

CHAPTER SIX

Owen

10 minutes earlier

Brandon passes out double shots of aged whiskey that he picked up during his semester abroad in Ireland. Now that's some dedication to save it for his wedding day.

"To my boys, thanks for standing up with me today." He raises his glass and we all follow his lead.

"And to you, for marrying the love of your life," Brad adds as he starts the clinking of glasses.

"I'm fucking getting married," Brandon yells like a rock star on stage.

We all down our whiskey, which never ceases to burn going down for me, whooping and hollering on the back porch.

"Not to get ahead of ourselves, but who's next? This is the best feeling in the world and I demand you all experience it!" Brandon might have partaken in two greyhounds this morning and Graham was generous with the vodka. We're going to have to slow the liquor train down so he's not giggling during the ceremony.

"James, you'll be soon, I can just feel it," he says, putting a hand on his brother's shoulder and looking him right in the eye. "But I wonder if one of these two might beat you down the aisle."

There's screaming inside the house. It sounds joyful and I can't see anything, so I assume the women are having some sort of bonding experience, likely booze-infused like ours, but I don't think Andi requested they all wear matching shirts. Unlike the groom, who had them custom made. I turn back to the guys.

Oh God, Brandon's pointing at Brad and me.

"Hey cousin, I didn't even bring a plus-one, I'm not putting a ring on anyone's finger anytime soon," I chuckle.

All the color drains from Brad's face. He brought a date. Someone who he's been seeing for two months, but they both had conferences and travel for work, so they've only been on four dates, and that includes the rehearsal dinner.

"Oh my God," Brad mumbles, his hand running over his face. "What if she catches the bouquet? I'm not ready to get married, man."

Graham steps in front of Brad, face serious. "If it looks like Ruby is going to catch it, I'll put my body on the line and will run interference."

This makes Brad burst out laughing while he's still a little pale. "You're a good man, Graham."

"I do what I can."

A phone buzzes on the table redirecting our attention and James grabs it. "It's almost time for the hair appointments, which means we won't have access to anything upstairs shortly. Does anyone need something they left up there? Everyone's suits are down here, but if you have your toothbrush, hair products, or even your socks aren't in this room, you're going to have to go without them until after the ceremony."

"Shit," I mumble. "My toothbrush is still up there. Is there anything else I should grab while I'm gone?"

"Be sure to grab Graham's shirt so we're all matching when we help outside, I want at least a dozen photos on my phone before we get dressed."

Graham groans at the groom.

"If I'm wearing the 'mantivities' shirt, then you are, too," James says.

"Do they have to be so...neon?" Graham whispers.

I look down at my own shirt. It's ridiculously garish in the color choices, which made it clear Andi wasn't the designer.

"They most certainly do," Brandon says, stumbling just a little as the guys make sure he's steady immediately. "If they weren't neon, how would they glow in the dark?"

"We'll be wearing our suits hours before it's dark," his brother notes with a bit of a frown.

The groom opens and closes his mouth, clearly taking a moment to let that fact sink in.

"Let's get you some coffee, big guy. Poppy had some sent over from that place in Honey Cove you love," Brad says.

"Bobbi's? Oh man, this is the best day ever!"

If Graham didn't have one of Brandon's arms over his shoulders, I think our groom would be beating his chest in celebration.

"I'll be right back and I'll keep my eyes down just in case Andi is out and about," I say, zipping up my hoodie to hide at least a little of my shirt.

It looks like another delivery came while we were on the porch and there are women I don't recognize sorting things among several tables. We've been told, in no uncertain terms, which parts of the house we are allowed to occupy once eight o'clock hits and it's half past, so I do my best to blend into the background.

Holy shit.

I stop in my tracks, my heart thundering in my chest.

Who is that?

My god, she's stunning.

Wavy auburn hair that's not-quite red hits just below her chin, exposing her slender neck. Even from the side, her brown eyes have a sparkle that shines through her tense posture. She's wearing running shoes and leggings that accentuate toned thighs. I'm already wondering what's underneath her loose-fitting shirt. Jesus, I must be more tipsy than I thought. Who is this woman?

Then I see she's got a death grip on a rolling suitcase. Must be the famous Poppy. Damn.

"Do you need something, Owen?"

"Sorry, Aunt Mae, I was trying to sneak through to get my toothbrush unnoticed. You look incredible, has Brandon seen you?" I ask.

"You're too kind, I haven't even changed into my wedding outfit, yet," she says, blushing. "And no, I'm not supposed to see my baby boy until we do the family photos."

"Well, he's going to cry, you do know that, right?"

"Oh, stop," she says, primping her hair. "Your mother said the same thing when we video chatted."

"It's true."

"Well, either way, you had better pop upstairs quickly, before it's time for Andi to get into her dress."

"On the double," I say, turning faster than I intended and feeling the effects of the whiskey before righting myself and almost running into who I assume is Poppy.

She must think I'm an absolute lush. Instead of likely embarrassing myself, I take the coward's way out, mumble something about the stairs, and concentrate on taking them one at a time. I can hear her lug her suitcase behind her.

God, I must look like a complete asshole. She has both hands full and here I am just hopping upstairs without offering to carry a damn thing. On the bright side, I think Brandon would kill me if I fell down the stairs and with the level of tipsy I am and how hard I have to concentrate without turning around to see her. If I were talking to this woman, there's no way I'd make it up the staircase in one piece.

The woman who was almost my coworker. I suppose it's okay to find her absolutely stunning if I won't be working with her, right?

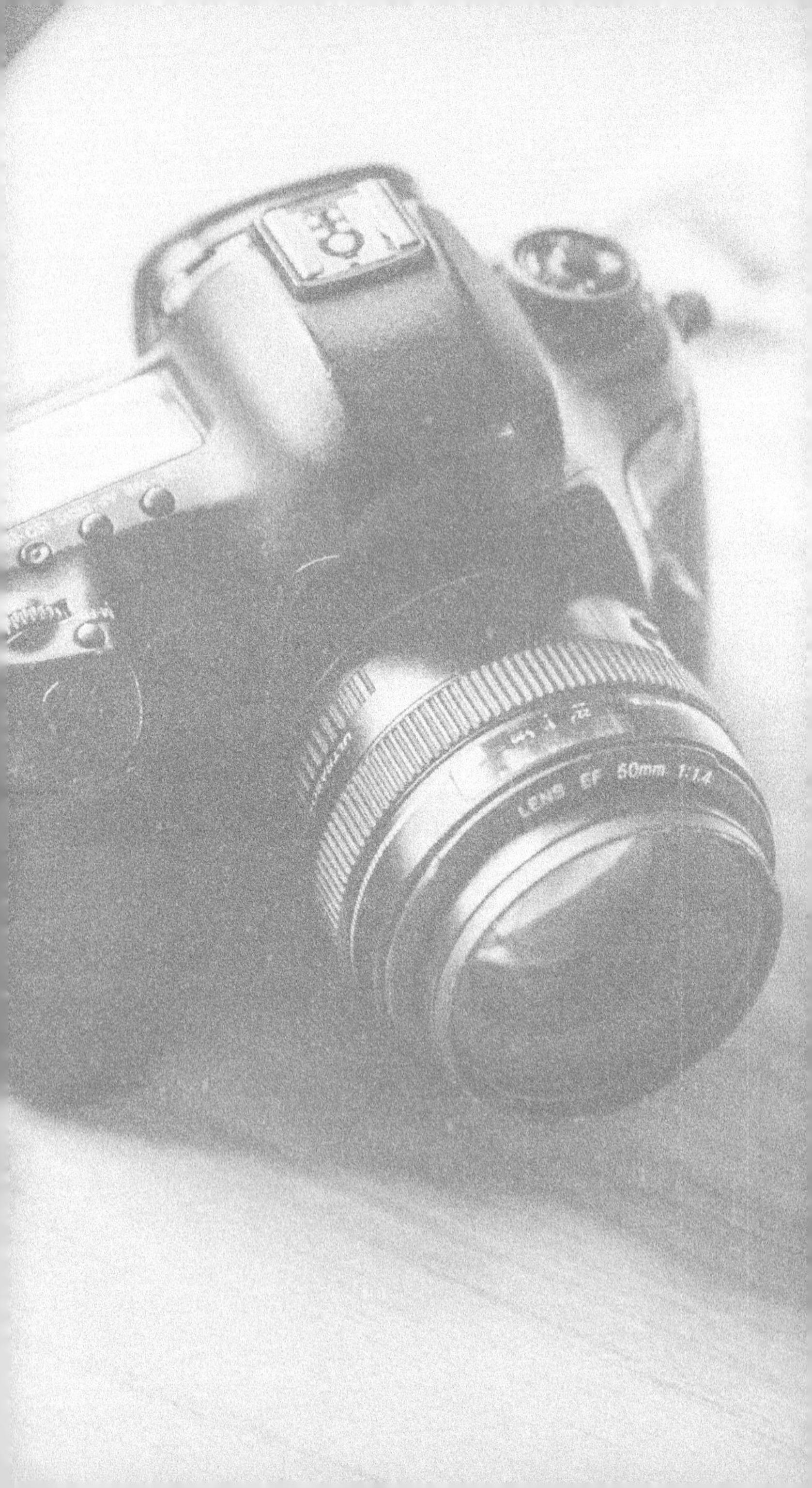
LENS EF 50mm 1:1.4

CHAPTER SEVEN

Poppy

Andi looks incredible—the lace and the mermaid cut of her dress are perfect for her style and shape. She's working it. Her hair lays in loose waves down her back with a pin holding some back on the side. She's a knockout and all her *assets*, as she would say, are on full display and look perfect.

"How are things looking out there?" Andi asks breathlessly as the other bridesmaids, stylist, and her mom fuss over the final touches on her hair and makeup. "Your parents have been amazing with helping us get everything set up."

"I saw them briefly for a quick hug, while they were buzzing around," I answer.

Suddenly it's a frenzy around her making miniscule adjustments. I wouldn't be surprised if a curling iron was tossed out from the fray. When they're satisfied, they all part and she begins to assess herself in the mirror.

Pulling the soft, gossamer curtains aside, I peek out at the backyard. *They have been busy.* White, pink, and green flowers line a cream stone walkway with draped chairs on either side. Twinkle lights hang over an arbor at the end. It's beautiful. I've been so busy helping Andi get ready, getting my own hair done by the stylist, and keeping myself calm that I didn't even think to look at what they had created for the actual wedding.

The chairs are filled, attendants are in place, there's an officiant looking man at the front, so I think things are a go.

"Everything is looking ready out there." Moving over to stand next to Andi, I brush a lock of hair off her forehead and wrap her in a hug. "You look beautiful. Are you ready for this?"

She gives me one of her pure joy smiles, her eyes shining and crinkled with feeling. Squeezing my hand, she turns toward the mirror, giving herself a last once-over, smooths down the front of her dress, then angles her body back towards the expectant group.

"Let's do this!"

Between all our fluffy dresses, heels, final touches, and dealing with that god damned narrow stairway, it still takes the whole bridal party ten more minutes to make it to where we need to line up.

I end up next to Lana, one of Andi's co-workers.. She's never been super friendly towards me, but she seems to support Andi, so I like her.

"I'm shocked you're here." She leans forward a little too closely, clearly enjoying her pre-wedding champagne.

"Why's that, Lana?" I know where this is going, but decide to continue the charade for a few more minutes. "Andi's my best friend, I wouldn't miss it." I fuss with the strap on my heel. Why didn't I choose sandals?

"Well, with everything you've been through, I mean. No one would have faulted you for not coming." She reaches out and rubs my arm consolingly.

I try to shoo her away gently, but she is relentless. "No, I'm doing alright," I say, smiling as widely as I can so that she knows how well I'm doing, *obviously*. But I worry I just look crazed now and like I'm trying too hard. *Too much?*

"I heard Steven is already engaged to someone too. I'll be honest, I went out with him a few times after you two broke up. I'm so, so sorry." Lana reaches down to hug me and it's all I can do to not throw my bouquet in her face.

"Lana, I don't know why you felt the need to say all that, can we please just leave it alone and focus on the wedding?" I restrain my face from giving her the look of disgust that desperately wants to make itself known. *Already engaged?*

After dabbing at her makeup in the hallway mirror, Lana nods and turns her attention back to our order and prepping to walk down the aisle.

Good lord, what the hell? I can't take any more of people's apologies and honesty.

Before I know it, it's time to walk and I'm standing at the front of the aisle next to Andi. She hands me her flowers and the ceremony has officially begun.

You held that together well, Poppy. I congratulate myself on not losing my shit with Lana. Refusing to talk to anyone seems like it would have been the right choice. This doesn't bode well for the rest of the night. Half these people aren't even drinking yet and I know it will just get worse as the night wears on. I may be branded as anti-social, but I think it will be the way to go.

Absent-mindedly I look out at the crowd. Andi's mom smiles at me and cries into her Kleenex. My mom and dad give animated waves. It *is* good to see them again. All the typical friends I'd expect are here. Blinded by the sun, I turn my attention towards the groomsmen, completely tuning out the ceremony. *Does anyone actually listen to these?* Suddenly I meet the gaze of the guy from the stairs earlier. I was so focused on getting by him that I didn't notice his kind smile or the way his lips look impossibly soft and full.

I am a little surprised I don't know who he is. He's in the wedding party. I thought I knew all of Brandon's groomsmen. He must have traveled in for the wedding. But, I have been pretty MIA the last half-year, so it wouldn't be *that* surprising I suppose, especially given my "no Honey Cove" rule. Andi should have mentioned a guy this cute though.

Snap out of it. You've sworn off guys. I give him one last look and he's still staring at me. I feel something heat up inside me, but I shush it down, reminding myself of my promise to make this time about me, not another man.

Looking away, my eyes catch on the groom's brother who is not actually looking at my face, but somewhere else. I glance down quickly to make sure everything is properly covered. *We're good ladies.* I mean, they do look amazing.

Andi *was* right about the dress.

CHAPTER EIGHT
Owen

Good Lord, this cake is delicious. I'm going to ask Brandon if this was a special order from somewhere local because damn it's amazing. The final bite is heavenly and even though I don't think I got frosting anywhere, I thoroughly wipe my mouth. This is the first time I've been sitting on-display during a reception. The groomsmen's and bridesmaids' seats flank the happy couple's on an elevated table. To say I'm eager to be moving around is an understatement. I've had too much time for my mind to drift back to the fact I need to tell everyone I'm moving back to New York soon. At least the bride and groom are enjoying their first dance.

Graham shifts in his seat, again.

"Everything okay?" I ask for the fifth time.

A sigh escapes him. "Yes. Sort of."

"Finally a real answer," I say with a smirk.

"See that guy over there?" Graham tilts his head to the right. "Blue suit with white shoes?"

"The one with the piercing blue eyes who's currently staring at you?"

Graham's head snaps to the right and he freezes.

"Relax, cousin," I tell him. "Go ask him to dance, Brandon and Andi's song is almost done."

"You have to, too."

"I'm not the one who wants to dance with him," I joke, getting a sarcastic smile out of him.

"No, you need to ask someone to dance."

I casually scan the reception hall before looking down the wedding party's long table. My gaze finds Poppy's for a moment before she looks down at her plate.

"Okay, I can't guarantee anyone will join me."

"Ask Aunt Mae if you need to."

I snort a laugh. "I'll check with the flower girl if my first attempt doesn't pan out."

Graham gives me a skeptical look. "You have one full song to be on that dance floor. Agreed?"

"Agreed," I say. "Now, go get him."

"Only if you go get her."

"I have no idea what—"

"You've been, subtly, checking on Poppy since the ceremony began," he says, cutting me off. "It wasn't obvious, I promise, but I can put two and two together."

It's still odd to see him be the astute one. I suppose that's what happens when you've lived away from your extended family most of your life and they aren't necessarily who you remember them to be from the last family reunion, but now you get to see who they've become.

"So?" His hand makes a circling motion to get me moving.

First, I look to see that the guy is still glancing Graham's way, which he most certainly is. Second, I make sure Poppy is still at her table and someone else hasn't swooped in. Everything is the same there too.

"Alright, let's go." I say. "But separately, this doesn't need to look like a mission."

"Fair point, dude. Whoever drains their drink last has to stand up first."

"You're on." We lift our half-full cups and the moment I nod, we both start drinking. Three gulps in and Graham sputters, but he manages to not spill on himself.

Graham curses under his breath, but takes a look at my now-empty cup and stands, patting me on the back as he passes behind me.

"Good luck, cousin," I say.

"Right back at you." He shakes out his arms and buttons his jacket.

Everyone claps as Brandon and Andi finish their first dance as a married couple. It's as good as I'll get for an excuse to get moving that looks semi-natural, so I check to make sure I don't have cake on my jacket as I stand, feeling just the right side of buzzed. And then I see the bride smile at the crowd, but it slips for a split second when she looks toward Poppy. I sneak one more peek at her. At the house, I thought she looked stunning. And then I saw her after she changed for the wedding. The dress hugs her in all the right places and flows off of her like it was made for her alone. The other women in the wedding party have similar dresses on, but not one holds a candle to Poppy.

The more I've seen today between her and Andi, the more I understand how much Andi meant every word of her bridezilla warning. They're clearly close, but there have already been moments where Poppy looks like she's just bracing for something to happen. Likely for someone to bring up that breakup. She does a great job hiding it, but there's a twitch in her cheek a few moments after the initial pleasantries are exchanged with someone.

Just after the ceremony, I overheard one of Andi's aunts greet her and then drop the "But how are you *really* doing, honey?" bomb on her. I took a step closer, feeling drawn to shield her from such a crap question.

I knew the aunt meant well and Andi's whole family clearly loves her best friend. But asking her about something that no person would want to talk about at a wedding reception? I'd call that a dick move.

Before I opened my mouth though, she just smiled and with a wave of her hand said, "Thankfully, I had some amazing travels as you might have heard, so I'm doing great."

And she's used a line like that a few times.

Not that I've been *overattentive*. Andi asked us to keep Poppy happy and that's what I'm doing. Asking her to dance will keep her occupied and away from people coming up to inquire about her time away. A little confidence surges through me while I walk over to her.

And as I get close, I second-guess myself. What if she just wants to be left alone? I think of Andi's worried look and how Brandon wants everything perfect for his bride. At least I know *I* won't be an asshole to her and ask her to talk about crap she clearly wants left in the past.

"Can I sit here?" I ask, shifting her attention from the dance floor to me. Sparkling brown eyes look at me in surprise.

"Sure, I don't think anyone is coming back any time soon."

Sitting down, I offer my hand to her. "I'm Owen, Brandon's cousin. I don't think we've officially been introduced."

Her hand slips into mine and there's a zap of electricity that I feel the moment we touch. "I'm Poppy, Andi's friend."

"You're—"

"Actually," she interrupts, "I don't mean to be rude, but can we just be Poppy and Owen tonight? Nothing else?"

I open my mouth to tell her that I worked at Honey Cove High School, but close it because the look on her face is almost pleading, like she needs to extend her time away from everyone a little longer.

So, I nod. "Absolutely. We can be anyone tonight."

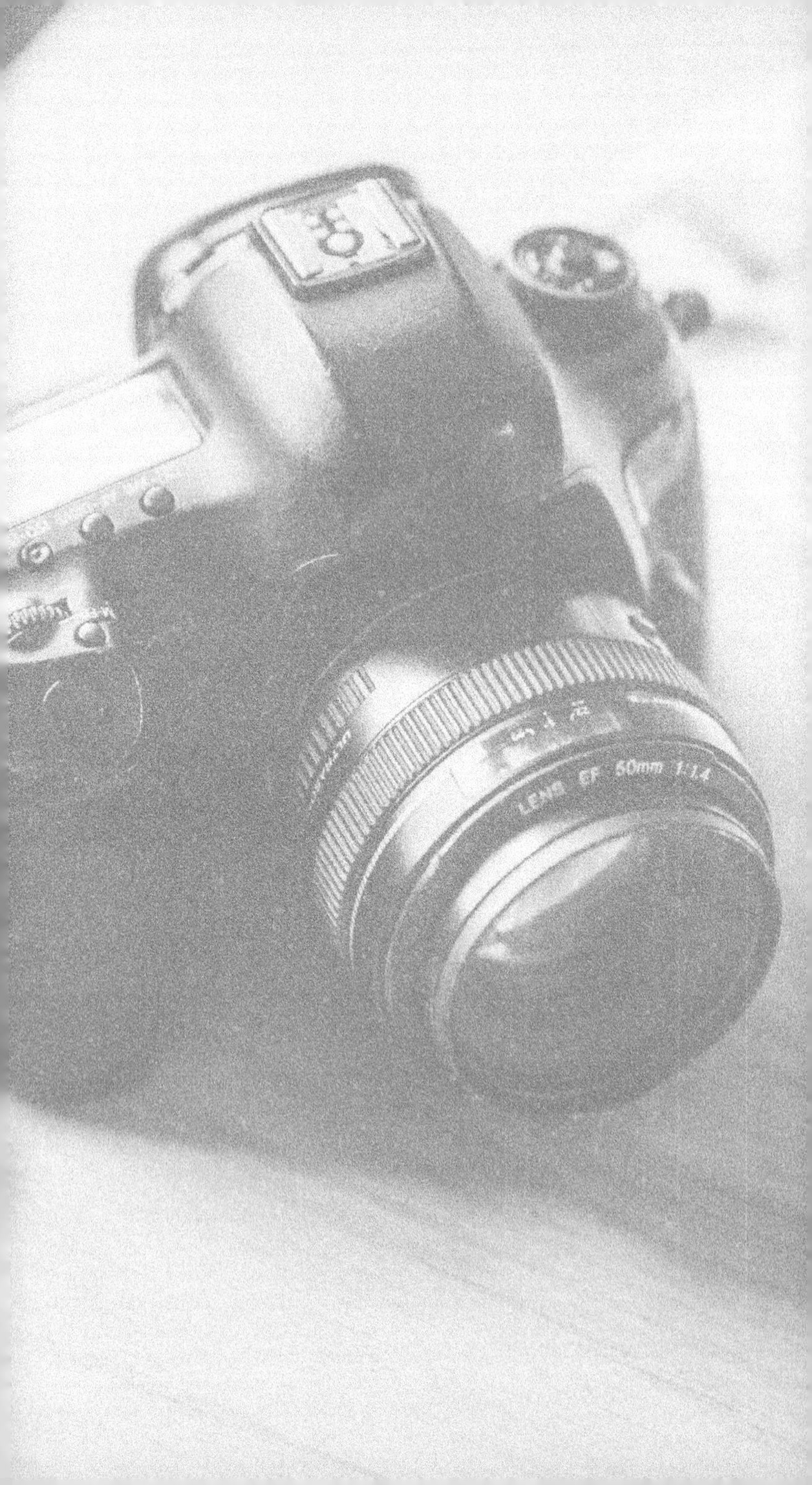
LENS EF 50mm 1:1.4

CHAPTER NINE

Poppy

I'm trying to keep my cool, but the room has started to spin ever so slightly and the man in front of me has the most gorgeous eyes. How did I not notice them on the stairs before? *God, could they be a richer shade of brown?*

What did he just say?

Looking squarely back at him jogs my memory. He's Owen and I'm Poppy, and we can be *anyone*. I'd like to be anyone tonight. The questions and stares have me already second-guessing if coming home was the right idea. "Would you like to get away for a little bit?" I ask.

"Away? Like from the tables or what do you mean?" His brow furrows most adorably and it's all I can do to keep from reaching out and touching the small wrinkles on his forehead. *Nope, that's not a normal thing to do.* Nodding, he motions for me to lead the way and I start walking towards the edge of the table area, where the lawn meets the stone walkway. Slipping off my heels, I saunter out into the grass, holding tight to my pink and bubbly champagne flute.

He moves to stand next to me and I feel him more than see him. He's tall, not towering, but a good amount of tall. And god help me, he smells amazing—like a summer breeze with a hint of cedar. I've been at peace with avoiding men for the time being, but if this is Brandon's cousin, there's not much chance he will be back in Honey Cove anytime soon. This *being anyone* is sounding more and more promising.

He meets my gaze for a moment before his attention flicks down towards my lips and I find myself moving towards him before noticing the hundreds of stars that have come out. My breath catches as I take it all in. The feel of the grass against my bare feet, the smell of bonfires in the distance, the cool breeze on my skin, and the gorgeous sky surrounding us have me taking a deep breath to steady myself.

"I've been gone for a while. Everywhere I've been has been in a city and I couldn't see anything like this. I don't think I realized how much I missed this until right this moment." Owen smiles back at me and I wrap my arms around myself, conscious of how odd I'm acting right now. He must think I'm a crazy person.

"They are beautiful." Moving towards me again, he gives me the slightest grin and his eyes grow heated, but before he can say anything else, he backs away quickly in an awkward, sudden movement which startles me. I stumble backwards, landing in the grass, as I try to discern what is going on. He's suddenly started making frantic noises and dare I say squawking? Andi had a parakeet when we were little and he actually is doing a great impression. *Who's the crazy person now, eh?*

"It stung me," he yelps.

"What happened?" Standing up, I venture towards him, but the flapping continues and it's difficult to get too close. Glancing around, I see that other guests have started looking over at us as well. I try to smile and wave that we're fine. *No more attention, please.*

"A bee, damnit." The jerking movements have stopped, *thank god*, and he's now cradling the side of his neck and looking quite embarrassed. "You know, I was going to be romantic just then. God, that hurts."

"Romantic, huh?" A laugh escapes my lips, which only adds to the dejected and ashamed look he's wearing. Although he brightens slightly at my jab. "Are you allergic?"

"No, I'm not allergic. It just took me by surprise. I didn't realize they were still active at night. I haven't been stung since I was a kid," he stammers out, still cradling his neck.

I give him a small smile, stepping closer to him. "Can I take a look?" Peeking at the sting as he tilts his neck towards me, the swelling is already obvious. "I think we should get something on this."

The look of alarm is instantaneous. "Does it look bad? What is it?"

"It's just a little swelling, but nothing a little ice can't help. Wait here." Stepping back onto the stones and into my heels, I walk over to the makeshift bar to ask for a cup of ice. Once I'm back in the grass, I hand him the cup. He winces when he presses it against his neck.

This close to him, I can see his freckles, the small scar across his chin, and the softest hint of gold to his irises. That warmth starts up in my core again and in this moment, I make a decision. I told him I'd be anyone tonight and I think that's just what I'll be. I haven't felt this comfortable with someone since being back and I'm thankful for the opportunity to just be, no matter what that means. And I don't think a one night stand is technically breaking my promise to myself, so I'm going with it.

"It's not often a guy can get rescued from a bee by a beautiful woman." Owen grins at me over the cup.

"Trying to be romantic again are you?"

"I had to try to salvage something here. After I'm done with this ice, can I ask you to dance or have I completely ruined the moment?"

Looking up through my lashes, I nod, ever so slightly and give him the most sexy grin I can muster given the situation. Maybe this will be a mistake, but maybe it's exactly what I need to shake Steven out of my life for good. And Owen couldn't be more attractive.

CHAPTER TEN

Owen

It would be inappropriate to kiss her right now. Especially since my neck now has water dripping under my collar from this ice.

Damn bee. Normally, I'm all for the little pollinators, but it picked a lousy time to sting me. Right now, I wish I could close the distance between us and see what it's like to kiss those rosy lips.

"Is the ice helping?" Poppy asks, reaching towards me.

"It feels a lot better." I let her take the cup from me and I hold still as she leans in to inspect what must be a nasty lump on my neck. She presses the dripping ice back against my skin, causing an involuntary shudder to race through my body.

"I'm sorry, did that hurt?" The concern in her eyes is clear.

"It's just cold," I assure her. "But I might warm up nicely if you'd dance with me now."

She glances at the tent and the little twitch is there and gone so quickly I would have believed my mind was playing tricks on me if I hadn't been watching her today.

"What if we danced here, in the grass? Just as Poppy and Owen," I try, not wanting this moment where she looks so free to go to waste. "We can hear the music and stay under the stars you've been missing."

Her sexy smile is back in full force. "That sounds rather perfect."

When her hand finds mine, it's like my skin is trying to memorize her touch. Each tiny piece of contact as I hold her, lights up my nerves. Nothing has ever felt quite like this woman.

The music drifts out into the night and I pull her closer, my arm wrapping around her waist like it was meant to be there. She relaxes against me, rooting me in place automatically, like my body doesn't want to lose any connection with her. So instead of moving around our grassy dance floor, we sway in place under the sky, looking up occasionally to take in the beauty of hundreds of visible stars that only a small town can provide.

She lets out a contented sigh and rests her head on my shoulder. "Is this okay?"

My arm pulls her closer, keeping her there in response and she lets out a sexy giggle. "I'll take that as a yes."

"It's a yes, Poppy," I murmur, resting my cheek gently on her hair. God, she smells incredible. "Without being a creep, what perfume do you use?"

"Oh man," she groans. "You're going to think it's stupid."

I look down to see her face, but she buried it in my shoulder to hide and my damn bee sting is still pretty tender. "Try me."

She peeks up at me through her hair which has fallen over part of her face, giving her a mysterious air that had my mind spinning with how she might look first thing in the morning. Her nose scrunches up in the most adorable fashion before she replies, "It's a poppy scent."

"Well, it's perfect."

"It's silly," she replies, shaking her head.

"It's you."

Her mouth screws to one side for a moment, like she's weighing the likelihood of me being genuine. She must believe me because she tucks herself against me once again, like she's allowing me to keep her safe from the outside world.

It's a stupid thought. We just met. But the underlying tension she's been carrying today seems to be gone and I can't help but smile.

The music changes to something upbeat and our little bubble breaks. Reluctantly, I let her take a step back and watch her gaze up at the stars once more.

"Thank you," she says. "I didn't realize how much I needed that."

We sit down next to her shoes, neither of us overly graceful, but there's a freedom in our casualness.

"I can assure you, it was no problem in the least. In fact, I might try to find you again for a repeat dance later this evening, Poppy."

She pauses putting on her shoes and looks my way, searching my face for...something. I'm guessing that trusting someone won't come easy after whatever her ex put her through. She seems like someone who might need to see consistency, but even more importantly, transparency. To see the real person behind the pretty words.

Something shifts in her expression. I don't dare move a muscle, afraid I might spook this beautiful woman. Then she leans towards me, her hand that I so recently held reaching out first. It's not until her fingers gently graze my neck that I release a sharp breath.

Damn, that still stings.

"How did I not think about this while we were dancing? The swelling went up even more and it has to feel terrible." The concern in her tone makes her even sexier, which seems like the worst thing to notice right now.

"I mean, it's not a lovely thing to have on my neck right now, but I was a little distracted," I say, trying to keep a little levity.

"Well, it looks downright angry, but I have an antihistamine ointment in my bags." Those fingers continue prodding near the most tender area with a calm confidence.

"You carry that with you?" I ask, one eyebrow raised.

"I picked it up while I was traveling, but haven't had time to unpack my toiletries."

"Then it's my lucky night."

Some of that sparkle returns before she says, "It just might be."

LENS EF 50mm 1:1.4

CHAPTER ELEVEN

Poppy

It just might be? Did I really just say that? I'm drowning here trying to figure out how to show Owen I'm open to *whatever* tonight, but I feel like I'm being more awkward than I thought I'd be about the situation. I'm definitely out of practice. I haven't been with anyone other than Steven for a long time. He and I were together for five years and before the infamous break-up, it was just high school romances that didn't feel like anything of consequence to me.

"Why don't we go grab that cream from my room and we can get you a proper ice pack from the kitchen inside," I say, reluctantly. Biting my lip I look up at him for a long moment before the mosquitos flitting around my head demand more of my attention. Those expensive citronella candles Andi insisted on aren't doing their job.

He searches my face, perhaps looking for the same confirmation I am indeed implying what he thinks I'm implying. After trying to figure things out he responds with a simple, quiet, "Alright, Poppy." My name comes out deep and a little gravelly as he says it and I find myself wishing he'd say it again and again.

As we move towards the patio, I feel a sudden wave of panic. "Wait, we should go up separately. My parents are here," I say, my throat tight as I look around to make sure they aren't watching all of this. I connected with them again after the ceremony but haven't been keeping tabs on what they've been up to. A lot of their friends are here and I know they're probably off having fun as well.

I'm open to being just Poppy tonight, but am not sure what they would think of my added extracurricular activities on my first night back in town. Especially with so *much* of the town here with a front row view.

He chuckles before adding, "Why would we need to hide that we're getting cream for my bee sting?" Owen raises his eyebrows at me, questioningly.

For a second I wonder if I've read this all wrong, but then he gives me a heated smile and I feel unsteady again on my feet. But this time it isn't just the champagne.

"Just," I give his shoulder a playful push, "go that way and I'll meet you in the kitchen. I'm going to let them know I'm leaving." Owen nods, taking off in a different direction.

While I scan the reception area for my parents, I can't help but keep glancing back at him as he heads towards the house. *Am I doing this?* Is this really happening? *Cut it out, this is normal. People do this all the time.* My mind is racing a mile a minute trying to think through the plan, while smiling at guests passing by.

I finally spy them standing next to a table, under the hanging lights and looking very much in love while talking with our neighbors. My dad's hand casually drapes over my mom's shoulder and she turns as I walk up to them. "Hi, sweetie."

Walking into my mom's open arms for a hug, I feel a little weight lift off of me. She and my dad have been so supportive through everything. While I've dreaded coming back to such a large gathering, I have been looking forward to spending time with my family and close friends again. Despite what happened, I love Honey Cove and really can't see myself living anywhere else.

"Hi, Mom."

She starts to tell the neighbors about my amazing trip, as if I was taking some sort of luxurious vacation. They smile and nod, but I know they likely already know the truth of what happened. After listening for a few minutes, I politely pull her aside.

"I'm going to head up to my room. It's just a lot coming back and being here with everyone. I'm feeling like I need a bit of quiet." Nervously playing with my necklace, I wait patiently for her to respond. I am an adult but for some reason, at this moment, I feel like I'm doing something I shouldn't.

She nods, pulling my hair to the side before pulling me into another hug. "You are so strong, sweetie. Can I stop by your place in a few days? I bought you some things for your classroom."

"Sure, I'd love that." After saying goodbye, I casually wind my way towards the kitchen and remind myself to breathe slowly. The memory of his soulful eyes and the way my skin burned at his touch keeps rushing back to me, making it impossible to calm my racing heart.

It isn't that I care if others know that I'm taking Owen to my room. But it feels like it would be best if they didn't know it *tonight*. I don't want to make a scene or have people thinking I'm a different person now, but I do want to *try* something a little out of my comfort zone and there's no shame in that. I also don't want to distract people from Andi and Brandon's night.

Once safely inside, I see Owen across the busy room and make my way towards him. Stepping closer to him, I find myself forced from behind, my hands finding their way to his chest as someone pushes past me to get back outside. He reaches down with his hand on the small of my back to make sure neither of us are bumped by the crowd that has seemed to take over the kitchen. Standing up on my toes I put my mouth close to his ear and whisper, "I'll go up the stairs, you wait for a while, then head up to use the bathroom. When the coast is clear, come to my room. Second on the left."

Then I'm off, leaving him *hopefully* awestruck by how alluring I am. Grasping the handrail to help me climb the stairs, my thoughts start to slow down a little. *Keep breathing, Poppy. You can do this.*

Once in the room, I'm not entirely sure what to do with myself. What if he doesn't come? What if someone sees him and makes a scene? I remember the cream I promised him and shuffle through my bag, dumping belongings onto the bed in my rush. In less than a minute, I've found it and pushed all my things back into the bag, clutching the cream close.

What do I do once he's here?

Has it been too long and he changed his mind? Biting my thumb, I turn off the lights and peek out the window to see if I can see him back outside at the wedding, but there's no sign of him. Before I can continue a more thorough scan, I hear the door click. Whirling around with a small, surprised gasp, Owen slowly closes the door and puts his finger up to his lips to quiet me.

Mouthing the word "Andi" he points his thumb over his shoulder, then smirks at me like he's trying to hold in a giggle. That starts me up and I have to hold my hand over my mouth to keep a laugh from escaping. Soon, we hear her soft footsteps going down the stairs and the rustle of her dress against the wall.

"What happened?" I whisper.

"I started to come over from the bathroom, but didn't realize Andi was in her room. She didn't see me, but I wasn't sure if she'd check on you in here." Nodding, I remember the cream and hold it out to him. He takes it and opens the cap while keeping his focus on me.

"Here, I can help." I dab some of the cream on his sting and find myself leaning closer into him than necessary. I can't help that he feels so good and there's something I love about the fact that we're *just* Owen and Poppy. He seemingly knows nothing about what has happened and I can just be me, without all that baggage.

"Thank you," he says, his voice deep again. Looking up at him, we lock eyes and my breathing becomes short, the warmth of his body sending a spark through my own. He sets the tube down slowly on the nightstand before leaning closer to me, slowly dragging his thumb along my jawline, angling my face up towards his. Shadows from the window and the party below dance along his face, bathing us both in a golden, flickering light.

The wait is agonizing. Owen takes a breath before whispering, "You are beautiful, just Poppy." His lips are an inch away from my own, his breath and touch sending a shiver through my body. "Is this what you want?"

It's all I can do to nod before he closes the distance between us. I relish the feeling of the softness of his full lips and press my body more firmly against him. My pulse skyrockets as he wraps his arms around me, pulling me in tighter still. All my nerves about tonight, every worry I had about coming home seems to disappear in the moment. Every thought and feeling focused on us.

I guess I am better at this than I thought.

CHAPTER TWELVE

Owen

She tastes like wedding cake and champagne and she's kissing me like I'm the missing piece of a puzzle.

We stumble backwards, falling on the bed with my arm softening our landing. Our lips part and her tongue finds mine again, and again. I have to suppress a groan because everything about this woman is mesmerizing, even in the dark.

Flipping her onto her back, we both scramble to remove my jacket and tie while trying to keep as many points of contact as possible. I'm already missing the feeling of her curves pressed against me as she untucks my shirt. Truly, I've never hated buttons more than I do at this very moment. I get the top few undone and stand up to pull it over my head, ready to fall forward and get lost in her kiss again, but the sight below me makes me pause.

"God, you're amazing," I say quietly, wishing the lights were on so I could see how she flushes when she's been kissed like this. Her eyes sparkle and her hair is disheveled, and I kneel on the ground in front of her. I'm so tempted to return where my lips could be on hers again, finding this position a little complicated because I'm so hard right now, but being able to drink in this sight a little longer is too much to resist. The only sounds now are our breaths as we try to catch them.

She props herself on her elbows to watch as my fingers run down the back of her soft calves, raising her foot so her heel is pressed into my bare chest. My eyes follow my motions as I undo the small buckle and remove one, taking care to lower her foot back where it was. When I finish removing both heels, I look back at her face and the hunger in her gaze matches my own.

My hands glide up her legs, gently lifting the hem of her dress.

"Is this–"

"It's okay," she says a little breathlessly, driving me more wild and lifting her hips. It takes all I have to lock my gaze with her because I want to see every inch of her that's being exposed, but she has me utterly captivated. When she sits up so I can tug the dress over her head, her perfume hits me again. Poppies. Something about that is so endearing, yet sexy.

Once she's free of her dress, I shake it out and drape it over the chair in the corner of the room along with my jacket and shirt in case we're heading back to the reception tonight. Not everyone needs to know exactly what we're up to. When I turn around, she has one eyebrow raised at me.

"Are you keeping those on too?" She looks pointedly at my pants.

With one hand, I pop the buckle of my belt and pull it out of the loops in one tug. Trying to not seem overly presumptuous, I toss my wallet on the bedside table. She takes a sharp breath, watching my every move while I remove my pants and socks. She backs up and repositions herself on the bed so she's in the center, allowing me to crawl over her and take my time looking at the way her black panties contrast against her tan skin. When my face is over her matching bra, I dip my head low to kiss her from her cleavage up to her neck until her fingers are in my hair, locking me in place right behind her ear.

The sounds she's trying so hard to stifle are driving me crazy. As my lips find hers again, my fingers slip underneath the bottom of her bra and she gasps when I find her nipple, pebbled already.

Finally, I settle over her only to have her lock me in place when she wraps her legs around my waist. Not that I'd ever complain about it, especially when I rock against her for the first time, my aching dick twitches and she moans, slapping a hand over her mouth.

"Do you think you can stay quiet for me?" I whisper into her ear, freeing my fingers and trailing them lightly down her stomach.

She nods vigorously in reply.

"Are you sure?" I ask, my voice dropping even deeper than usual as she loosens the grip her legs have on me so I have better access.

"I'm sure," she whimpers. "Please."

That word is my undoing.

My hand skates over her underwear and pulls it to the side, my fingers finding her soaked already as I sink one deep into her.

"Jesus, you feel absolutely amazing," I say before kissing her hard, showing her just how much she affects me. Something in me wants to taste her, but right now she's got me anchored against her with her nails close to leaving marks on my back.

Her moan vibrates all the way from the lip I'm nibbling on down to her core when I circle her clit, making my body tingle with anticipation. Every breath gets more labored as she quickly climbs closer to her release. My fingers move faster and she tenses so I pull back and watch her for a moment as her mouth falls open silently.

Then she tugs my mouth to hers as she unravels, effectively muffling the sounds of her pleasure. I swallow each one down while she rides out wave after wave until her lips smile against mine and she lets out a sigh.

Rolling onto my back, I tuck her against me, her arm falling across my chest and her head tucking into my shoulder as if we've been doing this for years.

I'm content to just hold her and stay here. But after only a minute or so, her fingers wander over my chest.

"I'm trying to be a gentleman and you're not making it easy right now," I say, my voice strained because her hand moves lower.

"Who said I wanted a gentleman tonight?" she asks.

"You'll have to be more specific with what you'd like then."

A confident smirk appears and she pushes herself to a seated position. "Does your wallet happen to have protection inside?"

"It might."

"Perfect."

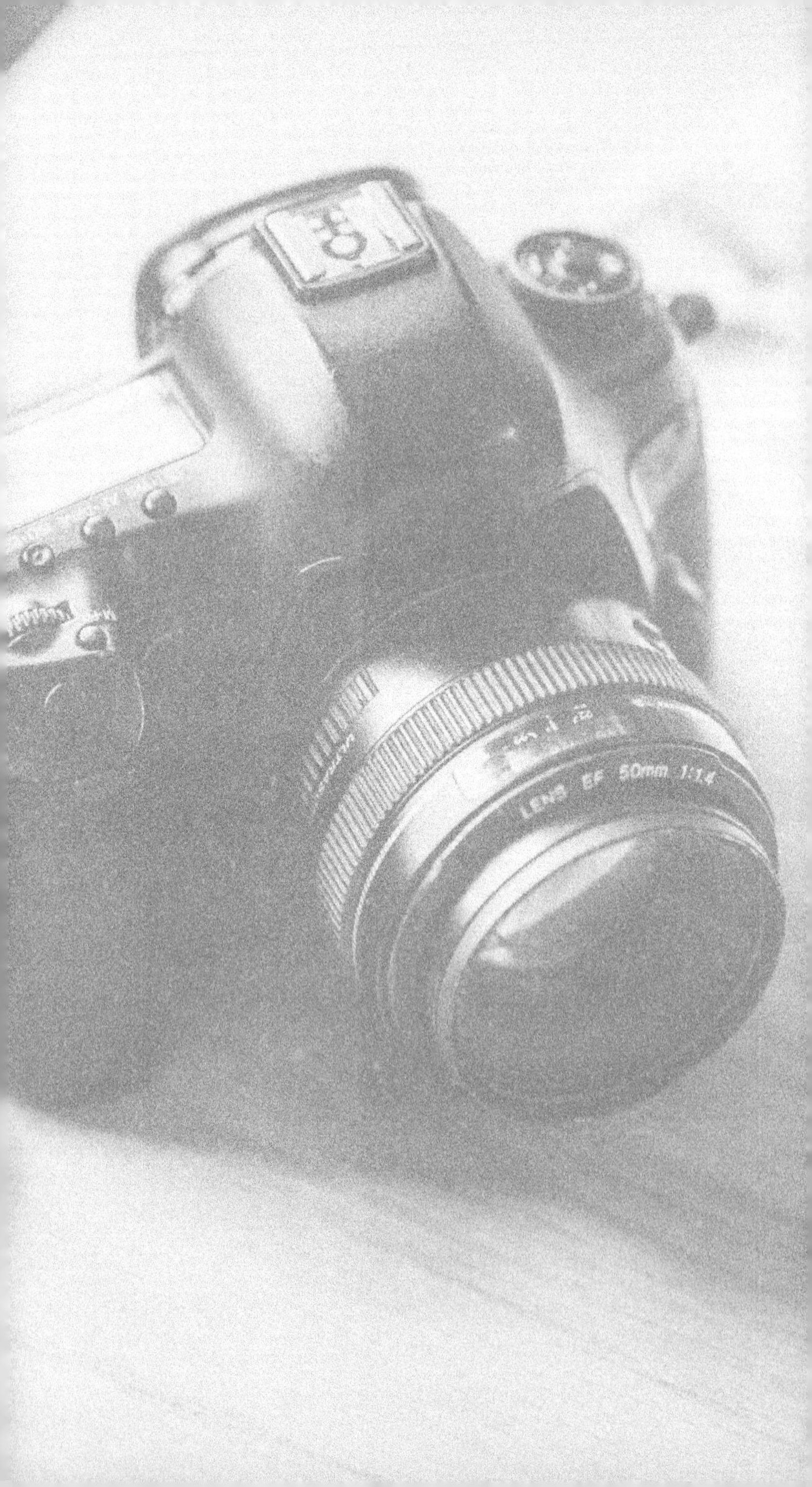
LENS EF 50mm 1:1.4

CHAPTER THIRTEEN

Poppy

Any lingering fears or nerves I had about tonight have completely vanished under Owen and his agile fingertips. I'm not sure what it is about him, but I feel comfortable despite this being a completely new situation for me. Leaning back against the soft sheets, I watch as he crosses the room to grab his wallet. The muscles in his back ripple with the movement, setting my core on fire again. His skin glows in the light from the party and the moment. I'm thankful again for the cool air inside as I brush away a bead of sweat off my chest.

Owen waves the condom at me, smirking.

"Let's see what we can do for you," I say, sliding myself over him as he sits back down on the bed. I can feel the warmth radiating off his body and he looks so damn hot waiting for me. He *is* quite the gentleman.

Leaning down, I kiss against his ear, eliciting a deep moan and a slight jerk against my hips. "I'll remember that you like that." Moving to his mouth, his hand finds my hair, giving a little tug that unravels me. I find myself frantically kissing him, trying to get more of him in this moment, but it's not enough. Pushing myself to the side, I rip at his underwear, freeing him in seconds, then I'm onto my own, but he stops me.

"Please, allow me," he says, a fire in his eyes that I can't pull my gaze away from. Relishing the feeling of freedom in this moment with him, I kiss him deeply as he leans over and reaches behind me. My bra is undone in one swift movement before he does the same with my thong. For a second, we take each other in. Our eyes raking over one another's bodies.

I see the small freckles on his face, the lines on his shoulders, his strong chest, and the curves of his arms. He is beautiful. All dark tones and shadows in the evening light. His hand gently tucks a lock of my hair behind my ear, then travels down to my chin before pulling me to him for a softer kiss. For a one night stand, he seems to be taking time to make me feel cared for. Doting on me in a way I didn't expect.

As he runs his hands down farther on my body, the heat builds and it feels like I might burst with how much I want him right now. Bringing my leg up higher, I tug him closer to me. He feels incredible as I move against him. Grabbing the condom, I push it onto him before straddling him once more. This time, I lower myself slowly, relishing the feel of him pushing inside of me. Gasping at the fullness, I double over, catching myself on the headboard.

"You feel amazing," I whisper as I slowly move up and down, grinding myself against him. His eyes roll back into his head and his hands find my hips, moving me in tandem with his own rhythm.

"You're gorgeous." His deep voice pushes me closer.

Our breathing becomes ragged, strangled as we climb higher together. He reaches out, making eye contact with me while adding extra friction to my clit and it's all I can do to hold back the scream that takes hold of my body. Owen groans and shudders as he finds his own release. Both of us fall against the sheets, our bodies tangled together, enjoying our moment of bliss.

Sunlight filters in through the window and I find myself blinking at the brightness, a pounding headache making it hard to think straight. Although my drinking last night has caught up with me, my memories are all here and I smile, seeing that Owen is still laying next to me. Watching the soft rise and fall of his back, I think through our night together. It was lovely. Perfect, even.

While I made the decision to do something out of the norm, I didn't expect to love the thrill and excitement of being with someone I didn't know quite as much as I did. The sneaking around just added to the anticipation even more, giving me a sense of freedom and of being myself that I haven't felt in years. Just the same, I find myself wondering where he is headed back to and if I'll ever see him again.

Glancing at my phone, I see that it's already almost nine and I have a million errands I need to run today. Staff are due back to school in less than a week and I need to make sure I have everything ready while giving myself some time to settle back in at home too. My mind reels a bit thinking of the tasks I still have ahead of me to clean Steven from my life here as well.

There's also the small matter of now having to make a presentation about my trip on the first day of staff development. I thought it was a great idea to post about my trip on social media, but my principal saw all my photos and one thing led to another, and now I have to make a presentation. My calm and serene wake up is now marred with anxiety over what comes next.

As quietly as I can, I grab my dress, bag, and other items. Deciding to leave Owen a note on the nightstand before heading out, I go back and forth with deciding what I want to say and how I want to say it. But ultimately kept it simple, leaving the cream for his sting next to it in case he needs more.

Thank you, Owen. You made my first night back in Honey Cove completely memorable.

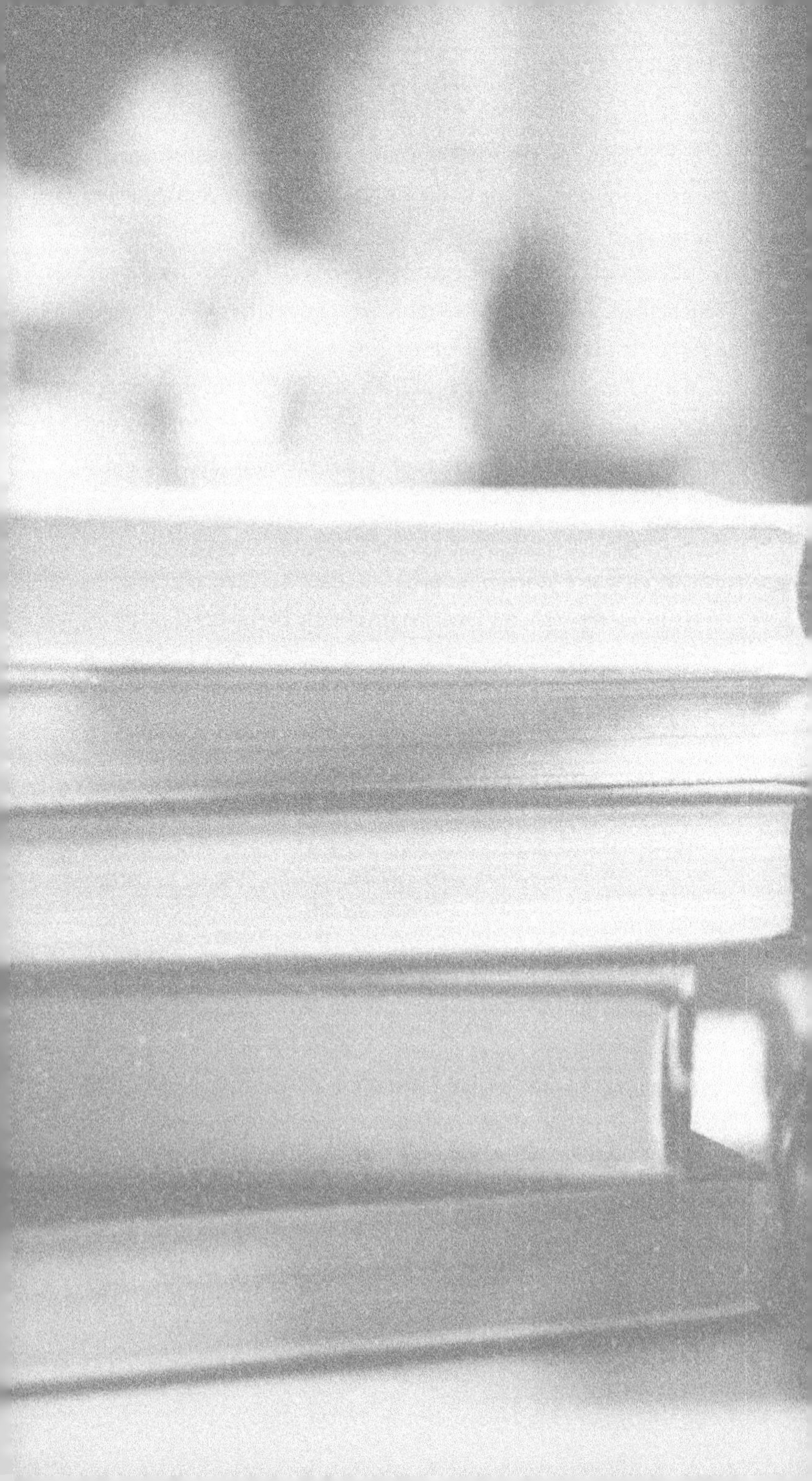

CHAPTER FOURTEEN

Owen

There's nothing like getting an unexpected phone call when you're packing up your life to begrudgingly move back to New York. Especially when that call is from Erin Matthews, the Honey Cove High School Principal, about the English position I applied for.

And was passed over for.

But the person they hired just backed out.

I *should* be ecstatic. This is exactly what I've been wanting, it's just a little dampened by the fact that I'm their second choice.

Actually, I already made peace with the fact I was leaving. Even my cousins, minus Brandon who is on his honeymoon, have plans to make the most of what was going to be my last few days here, starting with dinner tonight. At least I'm not very far into my packing. My shelves are still jam-packed with books even.

It doesn't feel real yet.

I'm staying here, in Honey Cove. My dream job was just officially offered to me.

My phone chimes.

Margerie:

> That's excellent news, Owen! I was preparing to list your apartment tomorrow, so if you'd like to continue your lease, I can drop the paperwork off this afternoon.

Whew. That's one less thing to worry about and, not for the first time, I'm grateful for a good landlord.

> I have a family dinner, so I can sign it on my way and save you the trip!

Margerie:

> Perfect, I'll have it ready shortly.

I can cancel the movers. I can celebrate with Graham and James. I can do this.

Okay, I can fake confidence.

Back-to-school faculty meetings are the absolute worst way to end the summer. But walking into the first meeting with so many people taking second glances at me makes it so much worse. Not only did my hire happen last-minute, but they haven't officially announced it because they're still finalizing the contract for a different position and wanted to share both at the same time.

Thankfully, people recognize me from last year and are putting two and two together, but a little heads-up to the staff would have been so nice.

"Owen," I hear over the chatter as teachers fuel up on the familiar terrible coffee from the staff room.

Turning around, I find Noah waving and weaving through a few people to get to me.

"I know I said it before, but I am so happy that you hadn't moved yet. We would have missed out big time." His voice and whole demeanor are so genuine that I fully believe it, even though the snarky part of my brain is trying to remind me that I wouldn't have been in the process of moving if they hadn't picked someone else first.

"Thanks so much, I was thrilled to get the call." It's true enough. But standing here and shaking his hand while people watch with interest, likely wondering what the heck I'm doing here, is a little awkward.

"A few people are stopping over at my place after we're done today for drinks and to unwind," he says a little quieter so not everyone hears. "Would you be able to make it?"

Noah really is one of the nicest guys I've met and saying no would be like turning away a puppy. "That sounds like what the doctor ordered, I'm in."

"Alright, I have to sit up front because I'm running the slides for Poppy's presentation which starts soon."

I freeze at the name.

"You are going to love her. She's the art teacher who was on leave last semester and I'll be sure to introduce you two today."

I think I nod because he trots up to the front row next to someone with auburn hair that falls just above her shoulders. Hair that I recently ran my hands through.

Oh god, how did I block out that Poppy, *just* Poppy, became my coworker?

Do I go up and say something to her? No, absolutely not. She's about to give a presentation and she doesn't need the guy she slept with the day she returned to town to say, "Surprise, we work together now!"

So, what then? I just watch her from the corner of my eye and wait until she sees me and wave? Jesus I have got to calm down.

There's a seat toward the back of the room that's open next to another English teacher. Perfect. It's not too close where she'll see me right away while presenting, but it won't look like I'm purposefully trying to stay out of her line of sight. And it's Beth. She's never one for idle chit-chat, but was so helpful getting me up to speed when I was learning the ropes.

Why haven't my feet moved?

Get a fucking grip and find that confidence you scrounged up for today.

One deep breath later and I'm off. Exchanging pleasantries with teachers along the way.

"Is this seat reserved?" I ask Beth, getting her attention which was solely focused on the novel in her hands.

"Oh, hi, Owen," she says, a smile on her face. "Nope, it's all yours. I can't tell you how excited we were when Noah said you accepted the position."

Settling in, I return the smile. "Thanks, it's been a bit of a whirlwind, but I'm really happy."

She leans in to whisper conspiratorially. "I'm *not* supposed to say anything, but you deserve to know that there was pressure from the district to have more tenured staff by the end of next year and the English opening was one of the few that had someone who qualified for only a one-year probationary period."

Wow, that's news to me. I carefully pull my messenger bag over my head with one hand while holding my coffee in the other as Beth fills me in.

"We all wanted the first offer to go to you because you're the best candidate for the position." She continues on as Erin stands up front and teachers fill in open seats. "It was an oddly backwards situation since most hiring committees consider the cost of the candidate's salary and we usually need to be fairly conservative with keeping those we make offers to within a lower range than someone with fifteen or more years would be getting. But that's neither here nor there and what's important is that we didn't miss out on the right person."

"Thanks, again," I say, meaning it fully. Beth might have shared more than she was supposed to, but that helps make sense of things. It lessens the sting a bit.

Notebook and pen now in hand, my foot shifts my bag under my seat and our attention is on the front of the room as the welcomes officially begin. Poppy hasn't turned around yet, but even from here I can see the tension in her posture.

"And now, we have Poppy Edwards sharing her explorations with photography over the past few months."

She stands a little stiffly with Noah ducking around her to load her program. Once she's at the podium, she takes a drink from her cup and looks out at the teachers watching her.

Honestly, she looks like she might vomit.

All I want to do is sneak her away so she doesn't have to do this. But that's unreasonable and she's a professional. I have no claim to her, we were just Owen and just Poppy, and just for one night. Maybe she's a nervous public speaker.

Who am I kidding? If Andi's comments were any indication about how Poppy felt returning to Honey Cove, she's terrified of what people are thinking of her needing to leave.

Now, instead of trying to duck behind people so I'm not in direct view, I sit still and send her all the supportive vibes I can from here and settle in for her presentation.

I can definitely be a supportive co-worker.

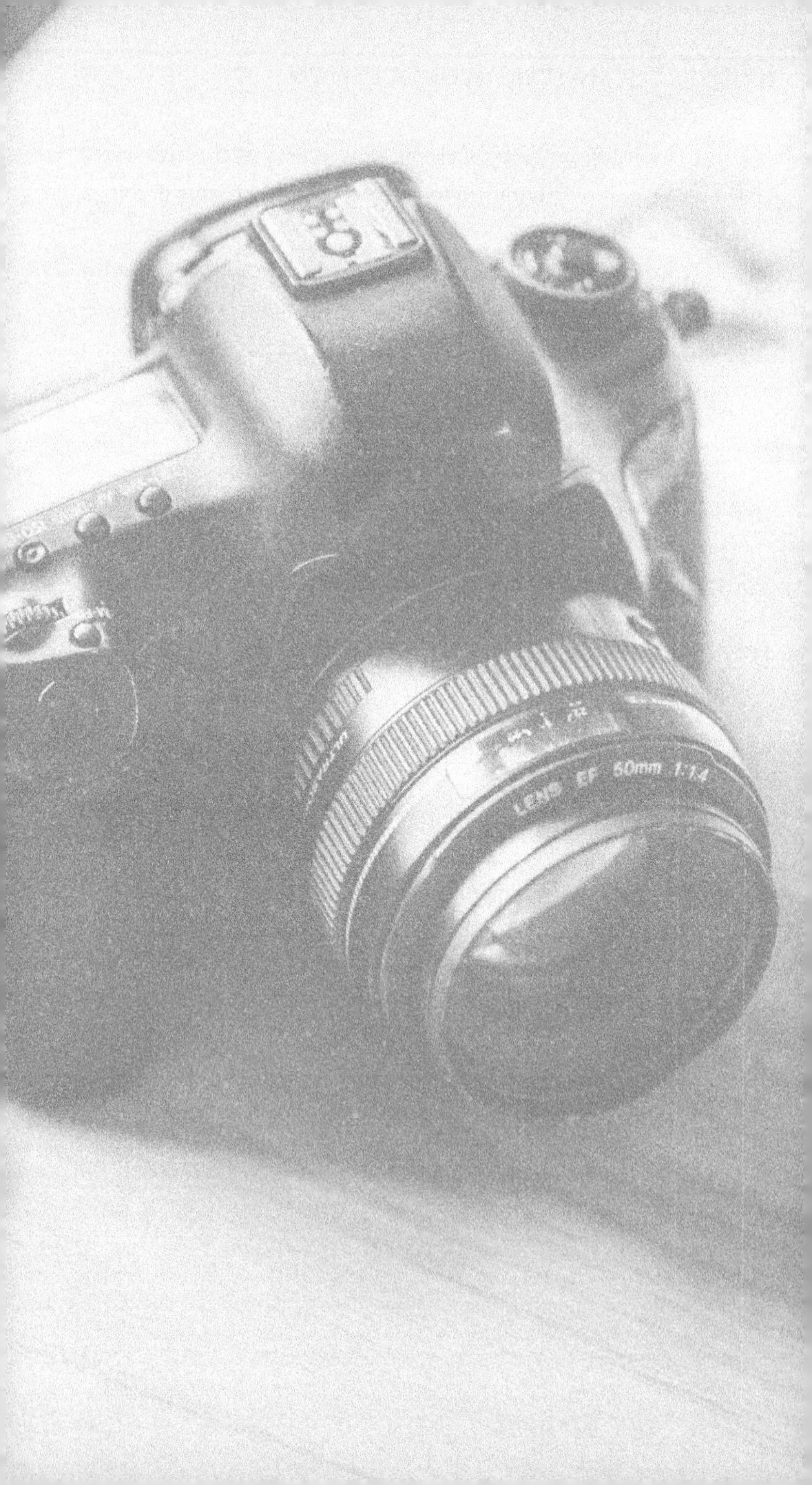
LENS EF 50mm 1:1.4

CHAPTER FIFTEEN

Poppy

Oh god, even at the best of times, I hate doing presentations like this. I know that I'm close with everyone here. They're supportive of me and all that, but I just despise feeling all their attention on me. Questions, I'm sure, milling about in their heads: *What did she do wrong? Why didn't Steven want her? Poppy can't seem to get a guy to put a ring on it.*

Closing my eyes and taking a deep breath, I breathe in the familiar smells of the library. The books, the stale coffee, newly sharpened pencils, the slight smell of peppermint gum that Noah always chews. When I open my eyes again, he is standing next to me, moving towards the computer to click through my PowerPoint for me. He gives me a warm smile before whispering in my ear, "You've got this."

We became close quickly when we were both newbies four years back. There haven't been too many hires since then, but it was nice to have a buddy to go through my first few years with. We were both learning so much and have become each other's go-to person for help talking through issues or about the latest staff gossip. It also helps that he has a kind heart and finds animal gifs as hilarious as I do, not to mention our coffee addiction.

Besides Andi, he's my closest friend here and with her gone on her honeymoon, it is nice to have a positive connection to keep me grounded through everything that has come with returning to work and town. He even offered to stand in for her and help me burn all my

Steven items if I wanted. I haven't decided yet if I'll take him up on that, but appreciated the thought.

"I almost forgot to give this to you. It's from Bobbi's." Noah is at my side again, this time with a large coffee. Bobbi's coffee is another one of the things I missed most while away.

"Thank you." My voice shakes as I respond and he takes notice, quickly giving my shoulders a squeeze.

"Hey girl, you can do this. It's just us." Noah waves out over the group of teachers. "Hell, if you mess it up, maybe it will give Ms. Neemeyer something to finally talk with Mr. Grube about. I think this is the year they hook up."

I can't help but laugh at our ongoing inside joke. Those two have been in love with each other for years, but it seems only those on the outside can see it. Sometimes you don't always see things clearly when you're so close to them, I suppose. *I can attest to that.*

My principal, Erin, nods at me as she starts her welcome speech that she gives at the start of every year. Sitting down to listen, I know I come after the new hires are introduced and look around to see the big deal English hire that apparently has years of experience when my gaze catches on *him*. *How is Owen here?*

She introduces him and I think I have a mental lapse as images of us together only a week before flash through my mind. Dancing under the stars, him on top of me, and the most amazing sex. I can't believe this. As soon as the vague hallucinations end, I feel my anger start to rise to the surface. *How could he do this?*

All that talk of being "*just* Owen and Poppy" was bullshit and he was using me. He knew who I was all along and my feeling of freedom was only a facade. Well, I will have *a lot* to say to him when I get the chance. Then his eyes meet mine and they're just as warm and rich as they were that night and I can't seem to remember what I was thinking.

"Poppy?" Erin's voice breaks through the haze and I realize everyone is looking at me. Shaking my head, I stand up suddenly.

"Sorry. Hi, everyone. It's great to be back and to see all your familiar faces again. As Erin likely shared, I was gone on personal leave for part of last year and took some of that time to work on my own photography."

I launch into my presentation, but my mind is perseverating on him. How did I let this happen? I was so stuck on feeling free and being *just* Poppy that I let myself get blindsided by a gorgeous man and his amazing smell. Somehow I push through the emotions rising to the surface and finish my presentation.

Hearing the claps of the staff clue me in that I'm done and I go to take my place next to Noah once more. "Um, what is it?" he asks. "You okay?"

"Yeah, can we talk after this is done?" I steal another peek at Owen unwillingly and find him staring back. He nods to me like that's supposed to mean something. Ripping my attention away, I look back down at the coffee I've hardly touched.

My mind is a blur of emotions and I can't seem to land on how I feel. *Did I make a huge mistake?* That night was supposed to be for me. For returning to Honey Cove undamaged and ready to strike out on my own without being tethered to anyone. But now, it feels like I've unwittingly done just that. When Erin lets us know we have a fifteen minute break, I grab Noah's hand and whip him out of the room with me.

"I need to talk to you, *now.*"

CHAPTER SIXTEEN

Owen

Where the hell did she go?

I gave her the "everything is going to be okay" nod. It was so clear that Beth asked me how I knew Poppy. Who knows what phrase I mumbled in reply, but I'm pretty sure it was about my cousin.

And then she just...disappeared. I can't even find Noah.

This is not how I wanted the school year to start out. Now I'm trying to not look desperate as I search for her and simultaneously field questions about why I'm back.

Which is worse: having the only girl you've connected with in a year duck out the first chance she gets when you see her again, or being reminded, again and again, that you aren't the rockstar English teacher with fifteen years of experience? God, between all of this and the shitty coffee, my stomach is in knots. Bobbi's was my go-to this summer and it spoiled me.

Beth lightly touches my elbow to get my attention while leaning in. "You look panicked."

It's a statement, not a question. Once again, she skips any chit-chat and gets right to the point.

"Sorry, I'll fix my face," I say, flashing her a smile.

"Don't apologize," she says gently. "Do you need anything?"

I scan the crowd, hoping to see one particular pair of brown eyes looking back at me. But, again, they're not here. Thinking about

Beth's question, I realize that getting out of the library might calm me down.

"I'm going to get some fresh air before we start our next session, but thank you."

She gives me a smile and nods to the door. "Hop to it."

Knowing that she'd tell me if there was a reason I shouldn't leave the library, I take the most direct route through the crowd and am already breathing easier when I reach the quiet hallway, tossing my empty coffee cup in the compost bin. I push open a side door for the building, and when a light breeze hits my face, I can feel myself begin to calm down.

No one else is here, so I lean against the stucco wall and tip my head up towards the sun. Rough bumps press into my back as I try to make sense of what just happened. It was as if a dozen emotions flitted across her face in less than a second, then they settled on something that looked like betrayal, which was gutting. Still is.

It'll be okay though. I'll simply explain everything to her. We weren't coworkers at the wedding. Hell, I was literally packing up my apartment just days ago.

It's almost time to get back inside, but I look around to make sure no one else is around and pull my wallet out of my pocket, tugging out a small piece of paper, the one thing I was going to take with me to remember those perfect hours we spent in her room. I've read it dozens of times already. But that night was memorable for me too.

Maybe that's all it will be.

What matters now is that we can work together, do our jobs, and put this behind us.

Okay, back-to-school faculty meetings in Honey Cove are officially just as bad as they were in New York. This next session seems to be taking ten hours even though it's not even lunch time, yet. At least it feels that way when Poppy's back is all I've seen of her since the last break. A back that I traced my fingers up and down as she fell asleep in my arms. Something that I should absolutely *not* be thinking about right now.

Beth is making an intricate pattern in her notebook, slowly creating a border around a page with only the date at the top. My notes are a bit scattered, but I feel a strong need to prove myself to everyone in this room, even after learning why I was originally passed over for the position.

Quietly, I pull my water bottle out of my bag. There's no way that awful coffee is worth another caffeine boost. I take a swig and place the bottle under my chair and make a note on the bottom half of the page reminding me to bring something from Bobbi's tomorrow. I briefly consider running over there during our lunch break today, but leaving partway through the first day of meetings might be counter-productive to my plan of proving I'm more than qualified to be here.

Finally, the presentation wraps up and Erin thanks him for his insights, switching over to a new set of slides. Teachers shift in their seats, trying to settle in for more time sitting in these uncomfortable chairs. At least we're not at the elementary school where most of the furniture is for small children.

We'll have some prep time coming up this afternoon, thankfully. I feel so frazzled by this last-minute change that it's like I'm being asked to coach cross-country versus teaching junior and senior English courses.

These are my favorite grades to teach and I'll recognize some of the students who were sophomores last year. I know the staff here, already. Well, most of them.

So why do I feel like I'm student teaching all over again? It's not like I haven't been on-track to get tenure before, I know what the probationary period feels like.

But this isn't New York. This is Honey Cove. It's a small town next to another small town next to another. There aren't fifteen English jobs posted within a thirty-minute commute. There's one.

If this is going to be my home, where I settle and finally really connect with my extended family, then this needs to work.

The stakes are higher here. My gamble on the sub-position getting my foot in the door for a long-term position paid off. Maybe not in the most ideal way, but it still ended with me here. That's what I need to remember. The shock of my hire, or more accurately the seasoned pro's change-of-mind, is going to be old news by this afternoon. I just need to stop reading into every look because they're not looks of sympathy. I hope.

"See you at lunch?" I ask Beth when we're excused.

"For sure," she says. "I'll meet you in the lunchroom in ten minutes."

"That sounds perfect," I say as she heads out. I was thinking of going to my classroom but I don't want to look like I'm being anti-social. God, I hate these little transition periods with everyone in groups.

I look up to find Poppy standing next to Noah who is talking to her, but her gaze is fixed on me. Even from here, I can see the strain she's trying to hide, just like at the wedding.

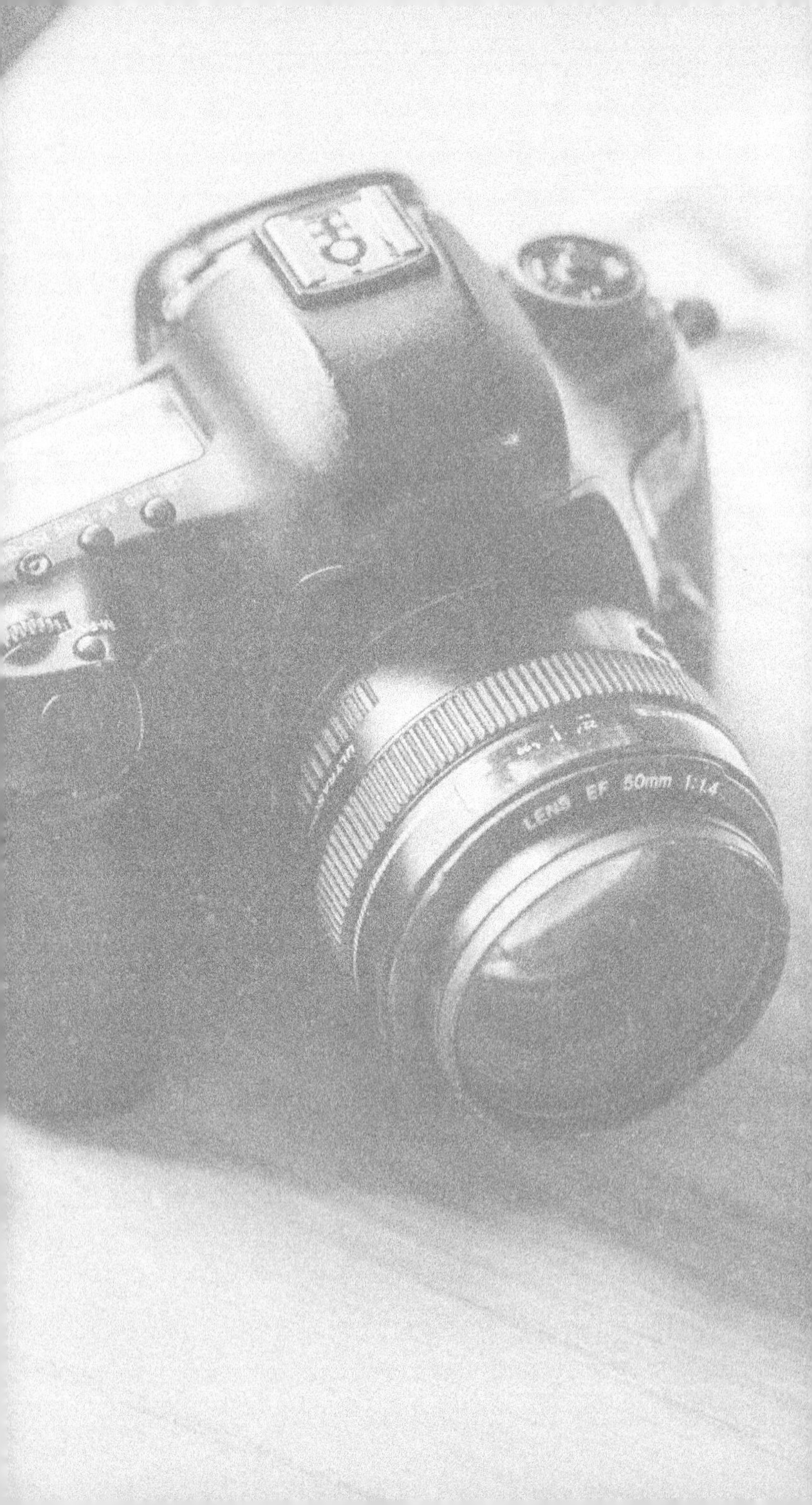
LENS EF 50mm 1:1.4

CHAPTER SEVENTEEN

Poppy

Noah grabs my arm and tugs me towards my classroom as soon as we're dismissed for lunch. "How was your group for that last session? Mr. Johnson wanted to compare tattoos, did you know he got one over break?"

"That's what you want to talk to me about? Mr. Johnson's midlife crisis? We have bigger things to deal with." His eyes narrow at me as we pass through the white doorway into my room as a large smile spreads across his face. The lights are still off and other than dropping off my lunch here this morning, I haven't been here. Flicking on the holiday lights I have hanging throughout the room, we go in, settling by one of the student tables. "We didn't get to finish our chat earlier."

I can hear Noah chiding me over not texting him about my first one night stand or about how Andi's wedding went, but my eyes are still moving around the room. *My* room. The last time I was here I was a completely different person and somehow being here again, I'm seeing the room with new eyes and new ideas for the year start pouring into my head. I *did* miss this.

"If you don't tell me right now who it was with, so help me…" Noah's voice brings me back to the moment. "You said I knew him before we got interrupted during the break?" He motions for me to go on, drumming his fingers on the wooden table behind him, covered in layers of paint and ink from years past.

"I missed you," I say, almost in a whisper before continuing, "I thought he was from out of town, but he's here today, at the training." I'm not sure why I hadn't clued Noah in to everything that had been going on for me the past week. I think it was another piece I wanted to keep to myself and transition back slowly.

His eyes go wide before he steps next to me, wrapping me into a big hug. "I've missed you too. But, you can't mean, Owen? Really?"

"Yes, but he was clearly playing me. I had no idea who he was. Only that he was related somehow to Brandon."

His laugh crackles through the room. "He's a great guy. He'd never do that to you, not on purpose anyway."

"Oh yeah, how would you even know what kind of guy he is?" Grabbing my lunch out of my mini fridge, I pull a stool over to the table he's standing by and sit down to eat. Noah grabs a protein shake—he's always trying to eat cleaner—out of his pack and sits as well.

"He was the sub for Ms. Gibs all spring." *What?* Maybe that's what Erin was saying about him when I was zoned out on remembering how his skin tasted that night. *How could Andi not tell me Brandon's cousin was working here?* I suppose I did tell her I didn't want any Honey Cove information, but this seems like a pretty big thing to not tell me. *How much did I miss?*

"And you and he became..."

"Friends, yes. He jumped right in here, really caring with the kids, and he even volunteered to do the lock-in for the seniors at the end of the year." He's still looking at me as if I've lost a chunk of my memory and can't be trusted. "How did you and he, you know?"

I take my time finishing a chip, unsure of how to respond at first, unsure how much of those moments I want to keep for myself. "He came up to talk with me at the reception and we had this whole thing of being *just* Poppy and Owen." I can see the smirk on Noah's mouth before hearing his laughter again. "It was cute, although it sounds a little silly now."

"I'm sure drunk Poppy found it cute." He takes a long sip of his shake, moving his eyes to look out the window while fishing a bar out of his pack.

"You love drunk Poppy."

"I do. What do you think you're going to do?" he asks.

Thinking for a moment, I run my hand through my hair before answering, "Well I was so angry when I saw him here, but after what you said, I'm wondering if he was somehow as in the dark as I was."

"He only found out a couple days ago that he got the job. He was preparing to move home and probably thought he'd never see you again. Did you like him?"

Feeling Noah's eyes on me, I try to pick my words carefully. This wasn't the carefree night of fun I thought it was. Now things feel suddenly serious. Owen *lives* here now, he has connections and friends. I can tell Noah's mind is already churning with ideas and I don't feel interested in any of that. I made myself a promise and would like to stick to it. This time is about me and finding my own way.

"Well yeah, he was sweet and he got stung by a bee and I helped him. But I'm not looking for anything. I can see where your mind is headed." I point a finger at him, letting him know I am serious.

"You know that also sounds absurd, right?"

"The bee? I am aware."

"Hey, I *am* glad to have you back. I missed you. And *this*."

A sigh brushes past my lips. I missed him too. While I don't love being grilled, it was warranted. Being back this week has been hard and I've, so far, avoided any unnecessarily intrusive conversations about my time away. Talking with Noah is like a breath of fresh air comparatively.

"Me too. Now enough about my sex life, fill me in on what else happened here. I clearly missed a lot."

CHAPTER EIGHTEEN

Owen

Of course she's not at lunch.

And neither is Noah. Damn, I wanted to catch up with him before today, but unpacking my essentials and prepping what I could for my syllabi took over these past few days.

Beth waves me over to her table with Mr. Johnson, which immediately brings me relief at not having to feel lost while looking for her.

"Owen, it's good to have you back," someone from a table with science and math teachers says.

Honestly, I can't pinpoint the voice between the four of them and they're all staring at me expectantly. As best I can, I give them all a nod and say, "Thanks, I'm happy to prove myself this year."

Happy to prove myself? Why the hell did I say that? It's not as if I didn't do a great job last semester. I now know that my interview process went really well and the reason I didn't receive the first offer was because of my experience level. I'm not some newbie fresh out of student teaching.

I'm damn good at what I do.

"Of course, I'd love to see it," Beth replies to something Mr. Johnson said and he's rolling up his sleeve, exposing his forearm.

"It's the view from the top of the mountain this summer," he explains to me.

Sure enough, wrapping completely around his arm, just below his elbow, is a panoramic view of a mountain range.

"He was just telling me about visiting the Tetons for the first time. He and Barbara took a few tours and are hoping to retire there one day." I send Beth a grateful smile at filling me in without getting a long-winded version from the source. My mind keeps trying to fixate on my "lack" of qualifications, which have never bothered me before, and wanting to worry about what Poppy must be thinking. Neither are helping me do my job.

I can't do anything about Poppy until I have a chance to talk to her. I can't do that until I see her. As far as my qualifications go, my experience, even if it's not fifteen years worth, has all been stellar. I'm not some prodigy, but I'm damn good at teaching.

Great, I've already spaced out as Brian points out the different peaks, naming each one and giving a small anecdote about something they saw or learned. By the time he's done, I'm halfway done with my lunch.

"How was your summer, Owen? It was your first one spent in Honey Cove, right?" he asks as he takes a massive bite of his sandwich.

"My family would visit over Christmas, and when I was younger, we'd spend a long weekend here during the summer. So I think it's safe to say this is my first real summer in Honey Cove and I love the change of pace from New York," I say, meaning every word. "This summer was plenty busy though. My cousin who lives in Maple Springs got married, and since we're all living around here, we kind of made the most of it."

"I grew up there, but I haven't met any Wrights in Maple Springs," he chuckles. "You might win an award because I thought I knew everyone in that town."

"My mother's family is here and she took my father's name when they married. My cousin is Brandon Taylor," I explain between bites of my sandwich.

"Oh, the Taylors," he says while clapping his hands once. "Yes, they have two sons, right?"

I nod and he continues into the little ways he's known them which gives Beth and me a chance to finish our lunches without having to talk much more.

Now I know why my colleague picked this table.

The damn printer is jammed again. Sighing, I open up the familiar door and pull out the section where most of the jams happen. This monstrosity has plenty of places where a torn piece of paper can be hiding though, so when I only come across half a sheet, I know I'll be digging around for a bit.

As efficient as this machine is, when it jams, it really makes a mess of things. But I just want to get in and out before everyone will be printing everything later this week so I'm less in my head about feeling unprepared.

"Oh." The word is softly spoken, but I didn't even hear the door open, let alone someone enter.

Poppy.

Her voice is unmistakable with its lilt. I disentangle myself the best I can without making a mess and look up to see her bright brown eyes. Her bangs frame her face and there's a blush starting to appear on her cheeks that remind me of that night.

"I was hoping to see you," I blurt before I second guess myself since she looks decidedly less angry than this morning.

"You were?" A little skepticism replaces her initial surprise.

"I had been passed over for the job. Erin called before the wedding letting me know they were going with someone else and I hadn't even told my parents because I didn't want to take anything away from the wedding." I can hear that I'm rambling but can't do anything about it. "I knew who you were, sort of. You were the art teacher who was on leave and Andi's best friend, but I didn't talk to anyone about your leave."

I didn't talk to anyone about your leave? What the hell is wrong with me? Groaning, I run my hand down my face as she stares at me.

"I would have never let anything happen without you knowing we were coworkers if I had gotten the job sooner. Oh god, not that I 'let' anything happen or normally 'let' something happen with a coworker." *Why am I using air quotes?* "I just...I don't regret anything and am not trying to make it sound that way, but even an English teacher can be terrible with words. We're coworkers now and I'd like us to be friends too."

She bursts out laughing. Her eyes widen in shock after the initial outburst and she claps a hand over her mouth to stifle the sound. I'm immediately reminded of how my mouth stifled very different sounds not so long ago, but those thoughts have to remain memories.

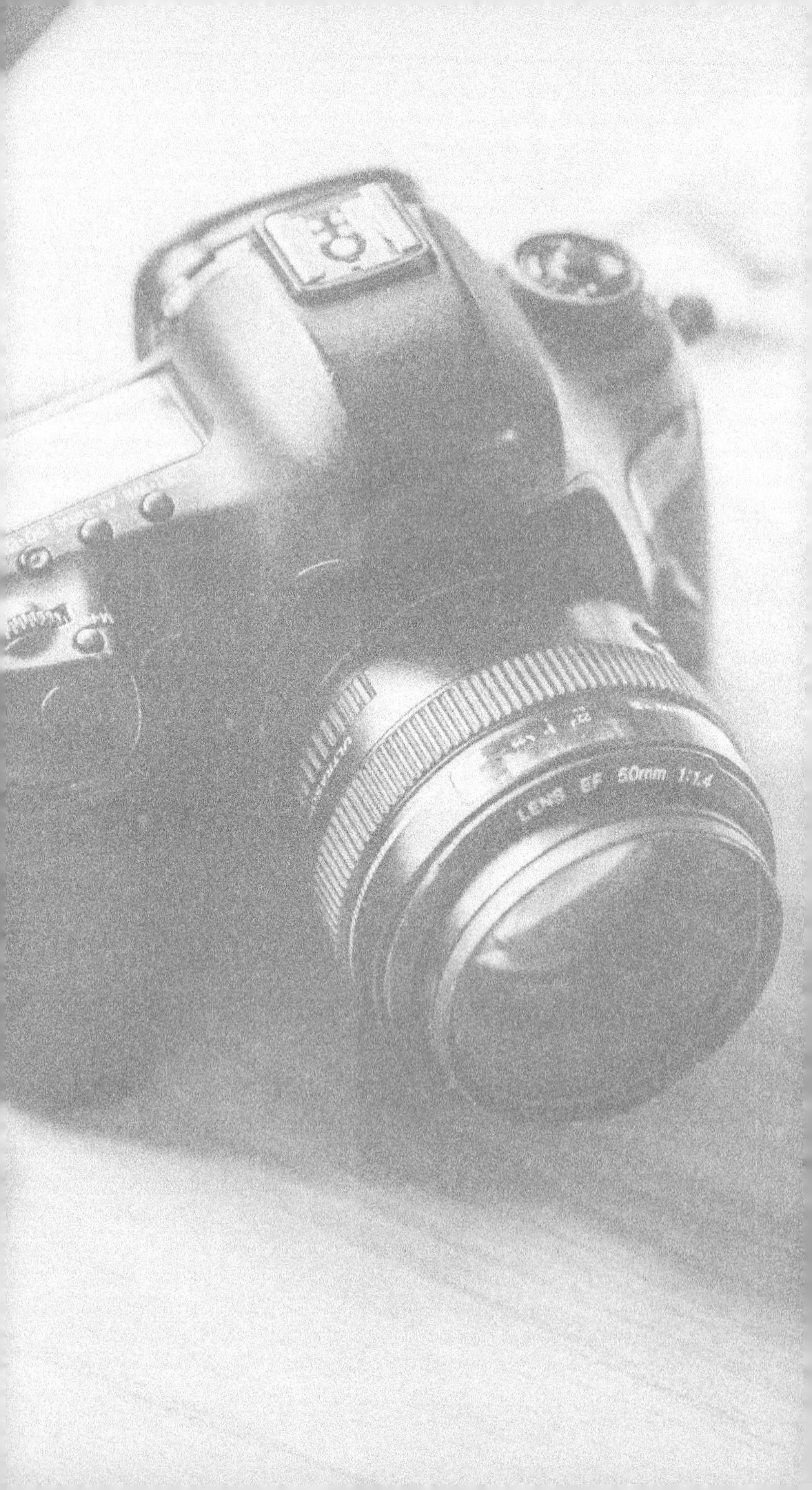
LENS EF 50mm 1:1.4

CHAPTER NINETEEN

Poppy

"I'm sorry," I blurt out, unsure of what just happened to me. "I'm not laughing at you, truly." Another giggle erupts out of me and I glance towards the copy room door, thankful it's closed. Shaking my hands out and fanning myself, I breathe slowly. *Get it together.*

"Are you okay?" he asks.

"I'm fin—" I start to say before catching his eyes and my involuntary laughter starts all over again. This time though, after the laughter starts to die down, I can feel tears sliding down my cheeks. Owen is wrestling with himself trying to figure out what to do, pivoting here and there. He finally decides to hand me a tissue box from one of the tables.

My head slides down the wall as I sink to the ground. My flats squeaking at the sudden movement. "Sorry." The word comes out slowly. It's the only word I can think of right now. Coming back has been a lot to process in and of itself, without throwing a gorgeous and kind teacher into the mix.

My feelings are all over the place and it's felt harder with Andi being on her honeymoon. It almost felt easier when I thought he was a jerk and I could be mad at him for what happened, but after finding out he thought he was leaving town, I can see his side of things too.

He moves to squat down next to me. "That was a lot I just threw at you, huh?"

Feeling more steady and like I can finally get a full breath in, I respond, "No, well it's all been a lot this past week. Andi's wedding, coming back here after everything, you."

He sucks in a breath, holding himself steady by grabbing onto the table next to us. The copy machine makes a grunting noise and I notice for the first time all the doors are open. *Must have jammed again.* "I *am* sorry about all this. Do you think we can work together? I mean, I suppose we won't see a lot of each other anyways, seeing as we're from different departments and all. And—"

"Shhh," I interject, holding a finger towards my lips. He tracks the movement for a moment before pushing himself up and looking at the copy machine. His nervous rambling is adorable, but it is also overwhelming me in this moment.

"Right, well."

"Yes, I think we can be coworkers just fine," I try to assure him. Pulling myself up to stand next to him, he turns and our arms brush as he grabs his papers. I'm shocked that his touch still burns my skin and makes me a little dizzy. "I did tell Noah, but it sounds like you guys are already friends." Pausing, I add, "I'm not sure we can be friends, though, it might be weird, don't you think?"

I don't want to hurt his feelings but I also just truly don't know if I can be friends with him after what happened between us. The night was amazing with all the things we did together and the way he made me feel. You don't just turn that off and forget about it because you have to work together. At least I can't.

"Yeah, we are. Not *us* being weird. Yes, Noah and I are friends."

My hands find my pockets, rummaging for something to occupy themselves with. The tears feel like they might start up again any time and his presence isn't helping anything. "Okay, I don't remember why I was in here, but I'm sure I'll see you at the next session."

I make my grand exit. *Totally alluring, Poppy, totally alluring.*

Heading back to the library for the afternoon sessions, I find myself a spot next to Libby, the building secretary. She's usually busy running the PowerPoints, or taking notes, or something for Erin. But she and I got closer last year with all the paperwork and things I had to get in order at the last minute for my unexpected leave. It's nice to catch up with her before diving into more planning for the school year.

"Welcome back," Erin calls out. "For this afternoon's session, we'll be working in groups on our goals related to increased literacy. Each group will have a member of our English team on it to help guide our discussions and help us know what data to track." She moves to the side so we can see the large lists of our groups broken down on the side. Looking over the list, I see that Owen and I are in the same group.

My heart skips a beat. Didn't we already have our awkward encounter for the year? *Can't that be enough, universe?*

Erin lays out the goals for our groups, when we'll be checking in, etc. before letting us know we will meet with our groups for an hour today and a few hours each day this week.

That's a lot of time to be "coworkers" with Owen. Grabbing a mug of cold coffee from the carafe, I find myself wishing for another drink from Bobbi's. Moving to the table where our group is assigned to meet, I see that almost everyone has already arrived. Only one open chair remains. Next to him.

He gives me that damned smile that could melt my heart into a million pieces before pulling the chair out for me. Is that weird? Did someone else see that and think it was weird?

Chill out, Poppy. You're acting like a high schooler yourself. Act normal.

CHAPTER TWENTY

Owen

God she smells good.

It's a great distraction right now because I'm reeling a little from Ms. Neemeyer. She came right up to me and I know she meant well, but she said, "It would have been so much easier if you had fifteen years of experience, then we could have just hired you right away. But I'm so happy we got you in the end. You're a real asset to this school."

Then she sat next to me and didn't stop talking to me until the table was almost full. I didn't even realize that the only open chair for Poppy to take was to my right.

Breathing in, my nose fills with the smell of poppies. I shake my head to get my mind off of our time in her room and focus on the calm and connection I felt with her under the stars. Maybe we'll get there again. Not connecting quite as *thoroughly* as that wedding night, but connections like that don't come around every day and not having her as a friend, just a friend, would be a shame.

All eyes are on me and it's time to get this show on the road.

"Okay," I say to the group while splitting the stack of papers in two, handing half to Ms. Neemeyer on my left and the other half to Poppy on my right. She just finished digging through a large brown bag and setting a spiral-bound book with "Lessons" written in sweeping letters on the cover. "The English department has broken down the main objectives and examples of the various literacy types."

I quickly find my groove and launch into the introduction I helped prepare late last semester. My eyes catch on the doodles Poppy makes on the margins of the paper even while she's taking notes. Vines with bundles of flowers snake around her page. Every now and then, someone asks a question and before I know it, we're in the brainstorming section.

The group is busy scribbling away and occasionally chatting quietly to someone next to them. At one point, she flips a page over and her arm brushes against mine. Sparks light up where her skin makes contact.

She mumbles an apology, but her cheeks get redder by the moment as she tries to look busy. But I can see that she's not really writing anything new. She's only adding serifs to what she already has and making it look like she's still busy and focused.

I bite back a smile. Seems I'm not the only one feeling *something*.

But I quickly sober. Dating a coworker—no matter the sparks, connection, and ease—is no way to start the school year. Especially when that person just wants to be coworkers.

"Here's to finishing the first day of back-to-school meetings in one piece," Noah says, clinking the neck of his bottle against mine as we sit in his backyard.

"And to you for forcing me out of my classroom at five," I reply.

"You've been too in your head today," he says after taking a swig.

"The transition felt a little like whiplash since I was already packing to move back to New York."

"Yeah, but you looked more uncertain today than you did your first day as a long-term sub in a town where you basically didn't know anyone."

I shift in my lawn chair and sigh because he's right.

"It seemed like I was the top candidate and I felt confident about the job. Then Erin called." He nods as I continue the narrative that's been playing through my head the last week. "I pushed that aside and enjoyed my cousin's wedding, letting it be my last hurrah in Honey Cove."

I pause, my mind taking me back to that dance under the stars.

"And then you got *another* call from Erin," he prompts, his eyebrows raised.

"Yeah, and then I got the call, which was great, of course. But..." I trail off.

"But it bothers you that someone else got the offer before you?" he ventures.

"Pretty much." As much as I'd like to confide in him about my history with Poppy, even though she mentioned he knows, I can't very well tell a coworker about it. Even if I trust the guy to not say a word to anyone. "I'm just feeling unmoored right now, but I'll find my confidence again."

"You know you're the best person for the job, right?"

Hoping I don't throw her under the bus, I say, "Beth might have explained the push from the district for new hires having more experience. I just felt like it was right and that things were falling into place to settle here for the long haul."

I take a sip of my beer, the cool crisp bubbles travel down my throat, and look around us at the view of the cove itself. His house is a bit up a hill and I can see half the town here, even my building and the boardwalk.

"It's a good thing Erin caught you before your things were fully packed," Noah says, trying to help me see all of this as a glass half full.

"You're right. I could have been back in the city prepping for another school year there." My last school in the city currently has two openings in the English department and the head of the department asked me to apply a few times. Since I left for Honey Cove, I'm no longer seen as an internal candidate, but I left on good terms.

I didn't want a backup job, which definitely looks stupid in hindsight. I wanted this small town.

Still do.

"I'm usually right," Noah says, smiling.

"So I'm learning," I reply, taking another drink and then picking at the corner of the label on my bottle. "Let's talk about something other than this last week, I need to get out of this funk."

"I have a date this weekend," he tells me nonchalantly, raising the bottle to his lips.

"And?" It's my turn to prompt him.

"And," he adds a pause for dramatic effect, "I matched with them online."

"Do I need to pry details out of you?" I growl good-naturedly.

"It's new territory for us to talk about dates," he says.

"How many dates have you been on since I moved here?"

"Zero," he replies without missing a beat.

"Dry spell?" I guess.

"Nah." He waves a hand dismissively. "I think I've moved through the eligible dating pool, which is one of the downsides of living in a small town. What about you?"

"No actual dates, either."

"Well, you'll have to let me know when your dry spell is over."

"I didn't say I was having a dry spell." That's as close as I will get to telling him about Poppy.

"So the opposite of a dry spell would be..."

"Nothing I'm experiencing." I laugh, imagining what he must have thought I meant. "Actually, I don't know the last time I went this long without trying to date. It wasn't necessarily easier in New York, but the big city offered a small likelihood you'll run into an ex, I suppose."

"Was that an issue before?"

"No," I reply. "Breakups are never a fun thing to go through, but things ended on respectful terms in the past. I guess I'm lucky with that."

"I'd say." He lets out a rueful chuckle.

"I'm sensing a story here." I settle in, ready for anything. "But we can focus on your upcoming date, if you'd rather."

"My upcoming date is with a vet who lives about twenty minutes away. I'll let you know how that goes, but the banter has been top-notch so far." He tries, and fails, to hide a smile.

"That sounds promising."

"I hope so," he says and then his smile fades. "But not all of my relationships ended amicably, unfortunately. So there's always a worry that things will go south again, I guess."

"But you're looking forward to this one?" I ask, wanting to bring back his hopefulness.

"I guess I am," he says, half of his smile returning.

While I feel happy for him, there's a little pang in my heart, realizing that for the first time in the past year, I actually am interested in dating someone. But she is off limits now that we work together.

Maybe I can live vicariously through Noah's dating life until I feel that with someone else.

However rare it is.

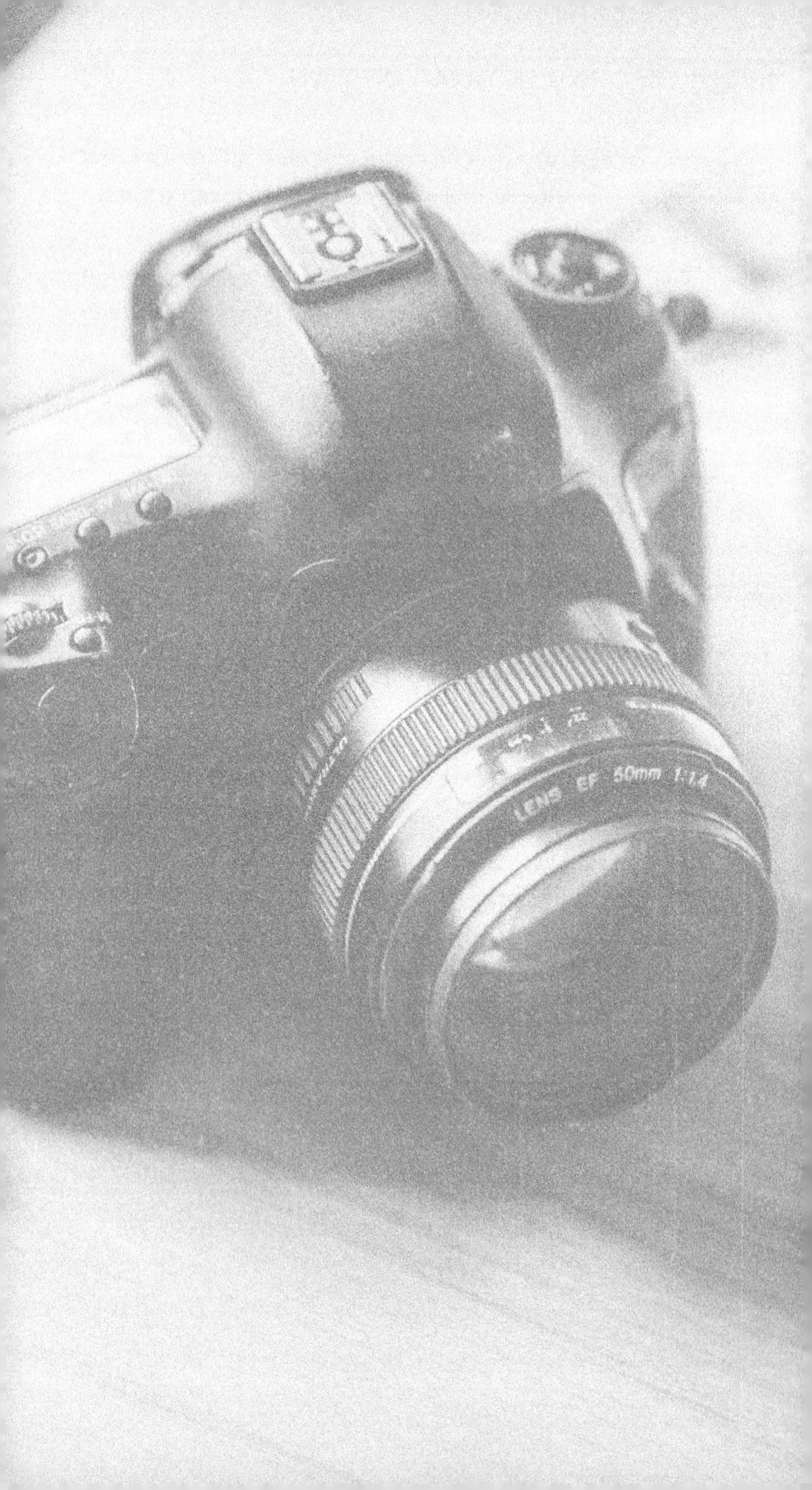
LENS EF 50mm 1:1.4

CHAPTER TWENTY-ONE

Poppy

"Oh my God, Mom," I yell out, jumping out of my car to help her as she struggles on my doorstep. With the amount of boxes she's carrying—and the large bouquet of dried flowers from Andi's wedding sitting on top—I cannot even see her face. As she peers at me around the boxes, I can see a slight furrow of her brow which tells me she has something she wants to talk about, and it isn't all about just bringing me presents and things for my classroom.

As I start taking the boxes from her, she breathlessly says, "Thank you, sweetie. I had so many things to bring you. Your dad just ran down to the bakery and will be back soon."

My heart warms at the idea of them both visiting, *I've missed our talks.*

"So it's a double team," I say jokingly under my breath as the scent of salt water on the air and this surprise visit from my parents reminds me I'm truly back in Honey Cove.

"What's that dear?" My mom turns back from unlocking my front door, and I can see the way the light shows her gray highlights and makes the stone in her long necklace sparkle. Both of my parents are getting older, but neither have let it slow them down. They're still busy in the community, helping with fundraisers and getting together with their friends. It's nice, something I hope for one day and one of the reasons I love this town so much.

"Nothing." I smile at her and reach out over the packages to give her a tight hug. "It's nice to see you, Mom." With the door now open, she flicks on the lights and we carry all of the boxes inside, setting them down on the coffee table in the living room.. Her eyes do a quick glance around the room and I remember she hasn't been back here since I've come home.

"The house looks good. Are those some new curtains?"

In the week since being home, I'd made a few changes. I want to make the space mine again and help it feel a little different. Nothing big, just *different*. The new floral curtains and boho-esque pillows are my way to stake some claim on this new chapter in my life.

I walk into the kitchen and grab some wineglasses, and I answer her. "Yeah, do you like them? I just wanted a bit of a change." Her eyes travel down to her hands, drumming them on my white countertop, then look over at where I have some of the prints from my trip laid out on the dining table. "Would you like red or white?" Wine with my mom has been our tradition since I was old enough, it's our "ladies' night" thing and for when we need to talk, which I am getting all the signals we do. I'm sure my dad heading to the bakery was also a covert way to give us some time alone.

"I do. Very pretty. And sure, red please." She pauses before adding, "The pillows are nice, too, they add a punch of color to the room." *A punch of color?* My mom must be really worried to be using phrases like that, usually she just sticks to "that's nice." My father is the decorator between them and is where I get my artistic side.

After pouring our glasses, we move over to the couch. She sinks into the gray, overstuffed fabric and moves one of the new throw pillows out of the way, picking mindlessly at the string details as I hand her the glass.

"Okay, Mom, out with it."

"What?"

"You clearly have something you'd like to talk about, so let's talk."
I think I know where this is going.

"Well, okay. I've just been worried about you after everything with Steven, and then at the wedding when you needed to leave early. Your father and I just want to make sure you're actually alright or if you need anything." She pauses, gauging my reaction before plowing on. "You know, your uncle John has dealt with a lot of depression and I just want to make sure you're alright. We're here to help however you need, if you want to talk with someone, we can figure that out together."

I can't help the smile that spreads across my face. While I haven't wanted anyone else prying into my life, my parents have always shown how much they care about me, and this is no exception. Their questions have never felt like burdens. Moving over to sit next to her, I lean over to give her a big hug. "Thank you, Mom, I appreciate you caring about me so much. I have been talking with a therapist virtually while I was traveling and am planning to keep doing it."

"Oh, I didn't know, that's great, sweetie. Is it helping?" Her eyes are wide, and she looks at me in anticipation.

"Yeah, I think it will take some time, but I like her and it seems to be a good fit. And while I wouldn't say I feel depressed, it has been a hard transition. Traveling was good for me, but I'm happy to be back now. I still missed Honey Cove."

"That's good to hear. Well, we love you so much and want you to know you can always talk with us."

"I know, Mom, thanks." After a brief pause, the sound of a car pulling up tells us that my dad has arrived. "I hope Dad got something good. Want to look at some of the prints from my trip?"

"I'd love that."

I reach for my work bag next to the couch and pull out the ones I developed this week. Handing her the pile, she starts flipping through them as I move to sit next to her on the couch. "Hi, my lovely ladies," my dad calls as he pushes open the front door, holding a box from the bakery in one hand.

"Hi, Dad."

"Come look at Poppy's pictures from the trip, they're gorgeous," my mom calls out to him, taking a sip from her wineglass and holding up the print.

"This one is looking out at Lake Ontario from the city. I loved the view so much." It was one of my favorite parts because it made it feel like home, staring out over the lake felt so similar to the view here in Honey Cove.

"I like this one." My dad still holds the bakery box, but has nestled himself next to my mom on the couch, looking over the pictures laid out on the coffee table.

"That one is from the CN Tower, it's the tallest building there. They even have tours where you can pay to walk on the edge, but I did not do that," I laugh, remembering the few minutes I pondered actually trying it.

My parents stay for a while, eating and enjoying looking over my photos and hearing about the trip. It feels so good to have this time with them and to feel comfortable in my space again. I *did* miss this.

CHAPTER TWENTY-TWO

Owen

Eight, nine, and ten.

My biceps start to shake just a little as I lower myself and drop to the ground, looking at the view of the cove. Damn, it's gorgeous even during storms, but today, the water looks as smooth as glass, reflecting every white cloud in the morning sky. I'm pretty lucky to have this view even standing in the doorway to my bedroom. Since I don't really have company over besides my cousins, I've taken to leaving the bar up.

Might be a sign that I'm not putting myself out there enough because I only shut the door to keep Samson out if someone is staying over. He'll meow at the door for a couple of minutes, and then curls up on his ridiculously plush cat bed I keep on a low shelf with stacked books filling the rest of the space, exactly as he prefers it.

For some reason, he gives every date I bring home the stink-eye. Well, not in the last year since I haven't brought anyone home, but the seven years prior, I suppose. He never has an issue with friends and relatives. Just people that might take his favorite pillow.

I roll out my mat and start my series of crunches, adjusting my position and dropping my knees to the right and then to the left as I go.

As if he knew I was just thinking about him, Samson trots towards me, making the little grunting noise he reserves for when he's approaching me to get a pet.

"One second, fur ball."

Per usual, he doesn't listen. Instead, he somehow manages to rub his face against mine each time I lower my shoulders to the mat. It's only another rep until I'm flat on my back and he's curled up on my chest, purring loudly.

"I woke up extra early and only had a few more reps left, and you still demand my attention?"

I scratch behind his ears and his eyes close, making him look like a big black and gray puffball. It seems like he's forgiven me for packing up again. He only peed on my shoes once, and those were sandals, a few days ago. His big cat tree in the sun room was in a box for probably two hours, but that was enough to get some serious cattitude from him for a few days.

"Okay buddy," I say, curling him into my arms and rolling up, then standing. "Time for me to get ready for work and for your breakfast."

Samson might be a longhair cat, but he's actually pretty petite and loves to sit on my shoulder while I get his food. Sure enough, when I open the cupboard above the sink, his claws grip my T-shirt, now covered in fur, and he maneuvers his way to my left shoulder. He squeaks out a little meow and the purring resumes as he tracks the bright label of the can.

The pop of the lid has him swishing his tail against my back. His bowl is in the drying rack and he leans forward, partially blocking my view as I scoop the food. He knows we're not done, yet, but I still have to nudge him back while I open the oil mixture for his joints from the counter.

"I know, I know," I tell him. "Almost done."

Once there are five drops distributed, I squat so he doesn't hurt his hips from jumping down, and put his dish on his mat next to his water. He eats like a gremlin, making so much noise between the purring and smacking of his mouth.

I shake my head, pet his back, and hit the shower, noting that I'm on my normal schedule even with waking up early. Apparently, I have some stress I'm working through because my workouts are getting longer.

Twenty minutes later, two breakfast bars in hand, and I'm out the door, leaving my cat sunning in his treehouse. I check my watch and see that I have enough time to grab coffee on the way as planned.

I'm not ready to resign myself to school coffee before the students even start. Thankfully, Bobbi's is just a few doors down the boardwalk from my building, so it's conveniently on the way to where I park.

Definitely one of the downsides of my place: street-only parking. But my views are better than anything I could have even imagined in the city. The sounds of the boardwalk in the morning feel so normal now. Even the seagulls.

The smell of the salty water is quickly replaced by brewing coffee the moment I open the door.

And there she is. Poppy. Looking gorgeous even as she rifles through her bag for something. Her bangs hide her face, but she looks a little flustered from here. I approach her, not that I could avoid her if I want my coffee since she's at the back of the short line, and clear my throat. Her search stops immediately and she looks up at me, capturing all of my attention for a moment.

"As your coworker..." I keep my tone light, but not mocking so she doesn't think I'm mad about her boundary to just be coworkers. I'll respect that, even if I'd like to be friends, or more than that. "I wanted to offer assistance to my fellow teacher, but I have no idea how to be helpful."

Her shoulders relax and she lets out a breath. "I think I left my planner back at my house and I was hoping, if I ransacked my purse, it might magically show up...even though I know I never put it in here."

I think for a moment. "Blue cover with colorful pages?"

"You know what my planner looks like?" she asks, one eyebrow raised.

"You were sitting next to me during the literacy introduction and you had it out," I counter. Her gaze softens, becoming less skeptical in a mini stare down. She lets out an adorable huff, slinging her purse onto her shoulder as we move closer to the register. "You had a big brown bag that you seemed to stuff things into throughout the day."

"Ugh, of course," she says, rubbing her forehead. "I had my presentation material with me yesterday. The bag is in my trunk."

"Problem solved?" I ask.

"Problem solved. Thank you, Mr. Wright."

"Owen, please," I say. "My students call me Mr. Wright, but my coworkers call me Owen."

Her lips purse and I fight to hold her gaze so it doesn't look like I'd like to kiss her. "Alright, Owen."

Oh god, I'm back to our night together. Hearing her say my first name at work might not have been my best idea after all.

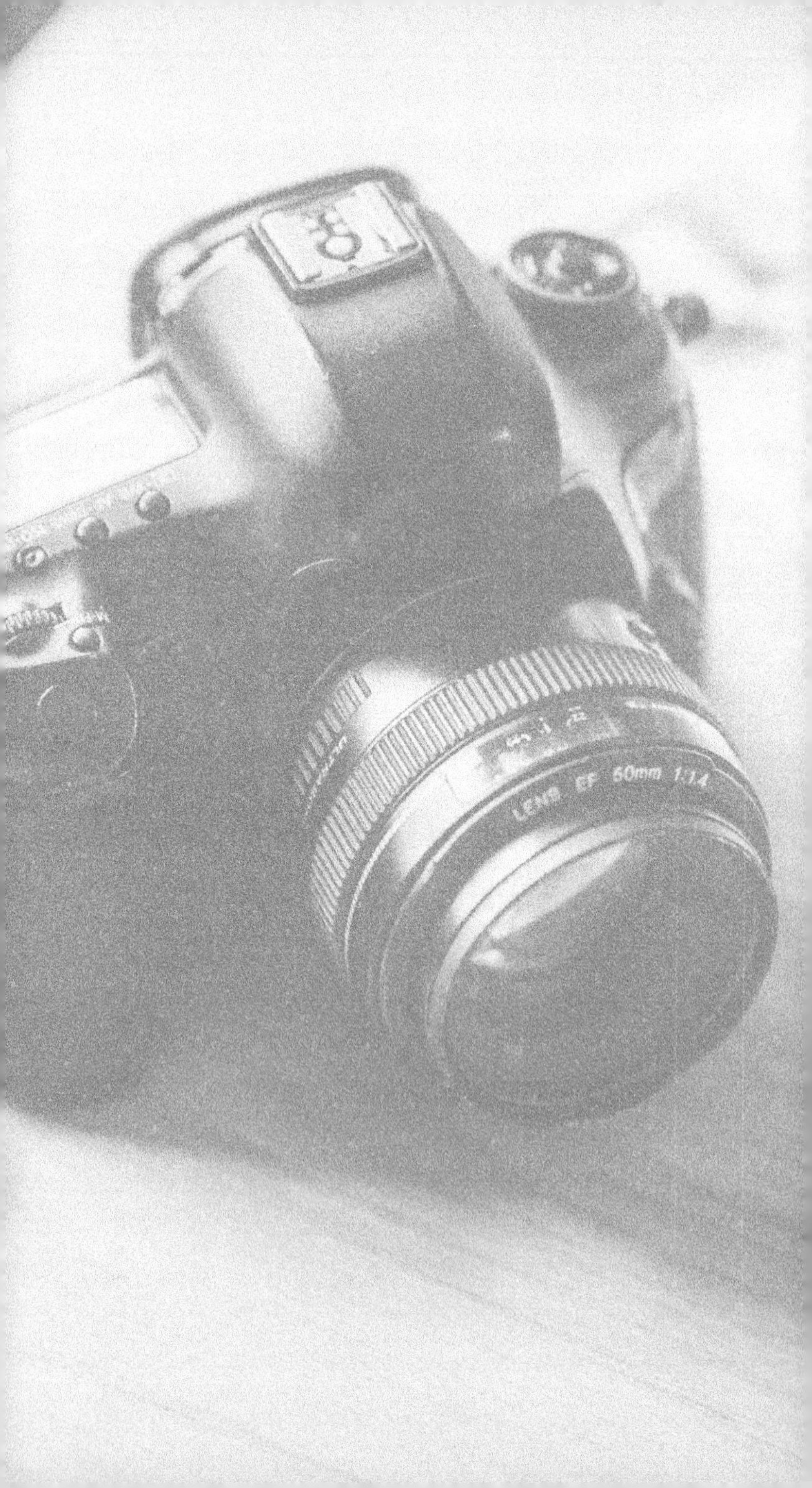
LENS EF 50mm 1:1.4

CHAPTER TWENTY-THREE

Poppy

Oh. My. God. I can't get any more awkward. First, I cried in front of him in the printer room and here I am frantically looking for my planner while in line for coffee. *He* had to remind me where I had put it and I'm not sure if I've ever felt so incredibly embarrassed. Even my sweaty bangs clung to my forehead in shame.

It's not that I want to impress him. It's just how many people have to work with their one-night-stand after the fact? My life has become a list of things I didn't plan for or think through and I'm not sure how to work my way around this one. *God, his arms look great in that shirt and he's always so sweet when I talk to him.*

"So, how are you liking Honey Cove?" I ask, then realize he's lived here for a while now. "I mean, how are you liking it now that it's more permanent?"

He looks at me as if he's unsure how to answer. "I didn't mean it has to be permanent, I'm not assuming it's permanent..."

"I've wanted to live closer to my cousins and in a smaller town for a while. I'm from New York, so it couldn't get more different. But I love it so far." He smiles and looks at me again. I'm a deer in the headlights taking in his gorgeous eyes and that warmth in my core starts up again, just like at Andi's wedding.

"That's good," I say, running my hands down my skirt and straightening my sweater. I thought this sweater would be nice for cooler fall days, but it suddenly feels too hot and itchy standing here next to him. Somehow my mind is racing to think of a reply while simultaneously being a blank canvas. Luckily, it's my turn to order and I step up to the counter, hitting my hip on the counter in the process. Grunting, I turn back and see that Owen's eyes are still on me. *Great, that'll bruise later.* "I'll take a large latte with french vanilla, please. Extra shot. And a large dark roast." *I should bring Noah something.* After paying, I move to the other side of the counter, shuffling my bag from shoulder to shoulder. Nothing feels quite right and I can't seem to get comfortable, continuing to bounce back and forth between stealing glances at Owen and the woman making my coffee.

Honey Cove is the best. You couldn't have chosen a nicer small town. So many options of things to say, but I can't seem to verbalize any of them.

Things are too out of sorts with him here and I'm not sure what to do to get my head in a better place. I don't regret sleeping with him; it was amazing. But, trying to work with him and find some sense of normalcy after all that has happened feels really hard. He stands near me at the pick up counter, repeatedly starting to say something, but neither of us seems to know what to do with ourselves.

He's impossibly handsome, champagne or not. And I can't quite seem to get my system to calm down around him. My drink is called at the same time as his. I reach forward to grab it and our hands brush as we both take hold of our cups. "Eh, sorry about that," I offer, ignoring the tingles racing up my arm.

"Oh, it's no problem." He holds the door open for me as we exit Bobbi's. "Wait, do you live around here?"

I'm caught off guard by his question, but I suppose it's fair seeing as we're both on foot and there are no cars parked around the boardwalk this early. "Yes, I live a couple streets down on Willow."

"This is me." Owen points up at the apartment building a few doors down from Bobbi's. *Shit. He lives close to me too.* I'm not sure this could get any more ridiculous.

"Nice, we'll have to meet for coffee sometime." I gesture towards the shop and wish I could die right there. "Not like a date, or anything, just like a work thing..." trailing off, I stand in disbelief at my own words. *A date? A date!*

He just smiles at me again, giving me a look as if he's figured me out. "I'll see you at work, Poppy." My body shivers at how he says my name, but I just wave and turn to walk back towards home. *I'm sure I'll just see him again in half an hour at school.* Do I want to see him?

What are you doing?

After recounting today's episode of *Can Poppy Embarrass Herself Any More*, Noah laughs and asks what I've been questioning myself since I first saw Owen here at the high school: "Are you interested in him? It certainly seems like he gets you all bothered." Another laugh.

"I can't be. We're coworkers and I am still trying to figure things out after Steven. That really messed with me, obviously, and I'm not sure I can do that again." Nervously fluffing my hair with one hand, I forcibly turn my attention to taking stock of the state of my supplies after last semester. It will be so good to have the kids back, and I'm sure it will work wonders to distract my brain from everything about my ex and worrying about when I'll finally run into him again.

"But what if you end up blissfully happy? Wouldn't all the heartache, tears, and struggle be worth it then?" Noah stands in front of me, gently looking at me, questioning my resolve.

"I haven't decided yet." Averting my gaze from his piercing stare, I continue my route of setting up the tables. "And who is to say that it would even be with Owen?"

"Who is to say that it isn't? He's a great guy, truly. I know the timing is off, but promise me you'll at least think about it?"

Sighing, I drop the last paintbrushes I've been counting before meeting his eyes, "I'll try to."

Erin's voice calls out over the intercoms, signaling the imminent start of our next session and my deliverance from having to talk or think about this for any longer.

CHAPTER TWENTY-FOUR

Owen

First day of school

Bracing myself for the smell of stale coffee, I open the door to the faculty lounge. But that's not the scent that hits my nose when I enter. It's floral and I recognize it right away as poppies. Sure enough, Poppy is here. Her back is to me and she's looking through packages wrapped in cellophane with little name tags on the counter, while holding her own cup from Bobbi's.

God, she looks amazing. A sleeveless silk-like shirt that ties at her neck shows off her toned arms. I'm already curious what it would feel like to wrap my arms around her when movement catches my attention. Noah's standing off to the side of the lounge, the only other person here, thankfully, with an amused expression on his face.

"Having a good morning, Owen?" His smirk tells me that I was staring.

It's like I stop thinking when I smell her perfume, hear her voice, or, lord help me, see her. Something about *her* holds my entire attention without giving me a chance to remind myself that we're coworkers. Period.

"We'll see, I finished off my coffee from Bobbi's, so I'm going to cross my fingers that water will be enough to make it through today," I say, feeling heat rise on my cheeks with my embarrassment as I walk to the printer.

The mischief in Noah's eye doesn't help that embarrassment lessen. Maybe I'm just reading into things and he's not acting like someone who's just waiting for two people to get together.

"Are you ready for today?" he asks, possibly having pity on me.

"Almost, I just need my updated syllabus," I explain, unlocking my job from the queue. "I was approved to test out a few options for audiobooks for more students, so I needed to make a few edits."

"That's awesome," he says, patting me on the back.

"Thanks, it felt like a big win for the students."

"Congratulations," Poppy says, picking up what looks like banana bread in the little package, drawing our attention as the printer churns out copies of my syllabus.

"What are you two doing Thursday?" he asks after a moment. "I feel like a happy hour will be in order after school."

I glance between the two. She pauses, so I decide to dive in since a happy hour sounds pretty ideal. "I'm in. Where would you like to go?"

"I'd be up for Calico Cafe, they have great specials on Thursdays." I'm surprised to hear her suggestion since we haven't talked again about being coworkers *and* friends. Or even coworkers who attend the same happy hour. "We could call ahead and reserve a table next to the boardwalk."

"Consider it done," he says enthusiastically as he strides to the door. "I have to run, but look for your bag, Owen, the parent association asked me to deliver some treats and they're delicious."

Just like that, as I'm gathering up my papers, it's only Poppy and me in the lounge.

"Are you feeling excited for the students to be in the building?" Damn, I need to work on my small talk.

She unlocks something from the printing queue while I staple my packets. "I think I am. The first day always feels a little frantic, but it'll be nice to hop into things with the students again. What about you?"

"Similar. Well, I'll be nervous for another few minutes. But once the students are here, I tend to get out of my head about everything I *might* be forgetting and just teach. Plus, my first class has a bunch of students I taught when I first got here in the spring, so I'm definitely excited to get to work with them again."

I take a breath, feeling like I'm going to really ramble if I don't slow down.

"I understand what you mean. I know you've already taught here, of course, but I remember what it's like to be the new teacher. Noah and I were hired the same year, actually," she says.

The door opens and most of the math department enters. They greet us and return to their chat as a handful of papers are spit out of the printer, claiming her attention.

As the other teachers get coffee from the carafe, I'm once again grateful I've been starting my day early enough to get Bobbi's before work. Even if Samson has been a little cranky when I begin my workout.

I count my packets once more, thanks to my first-day jitters, and then grab the little package with my name on it from the counter. The wrapper crinkles as I inspect the contents, grinning.

Definitely banana bread.

"Have a great day, everyone." I give them a wave with my banana bread and leave the lounge to the sound of echoed sentiments. A sense of calm washes over me while I walk the quiet halls knowing they're about to be filled with the sounds of lockers shutting and students talking.

I'm here, in the small town I hoped to land in, about to start off the school year teaching the courses I love, and making plans to meet up with two friends for happy hour in a few days.

Of course, now is the time that the little part of my brain that likes to doubt things every now and then reminds me of something: very recently, I was packing to move back to New York. This almost wasn't my reality.

When I get back to my room, I pull out my phone to make sure everything is on silent only to see I have a handful of new messages in a group chat.

Brandon:
> My wife and I want to say we hope you kick some serious ass today, Owen!

James:
> That sounds like the wrong encouragement. He's not engaging in combat.

Brandon:
> Correction: Kick some metaphorical ass today, Owen!

Graham:
> I'm on the other side of town from James and I swear I heard him sigh in exasperation just now...

James:
> I do not sigh in exasperation.

James:
> Brandon, go back to your honeymoon.

James:
> Owen, have a good one.

Brandon:
> My wife is currently ordering us breakfast.

Brandon:

> (did you see how I called Andi my wife twice today already?)

Graham:

> By the time Owen catches up, the first day of school will be over if Andi doesn't take Brandon's phone.

A huge grin spreads across my face. This is what I wanted. To be closer to my cousins. To be teaching what I love. To be making this my home.

> I fully intend to kick some major metaphorical ass, thanks.

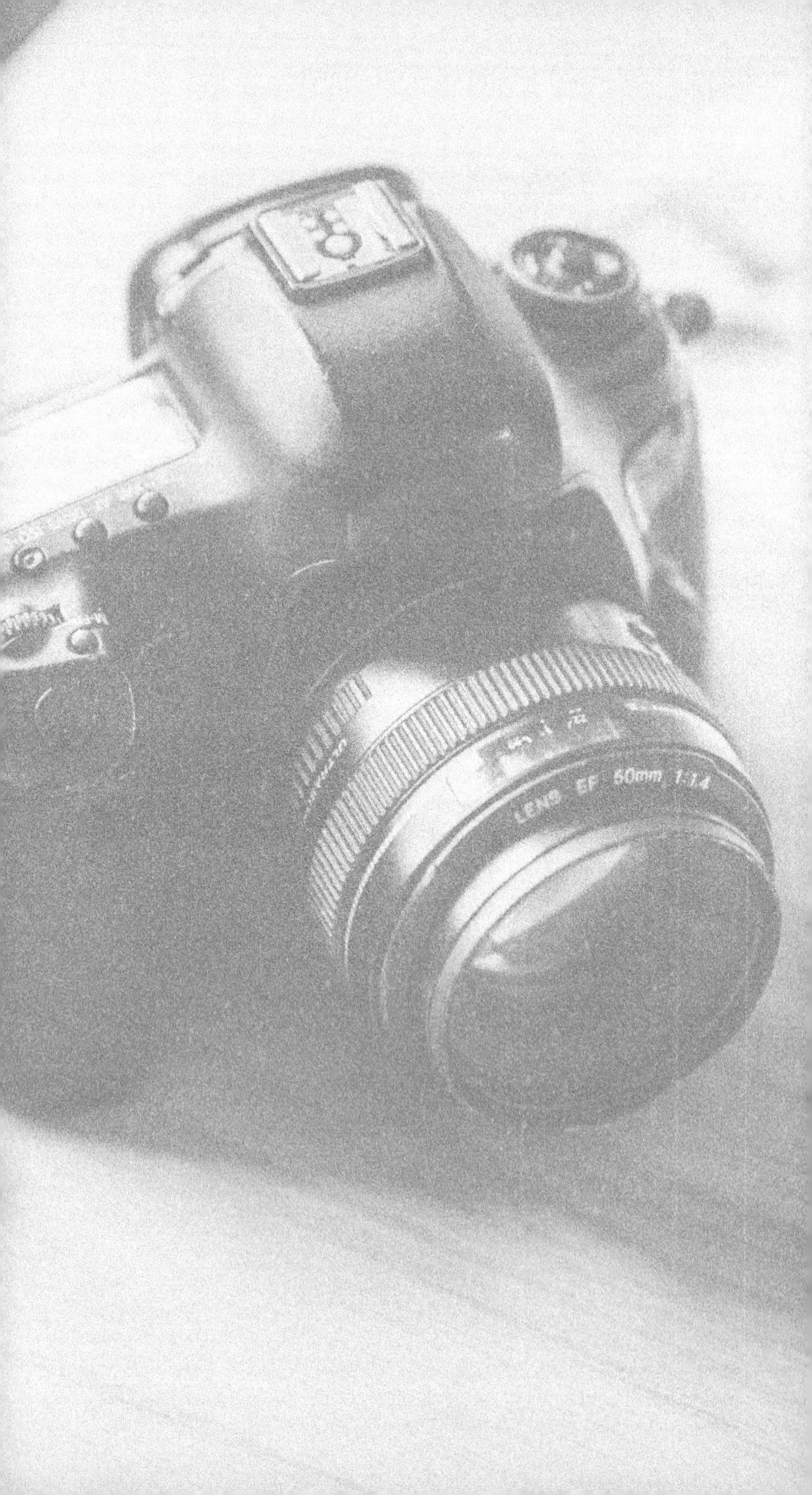
LENS EF 50mm 1:1.4

CHAPTER TWENTY-FIVE

Poppy

Before I can even take a full breath, I'm on my last period of the first day. Everything has felt like a whirlwind, from hearing about everyone's summers to meeting incoming freshmen, all nervously fidgeting with their backpacks and hoping to not be called on. It's been a better first day than I had imagined.

And it all started with agreeing to a happy hour with Owen. I haven't changed my mind, but I do feel like I need to relax my boundary of being *only* coworkers. He and Noah have been friends and that means something. Noah doesn't make friends with everyone and is a serious judge of character. I think it has something to do with being a school counselor and understanding feelings and all that. He just seems to *know and I trust his judgment.*

Even before things went south in my last relationship, Noah was subtly questioning me about it. He knew. I've been lucky that the subject hasn't come up with any students so far today. The town is only so big and even the high schoolers usually seem to know every detail of my life here. As I see Cicely Thompson enter my class for seventh period, I know I've spoken too soon.

Cicely's mom is friends with my mom and knows everything that goes on in town. She'd followed Steven's and my relationship closely, even taking to asking when he and I would be getting married regularly. Hearing her shrill shriek of joy as she sees me only confirms her enthusiasm is still intact.

"Hi, Cicely. How was your summer?" I beam at her, truly happy to see her again. There is something special about students you've had since they were freshmen. Watching them grow into seniors and seeing what they decide to do after graduation never ceases to do something for my heart, especially those with such a love for art like her.

"Ms. Edwards! I heard you were back and didn't believe it." She pulls me into a forceful hug before holding out a stack of Starbursts. "Do you want one?"

"No thanks, how are you? Ready for senior year?"

"I'm good. Glad summer is over though, my mom and her stupid boyfriend took me to some cabin in Canada for all of our break. I didn't see anyone." Her lips pout as she throws her backpack down onto the nearest table. I don't have assigned seats other than for freshman classes, and I think letting students choose their seats allows them to breathe a little more and have some say over something in an already heavily dictated day. She slouches down into the seat, relaxing in a way I could only dream of.

"That sounds hard, I know you like seeing your friends. I'm glad to see you again. And in Drawing 2, no less. It looks like you finally were able to fit it into your schedule." Smiling at her, I grab my notebook off my desk and quickly glance over the syllabus for the class.

"Yeah, Noah helped me work it out. It's the only art class I haven't taken yet." Cicely is a very talented artist and could do something more with it someday if she wanted to. She definitely has the skills to be a professional, even without further training. Knowing her, she spent almost all of her time at that cabin sketching and painting everything around her.

Before I can get another word in, Cicely leans in close to me, "I'm so sorry about what happened with Steven. Everyone is saying what a jerk he was and how much we hate him for it. He's being stupid, you're a catch, Ms. Edwards. Everyone says so."

I'm too stunned to speak. Not only is she bringing him up in my class, but she's saying that other students are talking about the entire situation. I knew it had the potential to turn into this given our small community, but no matter how much I hate him for what happened, I wouldn't want people turning on him either.

Physically, I take a step back, needing some distance from her and this topic. "Oh, he was just doing what he thought was best. Don't be too hard on him. It's been hard, for sure, but I'm moving on and it will be okay." Willing myself to believe those words, my attention is snagged by all the other students filing into the class and the two-minute warning bell.

"What he thought was best? No, he was being a selfish jerk. You don't have to be nice to him, Ms. Edwards."

I pull on my best smile, feigning that everything is okay and that I'm not secretly sweating through my silk blouse on the first day. I'm a seasoned teacher and this type of personal comment shouldn't throw me off like it does. *But*, it is Steven, and aside from my best friend's wedding I haven't had to navigate the fallout from what happened with him yet.

"It's time to take your seat, we're about to get started." Heart racing, I'm thankful for the bell. At least we can focus on the syllabus, and drawing for the time being. My mind can't help but wonder how many other students and their parents are talking about what happened to *poor Ms. Edwards*, and everything else that goes with it.

Cicely reluctantly sits down, but not before saying, "We've got your back, Ms. Edwards."

CHAPTER TWENTY-SIX

Owen

Samson is needier than usual when I get home from school today, probably because now that the students are back, my work days are longer. He's always wanting more attention when summer is officially over, so I'm not surprised he's rubbing against my legs the moment I enter the apartment.

"Hey buddy," I tell him, being careful that he's clear of the door when I close it. "Did you meow at the seagulls while I was gone or did the big birds scare you, again?"

He's purring so intensely that I can feel the vibrations while he covers the bottom of my pant legs with his fur. He'll get more comfortable with the change in schedule after another few weeks, but for now, I just have to be careful where I step when I first get home. At least until I get rid of my bag and put my keys away so I can pick him up.

Sure enough, as I toss my keyring on the table in the entryway, he's standing on his hind legs and pawing at my pocket, waiting for me to grab him. The moment he's in my arms, he rubs his face against mine and then settles in the crook of my arm to get scratches behind his ears.

"Alright, Samson," I say, fully aware I'm talking to my cat. "I need some help with what to change into for happy hour. I don't want to wear this button down shirt because, well, I look like a teacher and I don't need to remind Poppy we work together. So you're going to pick something out for me so I can stop overthinking this. Sound good?"

He purrs in response, blissfully unaware I'm leaving again. I lay out two options on my bed and then set him in the middle.

"Okay, feel free to roll on whichever one I shouldn't wear." As expected, when I reach my hand out to pet him, Samson makes one tight circle, tips his head down and flops onto his back for some belly rubs right on one of the outfits I laid out. I reward him with some extra pets and then change into a fitted navy tee and faded jeans that don't have hair on them.

"Even though perfectly clean clothes are now covered in your fur, this was a surprisingly efficient way to figure out an outfit," I say as he lays there with his paws in the air. "I'm sure you'll be napping again soon, but let's get you some exercise before I leave, okay?"

I hear his paws hit the wood floor of my bedroom as I walk to the sunroom, grabbing one of his favorite ribbons and playing with him for a few minutes until he decides he's done and hops into his cat tree to soak up the late-afternoon sun.

That view.

Damn, I don't think I'll ever get tired of it. The lighthouse sits at the end of a long jetty on the north of the town where the rocks reach farther out into the water. The waves are calm today, too, with just a soft breeze blowing the salty ocean air.

"Owen?" Noah's voice pulls me out of my thoughts as he takes a seat.

"Sorry, I was just soaking this in. It's so different from New York," I say.

"No worries, I get it. Why do you think I bought my house on the hill?"

"You do have some spectacular views."

"Absolutely." He takes a drink from one of the ice waters on our table. "Are things feeling more long-term for you or are you missing the Big Apple too much?"

"Honestly, besides my parents and some friends, of course, I don't miss much, which feels slightly terrible since I was happy there. I don't know how to describe it, but it was all fine." I pause, trying to find the words.

"It just wasn't *it*," he finishes.

I nod just as we hear "What wasn't *it*?" come from a few feet away.

"Poppy, you made it," he says, raising his arms in celebration as she sits down.

"You're making it sound like I'm late," she says, playfully rolling her eyes at him. "I'm actually five minutes early."

"I guess none of us wanted to miss out on happy hour," I say.

"Not one minute," Noah agrees.

Our server stops by to take our orders and we motion for Noah to start.

"Did I hear you have a new lager in, Kelly?" he asks, looking over the drink menu. I try to commit that name to memory for the future just like any time I hear someone's name around here.

"We do, it's just not on tap," she says.

"I'll take that and can we get a large order of nachos with plates for all three of us?"

"I'll have an IPA, please, Kelly," I say. "Whatever you have on tap."

"You'll have to remind me of your name, I know I served you during lunch a little while back," she says, scrunching up her nose in thought.

"I'm Owen."

"Owen, I'll do my best to remember."

I give Kelly a smile, saying her name over in my head a few more times while she asks Poppy what she'd like.

"I'll have your champagne greyhound, please."

I've never heard of a greyhound without vodka. I guess I should read their whole drink selection one day.

"Sounds good, I'll have your drinks out in a minute," Kelly says, gathering the happy hour menus. "Poppy, it's really good to have you home, again."

I notice Poppy's almost-imperceptible wince but she immediately smiles.

"Thank you, it's good to be back."

Our server gives her a smile and walks back into the cafe, and we all take a drink from our waters.

"So, what did I miss?" she asks us and then turns to Noah. "You said something just wasn't *it*. Did I miss talking about your date because I was only five minutes early?"

He chuckles at the alarm in her expression. "No, you did not. We can hash out that disaster after we get our drinks. We were talking about New York and Honey Cove and how you can be happy enough somewhere, but truly want to be someplace else."

"Oh," she says, blinking in surprise. "I guess I didn't know you missed New York."

"See, that's just it. There are some people I miss, but *this*," I say gesturing to the cove itself and the town, "is what I've been wanting."

She looks thoughtfully at me, her lips pursing just a little and her head tilting to the side. "You don't miss everything New York has to offer?"

"Especially with my parents living there, I'll still visit regularly, but I've always wanted to be out of the city." Sometimes it sounds ridiculous saying these things, especially not wanting to stay in New York since so many people dream of living there.

"And you have your cousins here, I remember you said you wanted to be closer to them," she says.

"Honestly, before I moved here, you probably knew just as much, if not more, about Brandon than I did with how little we got to visit each other." I look at both of them. "Noah and I have talked about how he chose Honey Cove, but Poppy, what brought you back?"

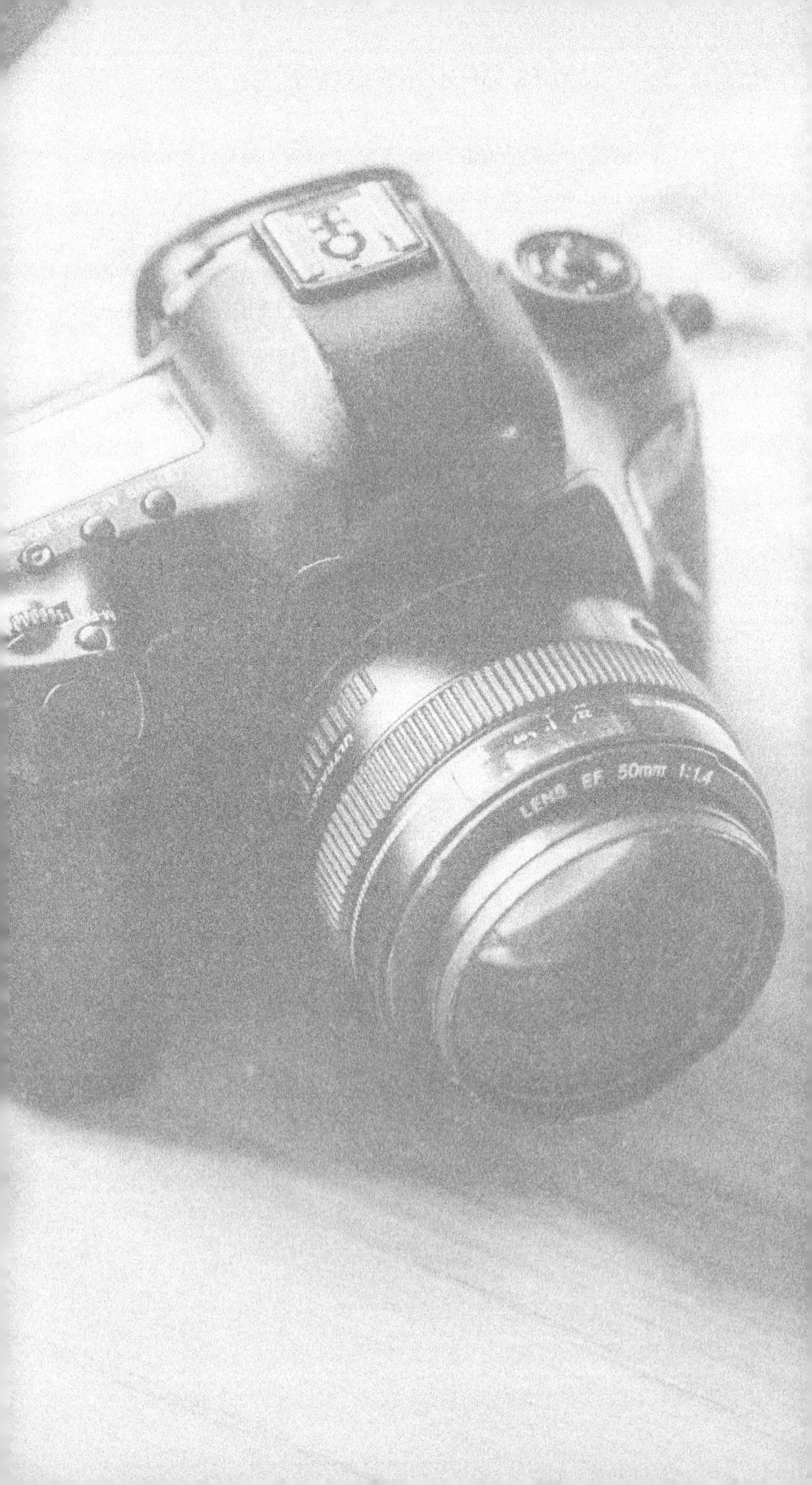
LENS EF 50mm 1:1.4

CHAPTER TWENTY-SEVEN

Poppy

So far this happy hour has been me constantly reminding myself that Owen and I can be friends, but sitting here, looking into the endless depths of his eyes, the small dimple on his left cheek, and the way his shoulders slope to meet his muscled arms, I'm not so sure. It's not even the fact that I'm clearly attracted to him, he's also kind, thoughtful, incredibly smart, and seems to notice the little things that no one else would. And I like that.

Kelly returns with our drinks. Handing me the cool glass, I see Noah take a long sip of his beer before both guys are looking at me. Physically pushing myself back from the table, "How did I end up here?" I look between the two of them, knowing I wasn't quite listening, but making my best guess. My thoughts were...elsewhere.

"Yeah, Poppy. Tell us your history," Noah croons as he sucks down more of his beer.

"I was born here in Honey Cove and have lived here all my life. I've always been here. So after I graduated, it was just a given that I'd come back." Shrugging, I sip from my glass, the sweet bubbles sliding down my throat effortlessly. "I love Honey Cove and I'm not sure I'd ever want to live anywhere else." I also came back because of Steven. That waiting atomic bomb I felt inexplicably tied to at the time.

Noah, sensing my nerves and what I've left unspoken chimes in, "I grew up here too, two years ahead of Poppy in school. You should have seen the school pictures. Next time you're over, I'll pull out the yearbooks."

A deep laugh rumbles out of Owen, "I'd like that." His smile fills his face and I can feel the warmth radiating off of him. *How does he do that?*

"I have nothing to hide," I say, raising an eyebrow and returning his full fledged smirk, ignoring the pounding of my heart filling my ears.

"I left for college, counseled at another school, but then moved back home to help my family after my mom got sick." He signals to Kelly that he'd like another beer before continuing, "She's doing well now, but I was glad to be home to help. And I've stayed ever since."

Noah notices that Owen and I are still watching one another and shifts the conversation. "Hey, Owen, do you exercise?"

My head whips around to glare at Noah, I can tell where this is going and it's clear he's ignoring all my requests and personal decisions to keep things platonic between Owen and me. I know I said I'd think about things, but this feels forward and meddlesome, even for Noah.

"I do. It's mostly body weight exercises, push-ups, pull-ups, those types of things. You?"

Before my mind can run off down that trail of imagination, Noah is answering. "Poppy and I run. You'd never believe how gorgeous the boardwalk looks in the morning sunshine. Especially this time of year."

I nod, confirming that we're runners to Owen before the inevitable comes out of Noah's mouth. "You should go running with us sometime." He excitedly looks between us, hopeful for the outcome he's been planning.

"Oh, sure. I could try that, I think." Owen eyes his beer nervously.

"Saturday. Meet in front of Bobbi's at six." Noah says it so decidedly, neither Owen or I argues with him at all. He drinks his freshly delivered beer and smiles to himself. *He's so proud.* I give his shin a much deserved kick under the table. Although in my flats, the effect is less than I'd hoped for.

"Anyways," I chime in, "How is your classroom feeling with students in it now? Anything you need?" I still cannot fathom how the year has already begun. I've blinked and the school year is in full swing. I haven't completely found my new routine here at home, but I am getting there, slowly figuring out what I want my day to day life to look like.

"Yeah, it's still coming along," he answers, slowly nursing his beer. "It doesn't feel as cozy as Noah's office or yours with the lights, but I'm trying to make it my own."

"We've had years to work on our spaces. If you want to borrow anything, let me know. I have too much stuff as it is. If you need an extra bookshelf or anything, just email out to the "all staff" email and I'm sure someone has one they're trying to get rid of."

"That would be great actually, I *do* need another bookshelf. And I need to run to the bathroom, I'll be right back." Owen has barely left the table before I'm hitting Noah in the arm.

"Why did you do that? You are unbelievable."

He smiles back at me, knowingly. "What? I thought it would be fun. Owen is a nice guy Poppy, even if nothing happens, we should be friends with him."

"*Even if nothing happens*. Something *already* happened, you jerk." Pointing a finger at him, I down the last of my cocktail before saying, "Promise me, no more meddling."

He holds up his hands in protest or submission, which I can't tell. "Fine, fine. No more meddling."

Somehow, I don't believe him.

CHAPTER TWENTY-EIGHT

Owen

Desks and tables are pushed back into their clusters after a lively discussion on our reading from last night. Some of the students are still debating the motives of the characters which makes me smile.

I hear one of the cross-country captains mention their upcoming meet and my mind goes right back to happy hour and what I agreed to this weekend.

Running.

I can run. In theory.

Well, I work out every morning, so I should be able to go for a run with two friends. Even if they are two friends who regularly run.

Right?

Maybe they don't run that far, or that often. There's a chance I might be less winded than either of them. Okay, that's highly unlikely since they run together and I...well I simply don't.

Why the hell did I do this to myself?

"A reminder that you don't have assigned reading this weekend, so I highly recommend dedicating some time towards choosing your region and time period. You need to have those to me by mid-week for planning out your final project this semester," I say over the chatter.

"Mr. Wright?" Cicely comes up to me, bag packed and everything while everyone else is gathering their things.

"What can I do for you?"

"I have a counseling appointment for going over my college applications, during my free period, but since we're done, I was wondering if I could pop by Ms. Edwards's room to grab a few samples of my art."

Poppy's smile as she talked with students earlier this week distracts me for a split second, remembering the genuine enthusiasm and care so obvious to anyone observing.

"Of course," I tell her, clearing my throat. "Let me know how the applications go. I know I didn't go to an art program and can't draw a stick figure, but I've been able to listen to some incredible artists at galleries in New York talk about their journeys."

Her mouth drops open a little in surprise. "I'm so jealous."

"We'll have to chat about your favorite artists sometime. In fact, maybe your final project in this class could be related to the intersection of the literature and art worlds somewhere."

"I will research that this weekend, absolutely," she says.

"Go get those samples so you're not late for your appointment, but we can talk on Monday."

Cicely nods and walk-runs out of the room.

A few students have other questions, but mostly, everyone is enjoying a few minutes to relax while I see what's new in my inbox and reply to a few emails.

"Alright, that's it for today. Have a great weekend, class, and I'll see you all next week."

With that, my classroom empties out, students telling me to have a good weekend too. These seniors have been a great group so far. Of course, there are a few who try to push back, but things have gone smoother than I planned, which is phenomenal.

My mind drifts back to the potentially terrible decision I made last night and I pull out my phone.

> *What can I do between now and tomorrow morning so I can keep up with two runners for an undisclosed distance?*

NOT FROM OUT OF TOWN

Graham:
> Why are you texting so early?

> It's 10am.

Graham:
> I had the closing shift at the bar last night, which means this is early.

James:
> The bars close at 10pm.

Graham:
> ...

> I feel like there's more to this story, cousin.

Graham:
> Says the guy who wants to learn how to run in one day.

> I know how to run, I just want to be able to do it for more than 30 seconds before I get winded. I haven't gone for a run since college.

James:
> Owen, drink water all day today and eat a bunch of carbs tonight. Isn't that what people do?

Graham:
> I don't think that will magically give Owen endurance.

Brandon:

What aren't you sharing, G?

Brandon:

And why is anyone running?

A friend invited me to go tomorrow morning. I said yes, and might be in over my head.

Brandon:

It'll be fine!

James:

You didn't get the route?

It was a happy hour, we didn't go into details other than where and when to meet.

Brandon:

I'm sure it'll be casual.

Oh, and the sunrise is supposed to be lovely on the boardwalk.

James:

The boardwalk in Honey Cove is long…

I'm all too aware right now of that fact.

Brandon:

Boardwalk running is the best!

Have you gone?

NOT FROM OUT OF TOWN

Brandon:
> Nope! But it sounds great and you'll be fine.

James:
> Aren't you taking off soon?

> Did you get the morning flight home?

Brandon:
> My wife was able to get our tickets switched to first class, she's quite crafty.

> That's amazing!

James:
> Is it just me or is Graham typing us the next great American novel?

> Maybe he fell asleep while in the middle of typing?

James:
> No, your text woke him up.

Graham:
> I had a date.

Brandon:
> WHAT?

James:
> With who?

> *Did your date have piercing blue eyes?*

James:

> *Wait, you've been typing forever, and that's all we get?*

Graham:

> *It was after I got home and they might have been woken up by Owen's text...*

Graham:

> *Yes, to Owen's question.*

Brandon:

> *They stayed over?*

James:

> *Of course they did. Graham said his phone woke them up.*

> *So the dance went well?*

Brandon:

> *What dance?*

Graham:

> *About that run you're going on tomorrow morning, Owen...*

James:

> *I vote for beers Saturday night at Maple's Moonshine. This conversation is getting ridiculous.*

> **I can make it.**

Graham:
> **I'm in.**

Brandon:
> **My wife is coming back to her first class seat, so I'm putting my phone away.**

Brandon:
> **But I'll see you all Saturday night.**

James:
> **I'll pick you up at noon. I'm tracking your flight.**

Well, if tomorrow morning goes terribly, then at least I can look forward to a night with my cousins.

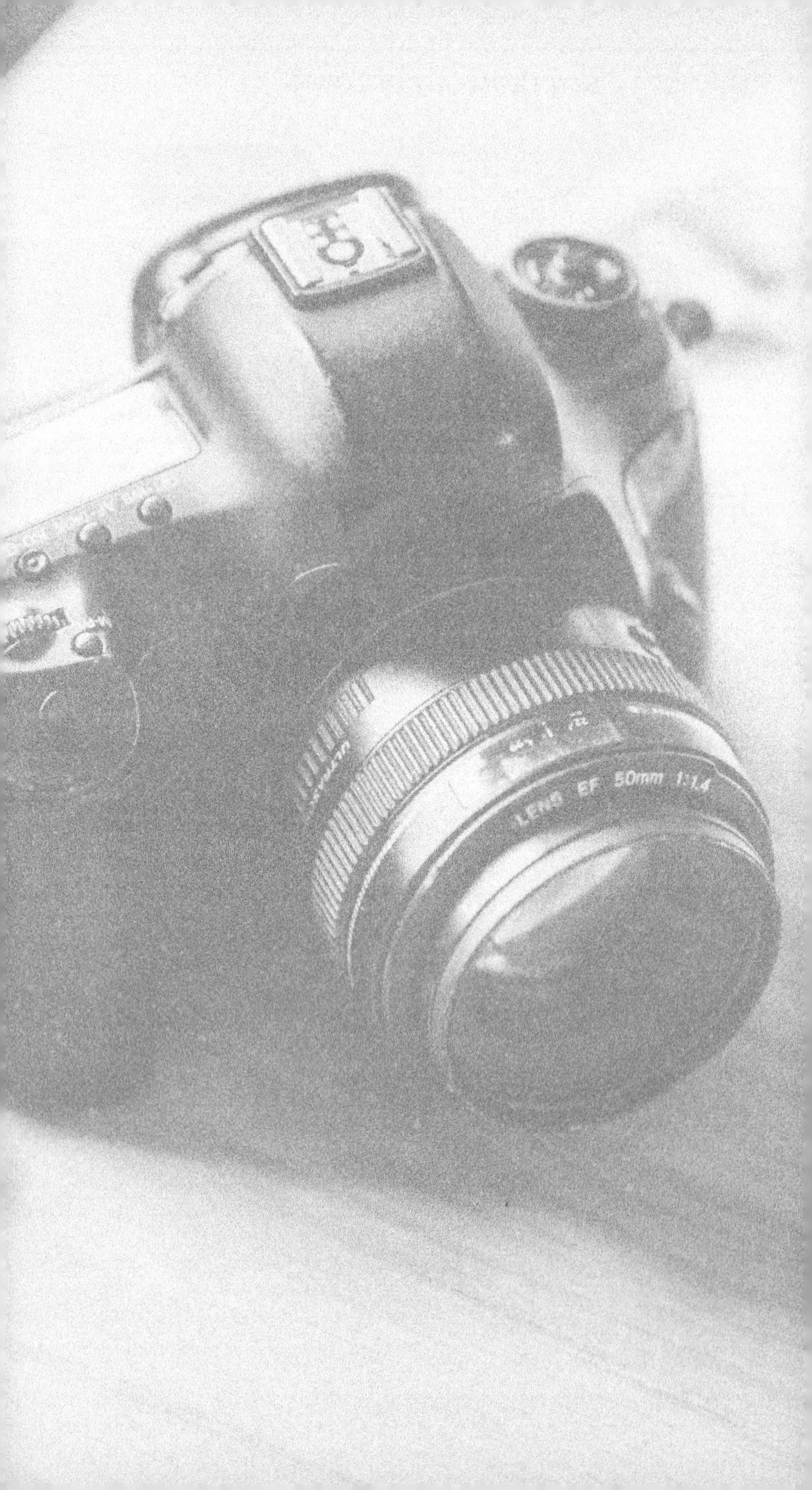
LENS EF 50mm 1:1.4

CHAPTER TWENTY-NINE

Poppy

Hearing the close of a car door, I'm out of my house in a flash. I'm sure my neighbors are less than enthused at the sudden, somewhat piercing squealing escaping my mouth, but at the moment I don't care. This is the longest Andi and I have gone without talking and while it was only a couple of weeks and we've texted a few times, it felt like ages. Even during my recent time away we talked or texted almost every day.

Andi's out of the car, running towards me, and also squealing. Wrapping my arms around her in a giant hug, it feels like I'm finally home. Between the whirlwind of her wedding, school starting, and everything else, it hasn't really felt like the Honey Cove I remembered with her gone. "It's so good to see you and god, you're so tan!"

"Laying on a beach for a few weeks will do that." Andi looks at me, fluffing her hair and dabbing at her eyes, "It's so good to be home and to have you back."

"Honeymoon not all it was cracked up to be?" I joke.

"No, *that* was wonderful, but you are here now and it's perfect." Her eyes glaze over a little more before she points and adds, exasperated, "Now get in the fucking car before I lose it and we're stuck here sobbing all night."

Walking around to the other side of the car, I hear Ms. Nelson from next door shout, "I thought a cat was out here dying, but it's just you two."

"Sorry, Ms. Nelson," we both call out in unison.

Giggling, we slide into our seats and Andi backs out, heading to our favorite restaurant one town over for margaritas and tacos.

"Now tell me all about the Keys. Was the resort nice?"

"It was lovely. Everyone was so helpful and there really is something to upgrading for newlyweds. First-class seats on the plane, a larger suite at the resort, and free drinks. I wish it was like that every time I traveled."

The rest of the ride over, Andi recounts every drink they had, telling me about the amazing bars at the resort, how beautiful everything was, long days on the beach, and how sweet Brandon was the entire time. Before we know it, we've arrived at the restaurant and are being seated.

"Here you go ladies, I'll be right back with some chips and salsa. Can I get any drinks started for you two?"

"We'll both have margaritas, please. On the rocks, no flavoring."

The waiter nods, and then it's just me and Andi again. Smiling, I think back to how much I was waiting for this while in Toronto and thinking through all my nightmare scenarios of coming back. It hasn't been nearly as bad as I thought it would be and I haven't even had a run-in with my ex yet, which has been fantastic.

"So," Andi starts, "You've heard all about my riveting days of sunshine and massages at the spa. How has it been for you being home?"

"It's been okay," I pause, thinking through everything that has happened so far. "Hard in some ways, but I redecorated my house."

"You redecorated?" Andi bites into a chip while her eyebrows raise. "Like, curtains and shit?"

"Yes. You don't think I can decorate?"

"You just haven't really, before. But I love that you did!"

I've gone back and forth on how to tell her about what else I've been up to and finally decided to just dive in head first.

"I may have hooked up with someone." Looking down at the chips and my napkin, I wait for it to register.

"What?" She chokes on the chip she was chewing and a few sips of water and deep breaths later, I continue.

"The night of your wedding..."

"Tell. Me. Everything."

I launch into my story of Owen, dancing under the stars, believing this to be my clean break from Steven before starting anew, only to find Owen at my presentation the first day back. Andi gasps and is both shocked and excited during the story, but doesn't add too much commentary, which is odd for her. After I finish, I wait for her to berate me with more questions or yell at me for my poor judgment, but it doesn't come. She's just eating chips.

"Okay, out with it," I prod her.

"Out with what?" She looks at me sheepishly.

"All your opinions. You must have thoughts on this."

"Well, Owen is honestly a stand-up guy. I haven't seen or heard of him dating anyone since moving here. I've only heard positive things about him from Brandon, aside from questionable taste in movies the one night he had the guys over, and I don't have anything to dish."

My eyes narrow at her.

"Seriously, you are an adult and if you're interested in him, why not give it a shot?"

Is this really her opinion? I waited all that time to ask her about this, prepared myself for her inevitable blow up, only for her to encourage me.

"Because this wasn't the plan. I wanted to come back and enjoy my small, quiet life on my own. Maybe get a cat."

"And that is fine if that's what you want to do, sweetie, but it seems like you are fighting this for some reason and I'm not entirely sure why. He's a good guy; it sounds like you like him."

Nodding, I glance across the dining room, unsure of what to say. *Would I say I like him? He's gorgeous. And kind.* I like that you know what you're getting from him. He wears his emotions clearly on the outside, from his yelling about that stupid bee to his babbling in the copy room, you know where you stand with him and he doesn't seem afraid to be himself.

"Listen, Steven was a shit guy. Seriously. I will be the first to say it. But, don't let him ruin you for any sort of relationship again. He doesn't deserve that power over you, so don't give it to him." Andi reaches out and puts her hand over mine where I've been absentmindedly twirling a napkin over and over again.

My eyes unexpectedly water at her words. And of course, that's exactly when the waiter is back with the margaritas. "Here we are, ladies!"

"Keep 'em coming," Andi calls after him.

CHAPTER THIRTY

Owen

Not starting the day with my workout routine feels odd. Especially since I'm up early and in athletic shorts and a tee.

I try not to pace outside my building, but I think if I stretch out any more than I already have, I'll somehow manage to injure myself from overdoing it. Instead, I unzip my pocket and pull out my phone. The group text is already open, but Noah hasn't opened the texts Poppy and I sent saying we were heading outside. To be fair, our messages were sent less than one minute ago.

It wasn't surprising to see a message from Noah pop up with an unknown number with a local area code. So now, I have Poppy's number. Which would normally be tempting for me to message outside of the group chat, but until I can be near her without momentarily forgetting how to function, I think I should steer clear of texting my coworker.

Once I'm done double-checking there's nothing new, I hear slowing footsteps on the wooden planks that make up the boardwalk.

When I turn, I'm not surprised to see that Poppy's jogging here, slowing to a walk before she gets to me. God she looks incredible this early in the morning. Honestly, she could have major bedhead and throw on a burlap sack and I'd still think she was stunning.

"Good morning," I say, noticing that she isn't very winded even though she lives a ways down the boardwalk. I'm never going to keep up on this run. As she nears, I see the smallest hint of sweat on her forehead, but that's it.

"Good morning is right." She gives me a smile that lights up her whole face. "I haven't gone running this early in the morning since I returned home and it feels amazing."

She looks out over the cove, and after a moment of watching her, I shift my gaze so I'm watching the sun rise over the water. There are pinks and oranges throughout the sky, and it brings a sense of peacefulness that can be felt deep in your bones.

"How often do you and Noah do sunrise runs?" I'm already kicking myself for not just letting this lovely moment continue.

"Maybe once a month when we're really motivated. We do try to get several runs in with each other every month. But, especially in the summer, it's hard to start the day this early, so we'll do mornings, just not before six," she explains. "Speaking of running with Noah, have you heard from him? Is he running late?"

"No, I haven't heard. We can message him to see how long he'll be," I suggest.

"Let's call him, actually. If he's warming up by jogging here, he easily misses messages."

As my phone starts to ring, Poppy asks me to put it on speaker phone. She leans in, tilting her head to one side to bring her ear closer to the phone. The smell of poppies is a little more faint than usual, but it's still there, bringing with it memories from our dance under the stars.

"Hello?" Noah's voice is scratchy.

"Why do you sound like this call woke you up?" she asks, her voice full of skepticism.

"Well, because my body slept right through my alarm, I would venture to guess."

"I've heard your alarm, it could wake anyone." The skepticism increases as her lips purse, waiting for his response.

"I must have selected the wrong time, when I set it. Sorry." He sounds anything but sorry right now. Judging by the look on her face, she agrees with my thoughts. "You two should enjoy the run while the sun rises. By the time I'd be able to leave my place, the purpose of the run would be nullified."

Poppy's eyes narrow.

"So, you're not coming?" I ask, suspicions raising that this might have been his plan all along.

"You go ahead without me this time, I'll be sure to double check my alarm for the next one."

I hear her mutter something like "unbelievable" under her breath. It seems that I'm not the only one who thinks there might be some meddling.

Suddenly, the thought of Noah planning out a sunrise run and purposefully sleeping in cracks me up and I let out a chuckle. Her gaze meets mine, a crease forming between her brows.

"Go back to sleep, Noah, we'll see you Monday," I say. "Just don't be surprised if you find your Bobbi's coffee switched out with the school's decaf sometime soon."

Poppy's mouth falls open before breaking into a smile as she holds back laughter.

"You wouldn't." I can practically see skepticism washing over his face.

"Oh, we would," she joins in. "Sweet dreams." She disconnects the call, mischief dancing in her eyes making it impossible to look away. "That was brilliant."

"It might be too cruel to actually do," I point out.

"Maybe we'll just replace half of his Bobbi's with the school's decaf, but not for a week or two so he's lulled into a false sense of security."

"Deal."

She holds out her hand to shake and when my fingers first make contact, I can feel those sparks. I wonder if she feels them, too, because something shifts in her expression and she bites her bottom lip.

God, I'd love to kiss her again.

Nope, I can't go there. We're coworkers. And, hopefully, friends. Nothing more.

Pulling my hand away is significantly harder than it should be, but I need a break in contact so I can get my head on right.

"Well, should we run?" Maybe that will help clear my mind. Physical exertion.

"Yeah, how about we go to where the jetty for the lighthouse begins?" she suggests. "We don't have to go all the way to the lighthouse, the rocks are pretty slippery with dew in the mornings."

"Not slipping on rocks seems reasonable." If my math is correct, that's going to be under two miles by the time we get back here. That should be good enough to reset and see Poppy only as a friend.

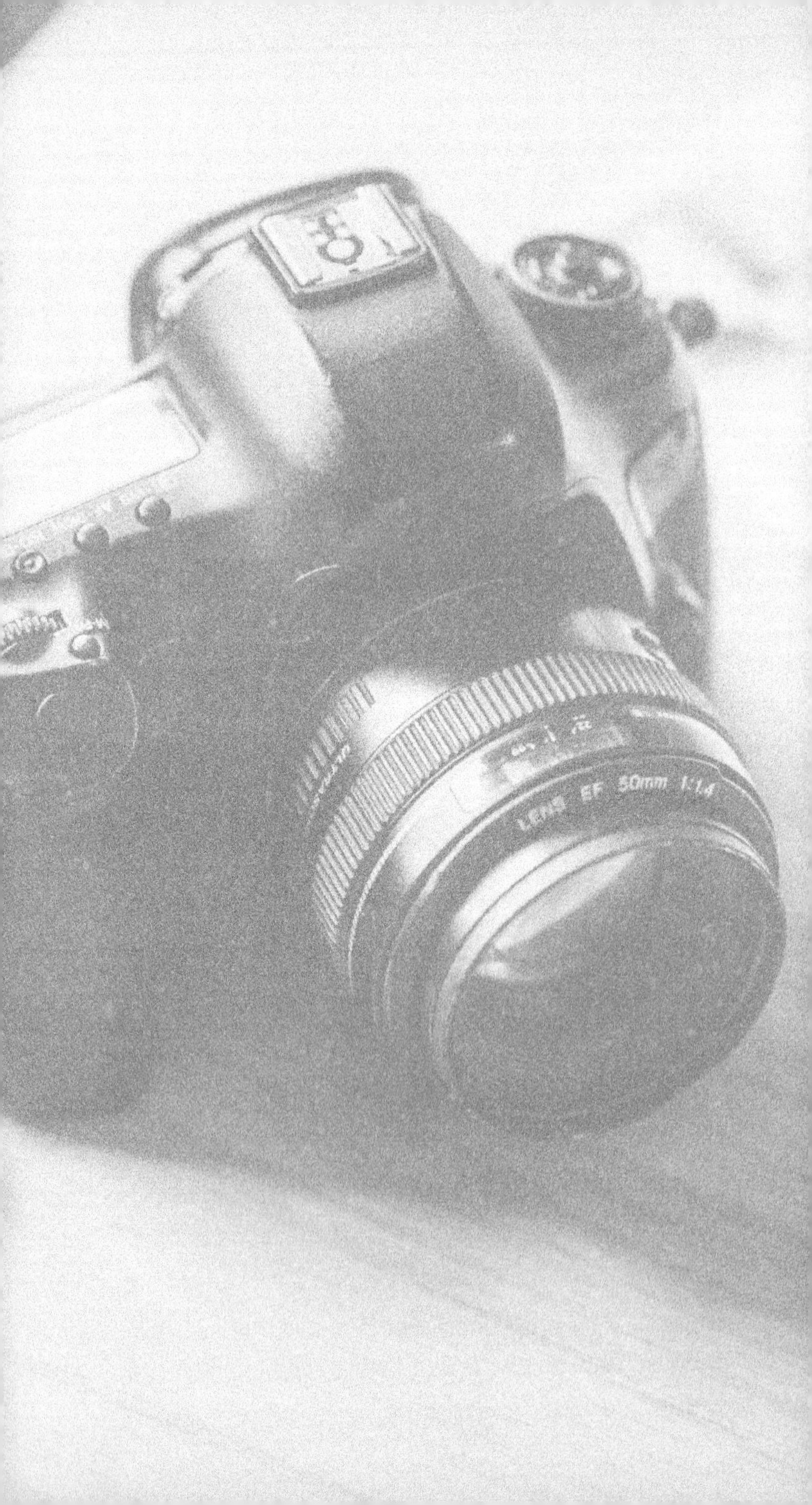
LENS EF 50mm 1:1.4

CHAPTER THIRTY-ONE

Poppy

The morning sunlight bouncing off the waves seems to be intensifying my already flushed skin. Pulling off my light jacket as I run, I quickly tie it around my waist before glancing over at Owen next to me.

"Getting warm?" he asks. *God, am I.* Why does my body respond like this around him?

"Yeah, the sun is bright today." *The sun is bright today? God.* "I love the way it makes everything sparkle by the boardwalk. Even the shops look glittery. It's one of my favorite things about living here."

Owen nods at me. He's a bit quiet after our call to Noah. He seemed to laugh off him standing us up, but maybe he was more uncomfortable than he let on. He glances towards me and I see beads of sweat slowly dripping down his forehead.

"It is beautiful." My eyes lock with his for a few seconds too long and I trip, catching myself just as I'm about to hit the boardwalk. He reaches down to help me up and my heart starts racing as the golden flecks in his eyes shimmer along with the waves, giving him an otherworldly feel. *Stay open, Poppy. You said you'd think about it. This is not Steven.*

I pull my hand away abruptly after standing and we continue down the beach. "Have you been able to see Brandon since he got back?" I break the quiet with a benign question, hoping this can somehow calm my nerves.

"Not quite yet, tonight I think. Getting a beer."

"Oh, nice." And it's silent again. What the hell am I doing? Thankfully we're only a block from the lighthouse at this point. This loop is pretty short and I usually do it three times when I run alone, but Owen already seems to be panting pretty hard, so we'll go for a light day today. "The lighthouse is just around this bend."

A few minutes later as we turn the corner I see that there are quite a few people on the pier and my eyes catch on one in particular. I'd know that baseball cap and shaggy blond hair anywhere. Steven. *Shit.*

I stop abruptly and Owen looks over at me understandably confused, "Can we actually head—" but before I can get the words out of my mouth, *he's* already walking towards us and has spotted me. Scanning the shops, I look for an easy way out, but find none. *I guess this is happening.*

"Poppy, is that you? I hadn't heard you were back." Turning towards his voice, I take in the beautiful woman on his arm, the ring on her finger, and his parents in tow behind them.

"Hi, Steven."

His mom comes straight over and hugs me, kissing my cheek. "My dear, I am so glad to see you out and about. We were so worried after you ran away when Steven broke up with you." She laughs like I overreacted over a missed date. After giving me an appraising once over, she adds, "But, you look like you're doing okay, I suppose."

My mouth is suddenly dry and I can't seem to get my brain to respond. But before I can actually form words, I hear a deep voice behind me say, "Babe, will you introduce me?"

Turning my body towards Owen, I can't mask the look of shock on my face. He looks at me sweetly, taking me in his strong arms and pulling me close to him. Feeling stronger and emboldened with him next to me, I say, "Sorry, this is Steven and his family. Steven, this is Owen." I open my mouth to elaborate on our relationship, but think better of it after remembering what a gossip Steven's mom is. If I actually say he's my boyfriend it will be around Honey Cove faster than a bee from a hive, but if she simply assumes incorrectly, well, then that will be something different entirely.

"How did you two meet?" Steven tentatively asks. I settle in closer into the crook of Owen's arm, lay a hand on his chest to really drive the ploy home. *This feels great.* I usually have a hard time feeling this comfortable with guys I've dated, but with him, it feels natural, easy.

"I teach at the high school," Owen responds quickly, sounding so self-assured and in that same deep timbre he used earlier. He glances at me again, sending me encouragement through the warmth of his gaze.

"Well, isn't that nice. Can we go back to the house, Steven? I'm chilled." The raven-haired beauty on Steven's arm finds her voice and she turns to make her way down the pier without a word to me.

"Bye, Poppy," Steven says quietly. His parents give curt nods.

"See you around, Penny," the woman says as she wraps her red manicured nails around Steven's neck, tugging him down into a kiss.

Once they're farther down the pier, I turn towards Owen, releasing a deeply held breath. "You didn't have to do that. They'll figure out we're not dating eventually." Running my hands over my face, I focus on slowing my heart. *You did it. You saw him and didn't die.*

"Oh, that's okay. At least I hope it was okay, it felt like the right thing at the moment."

"Yes, thank you." Looking out towards the waves, we stop and move to the fencing at the edge. Standing like that for a minute, my thoughts are racing, but there's one thing I know for certain: that did not happen the way I thought it would.

"I've rehearsed in my mind so many times what I would, or wouldn't, say to him when I saw him again." I don't know if my heart will ever fully heal from what he did to me, but it feels lighter now. We've officially seen each other again and I will never have to do that again for the first time.

"And I probably threw a wrench into that plan, huh?" Owen's melodic voice pulls me back to the pier and I involuntarily shiver.

"It never went like that in my head, but I think it was perfect. Thank you." Reaching out, I place my hand over his. He reaches as well, cupping mine in between his and I feel warm and tingly all over again. Between the glitter of the sun and the comforting feel of his hand in mine, I feel like a new chapter of my life is starting. The book is closing on Steven and opening on something new. I just haven't decided what that is yet.

"I just have one question, what in the world was that voice you were using?"

He holds up his hands. "I had to get into character, you know, a persona."

"Is that what you English teachers call it?"

"Something like that." He turns and we start walking back towards the main strip. I don't feel much like running anymore and enjoy the slower pace. Our hands brush against one another a few times as we walk and my heart resumes its quick pace at the closeness of him.

"Well, I liked it."

"What, the voice?" He looks at me, surprised.

"Yeah, it was sexy." I walk ahead of him a little this time, but can feel his shock just the same.

CHAPTER THIRTY-TWO

Owen

The tension is finally leaving my shoulders after walking south on the boardwalk for another minute. I keep stealing glances at her because, holy shit, she could have gotten so mad at me back there.

It felt like every fiber of my being was screaming to step in when she saw her ex. Hell, I was even able to let her handle it for a bit. She's a strong woman and was doing amazing, even if I could see signs of her discomfort. It wasn't until his mother said all that condescending bullshit that my control snapped.

Poppy looked like his mother had just slapped her across the face and her ex just stood there like this was a normal conversation.

What the hell is wrong with that guy?

But when she came into my arms after I opened my big mouth, it felt so fucking right. Even if it was just to get her out of a terrible situation.

She definitely looks calmer now. Playful at times. Her reaction to the tone I had when I stepped in has put too many ideas into my mind and each time our hands touch, I have to remind myself that everything back there was an act. That she's my friend. Friends help each other like that, right?

"Where's your head at?" she asks.

"Honestly?"

"Yeah, I like honesty."

I exhale sharply, still a little winded from the run and I wipe some of the sweat beading down from my brow. "Back there, it didn't feel like an act for me, and I'll work on that. I really respect you and want to be friends, if that works for you."

She stops as I mentally kick myself for saying *any* of that.

What the hell is wrong with me?

Her eyes roam over me, taking me in thoughtfully. A small smile begins to take shape and she simply says, "Let's just see."

And then she's walking again, leaving me baffled. *See what?* See if we can be friends or see if we are just coworkers? Or, was there something else behind it and I haven't been the only one feeling this pull?

How can she look so relaxed right now?

"So," she begins, drawing out the word as we near my apartment. Tension builds up inside of me, not knowing where this conversation might be headed. "When do we plan out Noah's coffee sabotage?"

I bark out a laugh.

"What? He's not getting away with this set up without a consequence. Otherwise he'll keep trying to meddle."

Would him meddling be such a bad thing? I wonder.

"Do you plan well on an empty stomach? Because I don't," I say instead.

"Did you bring energy bars or something? I didn't bring my wallet," she points out.

Taking a chance that she's open to friendship, I say, "I cook a mean omelet, but you'll have to put up with my cat to get one."

Some of her hair has fallen loose from her ponytail and I stop myself from tucking it behind her ear when a breeze causes it to brush across her face.

"What kind of cheese do you have?"

Hope settles inside me. "At least one shredded blend, sharp cheddar, a block of mozzarella, and fresh mozzarella."

"Impressive. I'm in."

"You're in for omelets in my apartment?" I clarify.

"Well, is your cat going to attack me?" Her hand goes to her hip, accentuating her natural curves.

"Samson is more of a lover than a fighter, but he might give you the third degree. He's never been fond of female guests."

An eyebrow raises, disappearing behind her bangs, which are somehow not plastered to her forehead. How have I not realized until now that she's not a sweating mess like me?

"Not that I've had many," I blurt. "I mean, I have had a good amount...no, the right amount. Actually, the amount doesn't matter, does it?"

It's her turn to laugh and I rub my face with both hands, simultaneously covering my embarrassment and wiping off the sweat that stopped dripping.

"I'm sorry, I'm not laughing at whatever that number is. You just got so adorable trying to backpedal."

"So, a very different response to the voice I used earlier," I say, laughing at my mini-ramble. But instead of laughing, she takes a sharp inhale and the mirth in her eyes shifts to something else. Something I saw the night of Brandon's wedding.

We're just friends. At most.

Before I get myself in trouble by talking more, I clear my throat, pull out my keys, and gesture to the door. "Shall we?"

"Let's meet this cat of yours, even if he doesn't like me, I love being around them."

"Do you have one?" I ask as we walk up the stairs side by side.

"I don't, but want to get one now that," she hesitates, "now that I'm done traveling."

"I'm sure Andi and Brandon would happily watch a cat for you when you travel, so you shouldn't let that stop you."

"Actually, Steven didn't like cats and before he and I started getting serious, or what seemed serious, I was still in college living in a dorm."

"Well, he might hide from you, but you're welcome to stop by and have all the cat-time you need with Samson," I say, unlocking the door to find the feline in question waiting just inside as we enter.

"Oh my goodness, he's so adorable," she coos at him, putting her hands on her knees to get a better look at him but not reaching out. "How old is he?"

I close the door and watch Samson look at her, glancing at me once, but not greeting me as usual.

"Hey bud," I say, squatting down and giving his neck a little scratch. He pushes his head back so I pet him more and purrs, but when he stands up, he walks over to Poppy. "He's seven."

She whispers a hello to him and slowly lowers herself so she's sitting crossed legged right in front of the door, holding out her hand so he can sniff her, still purring. Samson steps over her ankles and puts his front paws onto her chest, rubbing his face against hers.

"You said he'd give me the third degree," she whispers excitedly. "What is happening?"

"Honestly, I have no idea," I say, shaking my head in disbelief. "But he clearly likes you."

"I love him already and might sneak him home with me," she says, running her fingers through his fur.

"He might follow you home whether you like it or not judging by his reaction to you," I joke. "I'll give you two a minute and start breakfast."

Watching her with my cat feels way too natural and I need to keep my head on right. Poppy Edwards is in my apartment. And we're friends.

Nothing more.

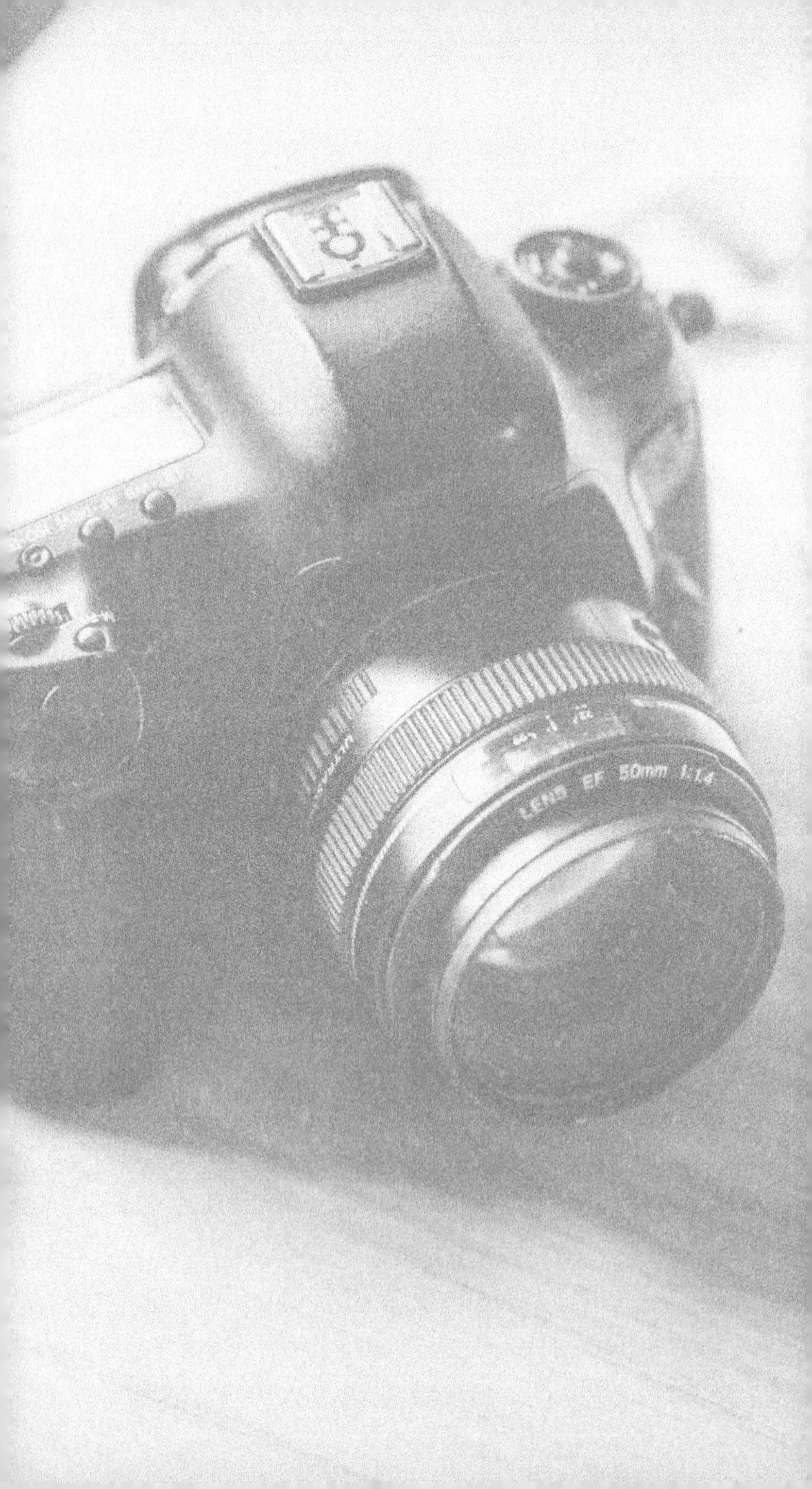
LENS EF 50mm 1:1.4

CHAPTER THIRTY-THREE

Poppy

"I may just be in cat heaven," I say between mouthfuls of the most delicious omelet I've ever tasted. Samson has insisted on sitting on my lap as I eat, which, fur notwithstanding, is quite comfortable. *I could get used to this*. Sitting here with Owen, and Samson snuggled against me, something feels right.

Despite our forwardness on the walk back, and everyone's encouragement, I still am worried that I'm jumping into something too early. Steven and I were together for so long and I was so head over heels for him, I'm nervous I might be rebounding with anyone I date next. No matter how kind they are or how great of an omelet chef they may be. And how cute their cat is. Leaning over, I give Samson a scratch behind his ears before stroking down his long and very furry back.

New chapter. It's time to stop comparing and thinking about what I may or may not be doing and just focus on the here and now.

"I'm still shocked he's sitting with you like that." It's hard to meet Owen's look and not feel the sudden intimacy of being here, alone in his apartment. I turn my attention back to my food before our stare can get too intense.

"How are things going for you at school, do you feel like you're settling in, er, back in, I suppose?" How do I keep forgetting he was here while I wasn't?

"Yeah, I think so. Everyone has been so helpful and welcoming. I felt pretty awkward after the whole being chosen second thing by the admin. I understand why, but it still bugs me." He wrinkles his nose up and shakes his head slightly, as if he's still trying to get over the sting of the situation.

"Everyone I have talked with believes you were always the right person for the job. I don't think it means anything about you or your teaching that the district was pushing another agenda."

He meets my eyes again and this time I don't do anything to lessen the chemistry between us. "Thank you," he says, his voice all gravelly again like when we were on the boardwalk. Without thinking, I reach out, resting my hand on top of his.

We both stare at our hands.

Is this okay?

Owen continues without addressing the issue of our hands. "You know, my grandma always used to tell me that things don't come to us always how we want them to, but they do come how they're meant to. It always seemed kind of cheesy to me, but as I've gotten older it really seems like she was right."

All I can do is nod. *I want to kiss him.* He's sitting with his back to the window, the sun a little higher now is shining around him, the transparent curtains muting it slightly. I'm not sure how much longer I can hold back what has been slowly building in me from the moment I saw him at the staff development day. *I want to kiss him.* Summoning all the self-confidence and sexy attitude I can, I stand up, and set Samson down on the ground.

Moving so my body is right next to him, I lean down, placing one hand on the back of his chair and the other on the table. Bringing my face to within centimeters of his own, my eyes search his. *Is this still what you want?* Owen reaches up, tracing his hand along my jaw, running his thumb over the corner of my lips. My heart hitches at his touch, racing at the thought of actually giving into whatever has been between us since Andi's wedding. With a sudden burst of confidence, I hook my leg over his lap and lower slowly onto him.

"Poppy?" he asks.

Before he can say another word and my mind can stop me, I lean forward, pressing my lips into his. He moves his hands to my hair, holding onto my now disheveled ponytail in a way that leaves me wanting so much more. That feeling of being myself is back. Freedom to do this or whatever else I might want to. He seems to accept me just as I am, knowing when to support me and step up, and when I need some space.

My lips part, allowing him more access, my tongue reaching forward to find his. But before they do, he pulls back. His gaze is smoldering, but his body gives a very different message, leaning away from me. "What?" I whisper.

"You have seemed so unsure about things and I don't want you to feel forced or like you want to hide whatever is going on between us."

"I don't." But he's right, I have been unsure. "Steven really…"

"Was awful to you?" he offers.

Nodding, I continue, "Yes, he made me wary. It isn't you, it's *anyone*. I thought for so long that he was my person, but he wasn't and that seems so obvious now, but I couldn't see it while I was in it."

"That makes sense."

"I like you. I am interested in seeing where this goes, but things feel…" I hesitate, trying to find the right word. "*Charged*, with you living here permanently. This is my home, too, and I'm worried about jeopardizing friendships." My mind goes to Andi, Brandon, Noah, and everyone else I'm close with.

"You think they couldn't handle it if it didn't work out between us?"

"No, they could, I think I just am nervous is all I'm trying to say. But I'd like to see where things go." He looks hesitant.

"What if we went out a few times, just as friends? No pressure."

No pressure? *We'll see.*

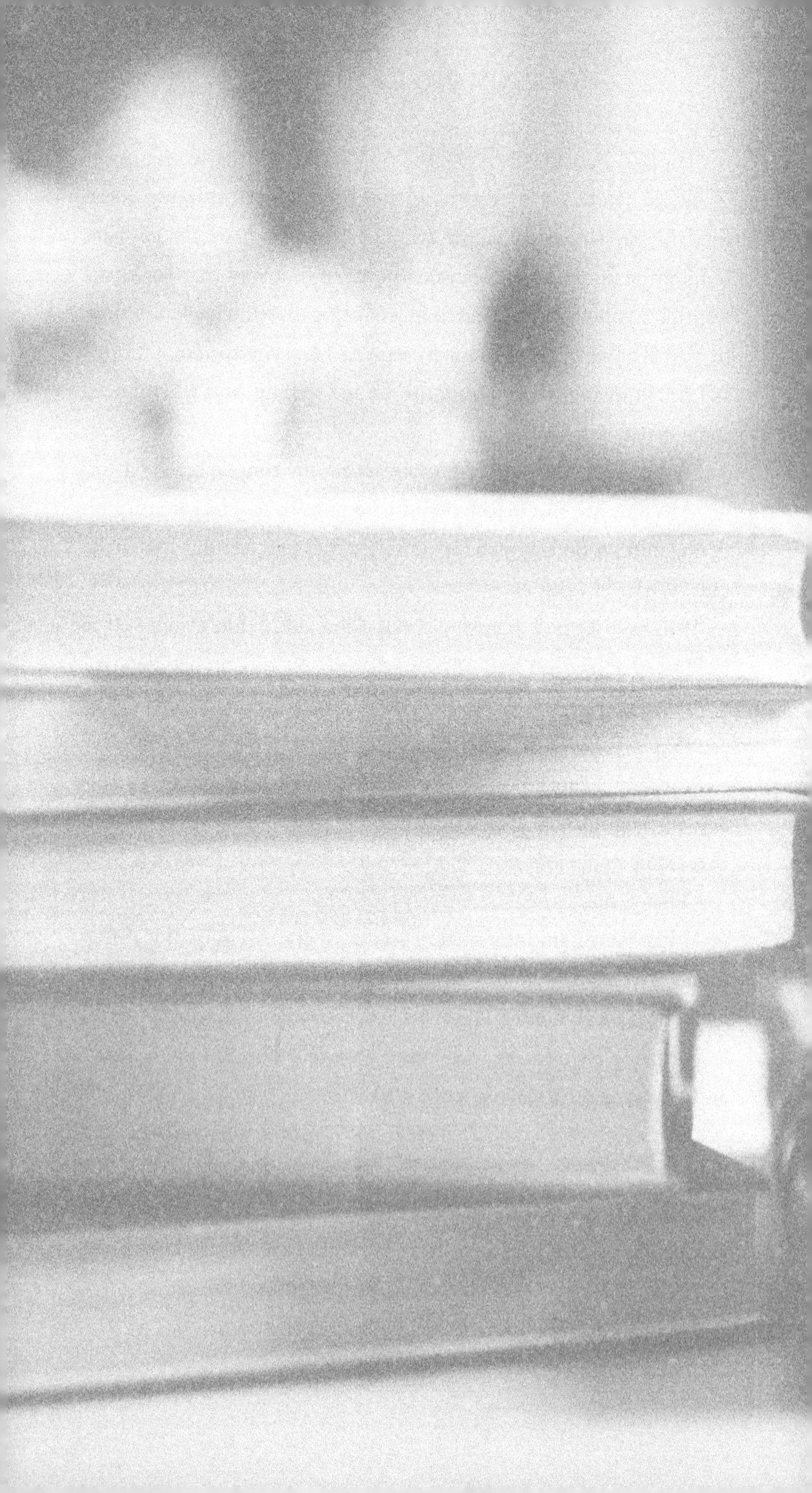

CHAPTER THIRTY-FOUR

Owen

"Just as friends?" she asks, one eyebrow raised as her fingers comb through my hair.

For the fifth time in the last minute, I'm questioning my sanity. Here I have the woman I can't stop thinking about straddling me in the kitchen. Kissing me like she needed to see if this connection was just as real for both of us.

And I pumped the brakes.

But now I know where she's at, so, even though I'm tempted to stand up and carry her the short distance to my bed, I have a footing to stand on. This isn't a one-sided attraction. She's feeling every bit of this as me.

"Well," I say, my hands trailing down her back and gripping her hips. "I'm not opposed to being friends who kiss every now and then, if that's what you're thinking."

She leans forward, closing the distance I created and my eyes fall shut just before our lips meet.

"Wait." My scalp gets a small tug when she tenses and I search her expression to see what happened.

"What's wrong?"

Small creases appear between her brows and she purses her lips. "How many friends are you kissing every now and then?"

Part of me wants to laugh in relief. Damn, I thought she had changed her mind and needed space, which I would gladly give her so she can work things out as she needs. But instead, I lean my head back to give the tip of her nose a kiss. "I'm not interested in kissing anyone but you."

I'm itching to find out if she's interested in possibly seeing anyone else, but we're just feeling things out. I can be open and honest about my feelings without pushing her into any declarations or commitments that are too much.

Those creases relax and her hands slide down to cup my face. "Okay then," she whispers, her lips brushing against mine which sends tingles down my spine.

This time, I'm the one who takes the lead, kissing her softly at first and savoring the way her lips react to mine. Then the kiss deepens. She gives a quiet sigh and lets me pull her flush against me as I lean back into the chair so more of her weight is pressing down on me. Just as her mouth opens and her tongue finds mine...

She giggles.

"Um, is everything okay?" I ask, feeling confused as she pulls back a little.

"Samson keeps rubbing against my leg," she says, her hand covering her amazing smile.

Leaning around Poppy, I look at my cat who is already happily rubbing his head against her calf as he purrs. "You've been on her lap since she got here, bud, I think it's okay that she's on mine for a minute or two."

With that, she lets herself fall forward to laugh against my neck. And everything feels *right*.

By the time I pull into the parking lot at Maple's Moonshine, I've managed to go from hopeful that this might really be something to thinking of all the things Poppy might worry about. We didn't even talk about school.

A drink with my cousins sounds like just the thing to help me from stewing over these thoughts.

The place isn't overly busy and I couldn't miss our table if I tried since Brandon is wearing the brightest tie-dyed shirt I've ever seen.

"Owen!" he calls out while waving me over. "I ordered you an IPA and our nachos should be out any minute."

"Awesome," I say, giving him a quick hug and sitting down on the other side of the table.

"So?" Brandon asks, his eyes expectant and on me.

Confused, I look at Graham and James who are also watching me like I have something to say.

"We're here to celebrate Brandon's return from the honeymoon. Why are you all looking at me?" My weight shifts as I squirm a little in my chair.

"Is there anything you'd like to share?" *Why is Graham asking me that?*

"Shouldn't you be asking Brandon, or did I miss something in the group messages?" I ask, partially joking, but still feeling completely lost as to why they're still watching me. "What?"

They can't know about the kiss.

Only Graham knew I *danced* with Poppy, and he was occupied for the rest of the wedding night, so they can't know.

"Your run, man," Brandon says. "You look like you're in one piece, so how was it?"

"Yeah, we may or may not have placed bets on how far you made it," Graham adds.

Relief washes over me. I'm not trying to hide anything about my attraction to her, but I didn't want to overstep or overshare when it was just supposed to be one night.

"We ended up running to the start of the lighthouse jetty and walked back. I can't imagine I'd be able to move well if we ran both ways, but I was definitely the weaker runner."

"Who'd you go with?" James asks.

"Andi's friend Poppy was the one who made it. Our friend Noah arranged everything but accidentally slept in." That sounded casual.

Graham's mouth opens, but thankfully the server sets down the nachos right as he's about to say something. I need a moment before I talk to anyone about what may or may not be going on. Poppy told Noah about the wedding night, and I'm guessing she's talked to Andi.

Taking a sip of the beer the server hands me, I steel myself. Telling them is putting my trust in them and bringing them into my new life, and that feels right. So, before my youngest cousin has a chance to possibly broach the subject, I take a breath and talk. I start with the wedding and work my way up to this morning.

Leaving some of the details out, of course.

"I knew it," he says, slapping his hand on the table. "You could barely keep your eyes off of her at the wedding and you both left way too early."

"Oh come on, I wasn't that obvious, was I?"

"I didn't notice anything," James offers. "But I also didn't realize that you ducked out early, so that might not mean much."

"And you like her?" Brandon says, fairly subdued for him.

I almost brush the question off and say that it's too early to know. But I'm not asking her to marry me tomorrow and that's not what Brandon means. "Yeah, I do. She's pretty amazing."

He nods. "It all makes sense now."

"What does?" James asks, never one to worry about seeming oblivious.

"Poppy and Andi went out for drinks the last night and when Andi came home—"

"I think you mean 'your wife,'" Graham butts in, earning a laugh from all of us.

"Very true, thank you, G," Brandon says. "When my wife came home, she was giddier than usual. I always let her tell me what she'd like in her own time when it comes to her chats with Poppy, but there was something different. At best, Andi tolerated Steven and she did everything she could to support Poppy. But after he ended things, Andi was heartbroken for her and was worried he might have hurt her enough for her to close herself off to someone who was actually good for her. And after she got home last night, she said, 'I think she's ready again,' squealed, and jumped into my arms."

"That makes no sense."

Graham gives an exasperated sigh. "James, Brandon is saying Andi was likely talking to Poppy about Owen."

"Ohhhh, I get it now," James says.

As Graham gets Brandon to tell us about his honeymoon, I find that the only thing I can do is smile and fill a plate with nachos.

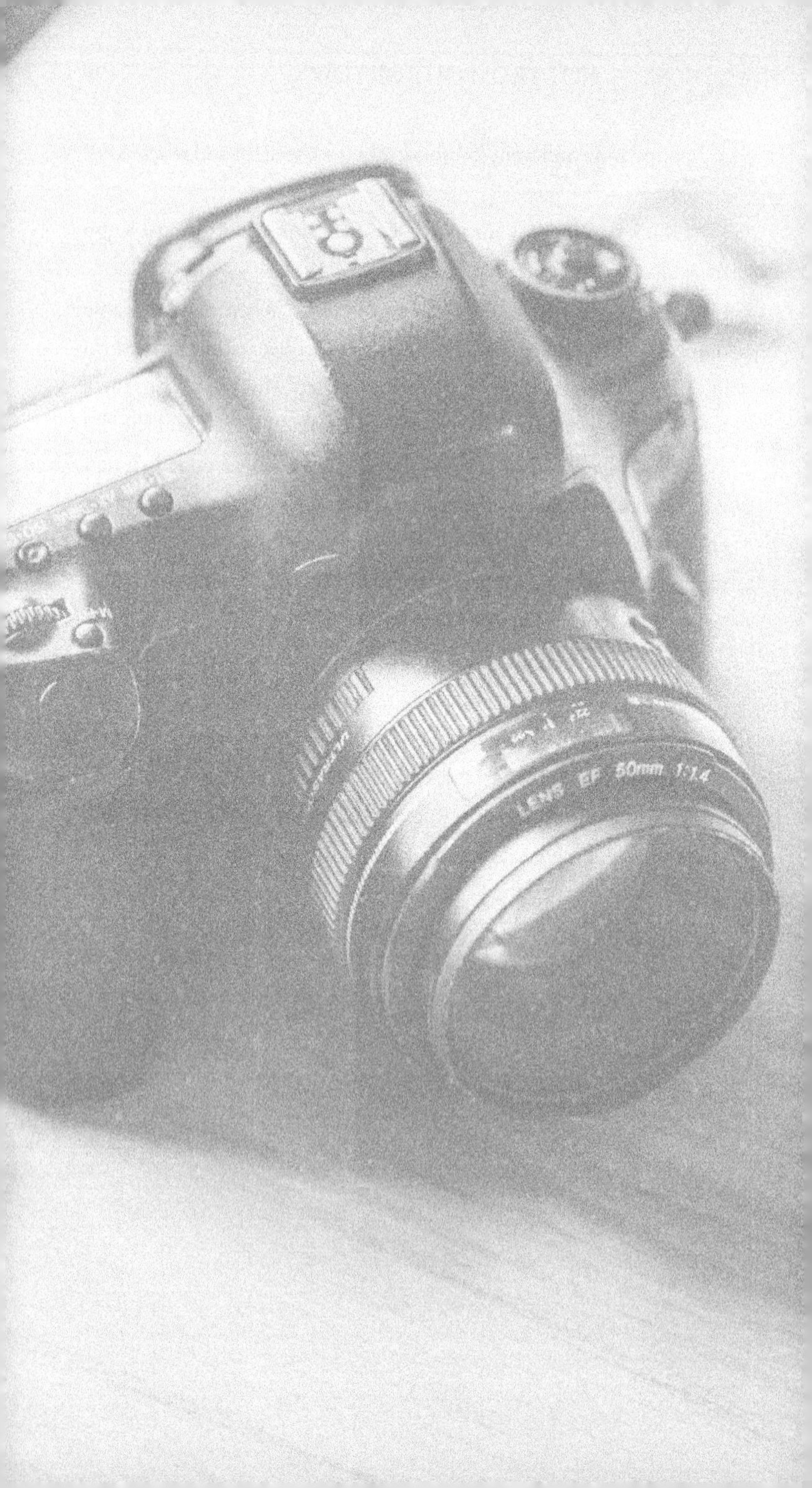
LENS EF 50mm 1:1.4

CHAPTER THIRTY-FIVE

Poppy

Running my makeup brush over my cheek, I add the final touches to my look for the evening. Standing up and moving to my full length mirror, I brush my hands over my outfit. It was expertly chosen by Andi over the course of an hour-long video call. It's hard to know how to dress for your date when you don't actually know where you're going. I fiddle with my earrings for a bit longer before heading downstairs. *Is it even a date? We had said as friends, but it feels like a date.*

After our spontaneous kiss at his apartment, Owen and I decided that he got to pick the next date since running was my thing to begin with. My mind wanders as I try to think about what he might choose and realize that aside from coffee and teaching English, I don't know much about his hobbies.

A knock on the door pulls me from my thoughts. Opening the door, my gaze lands on the huge bouquet of flowers in his hands. "Thank you so much, that was sweet."

Owen steps into the room as I grab a vase for the flowers. *He looks nice.* "You're welcome. In our family we tend to bring flowers to any occasion." He laughs like it's a joke and I don't quite understand. "My dad is a florist."

"Oh, that makes sense. Well, I love them. Are you taking me to Bobbi's for our date?" I ask him quizzically. "I already know you like coffee."

He scoffs at my question, but reaches down to grab my hand as we head out of my house and walk towards the boardwalk to officially begin our date. We *had* said as friends but I called it a date earlier and he seemed to go with it.

"I'm not taking you to Bobbi's." He gives my hand a squeeze, and we keep walking together in comfortable silence. The weather seems to have finally turned to fall and the ocean is responding in turn. Where just a few days earlier bright sun and warm mist crested onto the boardwalk, today a gray sky blankets the cold water.

I pull my sweater closer to me and smooth down the front of my dress, then fiddle with the clasp on my purse. *Calm down.*

"We're here. You chose running, and I chose books. I know it's a little cliche for an English teacher, but I can't help it." The browns of his eyes dance, reflecting the lights from the bookstore window.

"It's not cliche, I love that you enjoy reading."

His smile brings some warmth to my face before we head inside. I've been by Honey Cove Books a few times over the years, but am excited to explore it more with Owen. "After you," he says, holding the door open for me like a gentleman.

He says hi to the shop owner as we walk in. *He's clearly been here before.* I recognize Grace from school—I think she was a few years younger than me—and wave as he leads me farther back into the building. Shelves and shelves of books line the rows and the smell of old paper and leather hangs in the air.

"This is my favorite section," Owen declares proudly.

My eyes catch on the plaque that says "fantasy" before looking back at him in shock. "I had you pegged as a poetry kind of reader."

"Now why would you say that?" I move closer to him under the guise of looking over a shelf of books, but lean back into him as I shift in between him and the bookshelf. I'm continually shocking myself with how forward I am with him. What felt uncomfortable and awkward with others, somehow feels natural with him.

He leans down, lips skating against the curve of my ear, sending my heart into a frenzy at the feel of his warm breath along my neck. *Definitely a date.* "Just thought that seemed more the English teacher type, that's all. What genre would you guess is mine?"

Turning around, we're inches from each other. He leans forward, placing a hand on either side of me against the shelf to my back. "I just have one question before I can say with certainty."

"Yes?" I say, breathless and exasperated at how much this trip to the bookstore is turning me on.

"Where is your favorite place to be?"

"Honey Cove." *No question in my mind.*

"Really?" he moves farther away from me, clearly surprised.

"Of course, you seem surprised?"

"I just thought with you traveling and your love of photography, that you might prefer somewhere else. Somewhere different." He starts walking down the aisle again, clearly leading me to our next section. I miss the feel of his arms around me, but don't mind his arm slung casually around my shoulders either.

"I love Honey Cove. I do love to travel, but Honey Cove is home. "

He waves his hand as he stops by another sign. "Your genre, my dear."

"How did you know?" We're standing by the autobiographies and he looks very proud of himself.

"You like to travel, but like to be able to return to Honey Cove. You like a taste of what's out there. You like to look at things through a lens or through how others see things." He says it so nonchalantly like it's the easiest thing to see in the world. My face drops.

"Is that how you see me?"

"I meant it in the sense that you are a homebody. You look at things through other peoples' eyes because you already know yourself and know what you think. You already have that part figured out," he trails off. "That's what I meant."

Hooking my hand back in his and looking into his warm face, I nod. I am not sure anyone has quite put it that way before.

"And, I saw you carrying one when you got to Andi's house that day of her and Brandon's wedding." He lets out a quiet laugh as I pretend to push him.

"You cheated then!"

"No, I would have known anyway."

"Oh yeah, how?"

"Because I already feel like I know you. You are always true to yourself. You say what you mean and you are clearly in love with this town and those you care about. You look at things through a lens, yes, but it's because you're finding the beauty in what is out there. Books like that are always about the things people love and what's made them who they are, finding the beauty in the hard to reach places."

My breath catches as he pulls me closer to him. Standing up on my tiptoes, I silently curse my choice to wear flats today, I lean forward to kiss him and feel him envelop me in his arms. I don't know if I've ever felt so seen by someone before and it feels a bit unnerving. *If this is what a first date with Owen is like, my heart better buckle in for the next.*

CHAPTER THIRTY-SIX

Owen

I know we're going to have to stop soon because we're in public, but, thankfully, no one else seems to be looking for an autobiography right now. Her soft lips caress mine as we're surrounded by books. My arms tighten around her waist and I lift her off her feet and spin us around in a circle, causing her to let out a little squeal of surprise.

Something about just being with her seems to unlock a new sense of joy in me. I don't know the last time I felt this free to really be myself.

"You ready to pick out a few books?" I ask, setting her back down, but keeping my hands on her hips.

Her fingers are locked behind my neck as she looks up at me, her cheeks a little flushed. "What am I picking out books for?"

"To read."

"Are we sitting on the floor here and sampling them for our date?"

There's that word again. She's called this a date before and each time I hear it, something stirs inside of me.

"We could if that's what you'd like to do," I say. "Or, we can get a few and read on the beach."

"Oh, I love that idea," she says, tugging me down for a quick kiss. One hand travels down my arm until she has our fingers entwined, giving me a tug. Happily, I follow her as she scans the shelves until she finds a book by a photographer who has done various projects where he takes photos of a specific neighborhood, and then creates public installations within that same area. We continue on and I offer to carry each book so she can browse while still holding my hand.

"Okay, let's go get yours now." Her smile is infectious as she pulls me back to the fantasy section.

There are three books that I've been meaning to read and I make short work of pointing them out to Poppy so she can grab them with her free hand and add them to the stack. We'd probably look ridiculous to anyone walking by, but the store is pretty quiet on Sunday afternoons.

"That's it for me. Are you ready to read on the beach?" I ask.

"Absolutely." She lets go of my hand and sorts through the titles we have and starts pulling out hers.

"What are you doing?" My hand covers hers.

"I'm getting mine to check out," she says matter-of-factly.

"Nope," I say, pulling the stack away from her. "I planned the date, I get to buy the books."

When she opens her mouth to argue, I add, "You can buy books the next time we come here together."

"Next time?" she asks, that sexy smile appearing.

"Next time."

By the time I've paid Grace for the books, Poppy is frowning and looking towards the windows at the front of the store. More specifically, at the rain coming down in buckets.

"I don't think our books will hold up well if we try to read them on the beach," I say, putting my arm around her and resting my hand on her hip, giving it a light squeeze.

"My place is about a mile south once we get back to the boardwalk," she offers weakly.

"Well, if you'd like to be a little drier, we could go back to mine and you could get some Samson cuddles."

Her eyes brighten at the mention of my cat and I chuckle.

"My place it is. Are you ready?" I ask, opening the door.

I catch a sparkle of mischief in her expression just before she runs outside calling, "Race ya!"

Cursing, I double check that the bag is wrapped around the books so they won't get soaked and follow her laughter all the way to the awning of my building. We're both dripping wet, our clothes clinging to our bodies.

Something shifts in the air between us, laughter dying out as we take each other in. The need to hold her, touch her, kiss her, hits me full force and I take one more step. My fingers tangle themselves into her hair and I kiss her.

The moment our lips crash together, I almost drop the bag of books. The kiss is searing as her nails dig into my back to keep us flush. A flash of lightning quickly followed by a loud boom of thunder startles us out of the moment.

Not wanting to fully let her go, I hold her hand and then pass her the bag of books. Pulling my keys from my pocket, I get the entrance open and we fly up the stairs to my apartment. No one is in the hallway, so I spin her and press her back against the door and kiss her neck while I fumble to unlock the door.

Samson greets us right when we enter and I give him a quick pet, then, in record time, set up one of his toys that he loves. It takes a moment to get his attention away from Poppy and I move the contraption into the living room just as she kisses me again.

Peeling off her sweater and leaving it on the kitchen table next to the bag of books, I walk her backwards toward my bedroom. I wasn't planning to bring her back here for our date, but for the first time since moving, I took down my pull-up bar after my workout this morning.

My shirt is off before I shut the door, making sure it latches so Samson can't push it open. Her shirt follows suit and I take a moment to appreciate the view of her standing in my bedroom, her hair soaked and her face glistening from the rain.

She's absolutely stunning.

Just as she reaches for my belt buckle a meow comes from the other side of my door. Followed by another. And another. We both look at the door and see a little gray paw reaching through the little gap between the bottom of the door and the floor.

"Does he normally do that?" Poppy asks, her chest rising and falling fast.

"Nope," I say, shaking my head.

The meowing gets more and more insistent as we try to wait him out until we're both laughing at his utter insistence to be near us. Finally, we give in to my cat's demands and put some dry clothes on, confirming a hunch I had that she would look amazing in my sweatpants and tee.

Much to Samson's delight, we snuggle up on the couch with our books to read.

I vow to find a toy that will distract my cat for at least thirty minutes before she visits again.

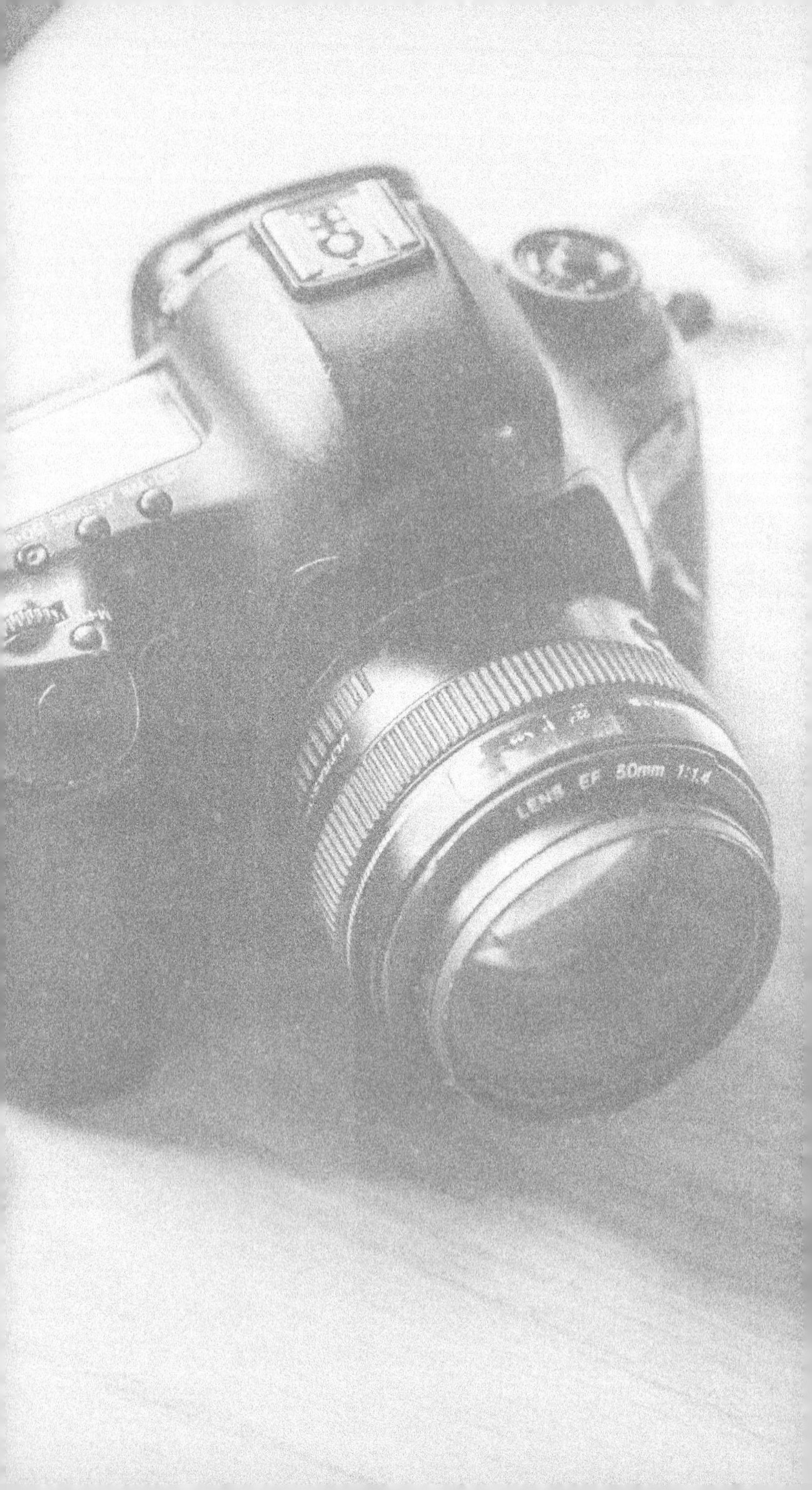
LENS EF 50mm 1:1.4

CHAPTER THIRTY-SEVEN

Poppy

Cockblocked by a cat. I'm not sure that I would have guessed that was in the cards for our date today, but Samson clearly has his own agenda here. He's currently snuggled up on my lap, in a sea of blankets, and getting all the pets he could want. I'm enjoying it just as much as he is. Being able to just be quiet and bask in Owen's snug apartment is surprisingly perfect for our date.

"What a little prince you are, sweet Samson," I coo at him as he looks up at me with his big eyes. His purrs loudly cut through the silence of our cozy reading time.

"Would you like some tea?" Owen offers, shuffling over to the kitchen. "I'm still cold from the rain."

"Sure, what do you have?" I make a move to get up, but Samson gives me a look that keeps me in my place on the couch. *This cat knows what he wants.*

"I've got an Earl Grey or a Jasmine?"

"Jasmine for me."

Owen starts filling a kettle before turning on the stove. The familiar clink of mugs as he gets them down from the cabinet only adds to the warm and comfortable feel of his apartment. Soon, the kettle whistles and I scoot Samson to the side. He looks at me sleepily but accepts.

Walking up behind Owen as he works at the counter, I wrap my hands around his waist, burying my face in his back. This is so new with him, but also feels like we've been doing this forever. I feel a level of comfort with him that is unexpected, especially with this *technically* being our first date.

"Here you are," he says, handing me a cup. His voice has that familiar gravelly sound I've already come to like.

"Thank you." He eyes me. "We've read for a bit, want to watch a movie and order in some food?"

"That sounds great, we could get something from Calico Cafe." I hold my mug close, blowing on it and relishing the warmth of the steam against my face. While Owen pulls up the menu on his phone and puts in our order, I look at the pictures that line his bookshelf. They all appear to be of New York City. I knew that he had lived there, but didn't realize he'd be the type to keep so many architectural photographs displayed.

Once our order is settled, we both move to sit down and enjoy our tea. "I'm eager to hear more about New York."

He nods, sinking down into one of the cushioned chairs in a breakfast nook type space next to his kitchen. "New York is busy. It's loud. It's beautiful, especially at night. I loved the hustle of it all and the way I felt connected with the thrum of the city." He looks thoughtfully to the side, his eyes landing on one photo and lingering there. "But, it's also painfully anonymous and lonely. Aside from my family who live there, I didn't feel super connected to anyone. Friendships felt superficial because everyone there is so busy and focused on their own lives. I wanted something *more*."

"I can understand that. I feel the same way when I travel. It's fine for a little bit and there are things I love, but I always need to come home and be grounded again. But New York wasn't grounding for you?"

"No, it felt more like it disoriented me. I know people who love it and will never leave, but it just isn't where I see myself long term. Family has always been important to me and since I came here so much growing up, it felt like a natural option."

"And then the short term position opened up at the high school..." I say, understanding how everything fell into place for him to be here.

"Exactly, I took the plunge. And I think it's been one of the best decisions I've made yet." He looks across the table at me and I instinctively reach my hand across the honey oak table to interlace my fingers with his.

We're both startled by the ringing of my phone. "Oh god," I say, much louder than necessary, the sudden noise pulling me out of our intimate moment. Glancing down at it, I see that it's Sally from that hotel in Toronto. "That's strange," I add, before silencing it.

"What?"

"It's a woman from my hotel while I was traveling. We chatted a lot, but I can't imagine why she's calling me. I'm sure she'll leave a voicemail and I can check it later. Maybe I left something there," I trail off, not at all sure why she'd be contacting me.

"Do you want to talk to her? You can take it."

"No, it's fine. I'll call her back later." Putting my hand back into Owen's, I revel at the way my skin feels against his. "There's still a little time until we need to eat, I think it's time we stop letting Samson dictate our choices..."

CHAPTER THIRTY-EIGHT

Owen

That smirk does me in.

We both seem to know that Samson might decide his luxurious bed of blankets is missing his new favorite person. And he's already proved himself persistent at having time with her, so we quietly abandon our mugs of steaming tea and stealthily walk to my bedroom. I can't help but wrap my arms around her waist on the way and she lets out a soft sigh.

When we cross the threshold, Poppy closes the door, being careful to keep the latch from clicking loudly, as I kiss just behind her ear and down her neck. "You know we're going to make more noise than my door shutting, right?"

"Shush," she says. "I'm buying us as much time as I can."

A rumble of approval vibrates in my chest. "I'll take every second I can with you," I murmur, letting my senses focus on her alone. Even after the rain and changing into my clothes, I catch a whiff of her perfume while my lips graze her soft skin.

Today's date was supposed to be two friends hanging out and getting to know each other. Instead, it feels like the future I've always wanted. Walking around with her hand in mine, being able to drape my arm around her shoulders, and having her steal kisses from me in the bookstore are all fairly innocuous things for people who are dating. Casual, almost, even though everything with her is far from casual. It's easy to let go with her and each touch feels like it's igniting a fire inside of me while simultaneously feeling natural, as if we've been together for years.

My fingers slip under her shirt and skim over her stomach. I can feel her ribcage expand when she gasps as I brush the underside of her breast and nip her earlobe.

"Bed," she whispers, twisting around in my arms so we can kiss properly. Our lips crash together as we stumble to the bed, too consumed with needing *this*, needing each other, to focus on anything else than where we're touching. God, she tastes like Jasmine tea and something utterly addicting and unique.

Our shirts come off in record time and are flung somewhere on my floor, so different from our first night together. Everything now is almost desperate. It's only been a few weeks since we met, but it's like we've both been holding these flood waters back with a makeshift dam that we've finally let crumble. She shoves my sweatpants down as we tumble onto the bed in a heap of desire. As I kick them off my feet, she lifts her hips so I can slip hers down, kissing my way from between her breasts down to the top of her blue lacy panties, her fingers locking onto my hair.

"Condom?" she asks, already breathless.

"I don't have your pants all the way off, yet," I say, chuckling against her sensitive skin causing her to shiver and tug my hair so I'm looking up at her.

"I'm not looking to be interrupted by anything, no matter how adorable your cat may be." The heat in her gaze has me yanking her pants the rest of the way off.

Nodding to the right of my bed, I say, "Top drawer."

When she flips over to better reach the bedside table, I remove my boxer briefs and crawl over her, kissing my way up her back and unclasping the bra that matches her underwear. By the time she closes the drawer, I'm kissing the back of her neck and she rolls over to reclaim my lips with hers, pushing the condom into my hand.

We're all tongue and teeth in our kisses as she shimmies out of her remaining layer and I open the foil package, rolling the condom down my more than ready shaft. Her legs wrap around my waist as I reach down between us and feel how soaked she already is. Dipping two fingers into her, I coat them in her desire then rub a few circles around her clit causing her to moan my name and arch off my bed.

"Fuck, you're perfect," I say, my voice rough and deep as I line myself up with her entrance. Her hand wraps around mine and she guides me into her and it's somehow better than I remember.

Pushing deeper until I'm buried completely, I pause, staring down at this incredible woman. Her nails dig into my biceps and her plump bottom lip is caught between her teeth while she tries to be quiet.

"What's wrong?" she asks, her brown eyes filling with worry.

"Absolutely nothing," I reassure her. "I was just taking in this amazing view for a moment."

She blushes as I pull almost all the way out and tilt her hips with my hands, relishing in how responsive her body is to mine, and slam back in. She slaps her hand over her mouth to smother her moan and I bite the inside of my cheek to keep mine quiet. As we find our pace, she meets me thrust for thrust and pulls me down to her. Our tongues tangle and she devours my gasp as she pinches my nipple. My hand roams her body, memorizing every peak and valley and finding every place that makes her breath hitch. We're both building much too fast to explore for long though, so my hand slides down between our sweat-slicked bodies and makes circles against her swollen clit.

"Fucking perfect," I growl against her ear as I feel her body tensing and her nails digging into my shoulders.

"Oh my god, Owen," she pleads, her breath coming in short pants.

"Let go with me." My restraint is fading fast as a tingling sensation grows deep within me.

Then her back arches, pressing her chest into mine and her mouth opens into a perfect "O" just before she cries out and shudders all over.

Her walls flood with a fresh wave of desire as they clamp down on my dick, sending me right over the edge with her, slamming into her to draw out her orgasm. Her cry turns into a long moan while she rides out her pleasure, my fingers still working her clit as I fill the condom.

Poppy gives one final, sharp exhale and her body melts down into the mattress, her hair a glorious mess against my pillows. "That was..." she begins.

"Incredible?" I offer.

"Something we should have been doing these past few weeks," she says sleepily. I give her a long kiss before going to my dresser for a tissue to take care of the condom. Crawling back onto the bed next to her, she snuggles against me, tucking her head into the crook of my shoulder.

"Stay tonight," I say softly against her wild hair.

"But we have school tomorrow morning," she says with a groan.

"Stay tonight," I repeat, holding her close.

She looks into my eyes for a moment and kisses me softly, like we have all the time in the world. When we break apart, she whispers, "Okay."

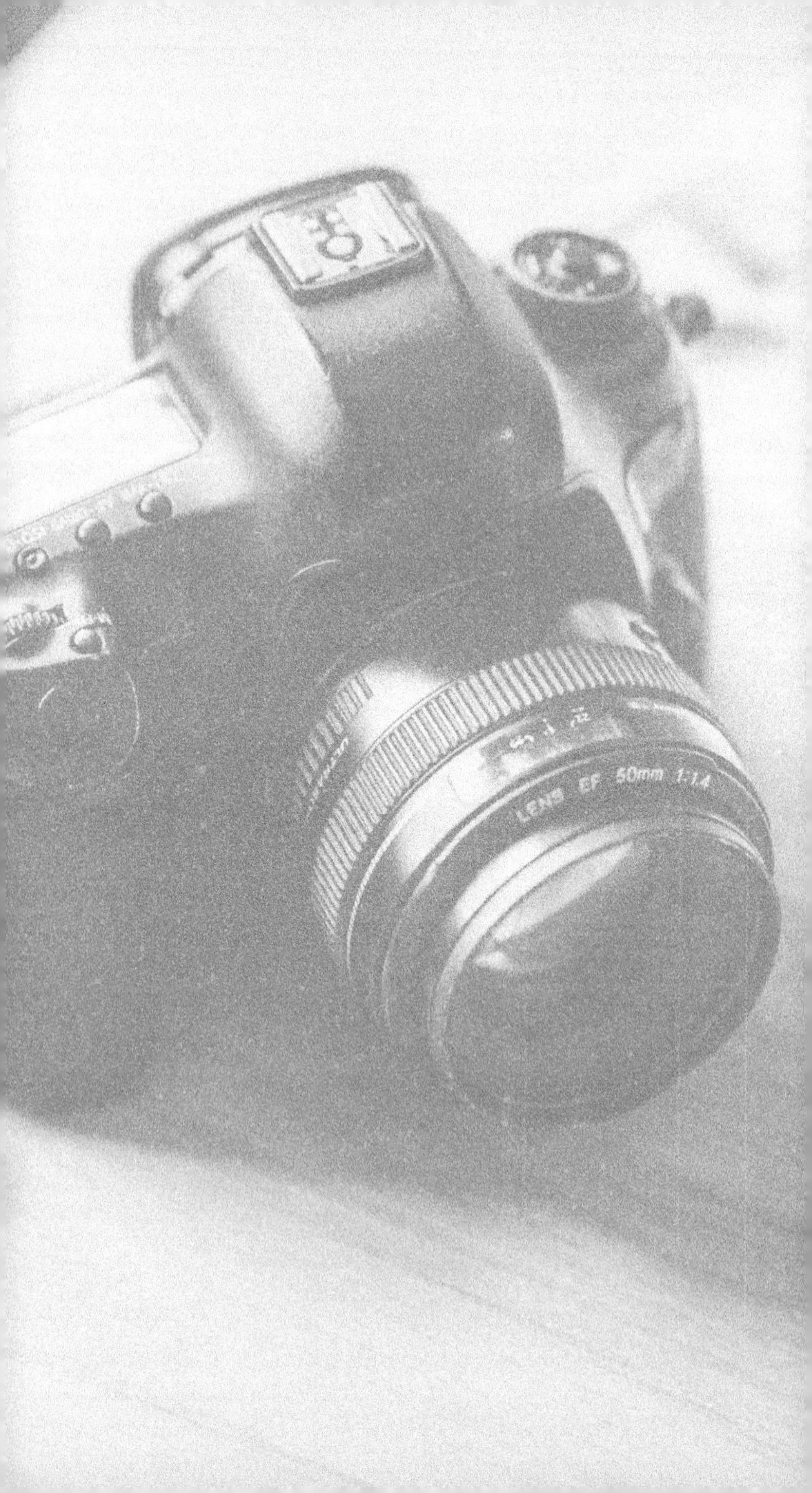
LENS EF 50mm 1:1.4

CHAPTER THIRTY-NINE

Poppy

Peeling myself away from Owen this morning was insanely difficult. Cocooned together in his bed with Samson snuggled on top was the most at home I've felt in a long time. Not to mention how soft his sheets were, the warm sunshine pouring in through his window from the sea, and the feel of his skin against mine.

After our "alone time" from Samson, we had a relaxed evening in with our take out from down the boardwalk and enjoyed a movie before falling asleep in each other's arms. I wish we could have had a more lazy start to the morning, but I suppose that's what we get for having our date on a Sunday. Ultimately, the roughly mile and a half jog home in my flats with the sunrise was the wake-me-up I needed to pull me from my sex and take out slumber.

I always thought things were good with Steven. Even from the beginning. But seeing how Owen treats me, even on our first "date," has me questioning a lot of things I had simply accepted as normal. Making a mental note to talk to Andi about it later, I unlock my front door and rush inside to shower and grab my things before the first bell at school. I've never quite had a jog of shame before...I guess there's a first time for everything.

My hair is wet, I forgot my lunch, and I'm sort of a hot mess, but I'm still riding my elated dopamine over how my night went. I think I feel okay about dating a coworker, but now that I'm here, at school, I'm freaking out about it a little.

Can I handle navigating the relationship as coworkers *and* as something more? Will we need to report this to someone? Did we even talk about what our title is? Are we just dating, but seeing other people? I'm not seeing other people. I hope *he* isn't seeing other people. He said he wasn't interested in kissing anyone else, so that bodes well. *God, I need to stop.*

I nibble on a stale bagel I snagged from the teacher's lounge this morning. It was leftover from some sort of potluck or parents' thing. The questions won't seem to stop. I haven't dated, like actually dated for so long, all of this feels new to me again.

What will our coworkers say? Will they think this is a rebound? It's been a while since the *incident*, but I suppose people are still talking about it. I see some whispers and looks when people think I'm not watching, and students still ask me about it. Especially those that know my ex or his family.

The kids were so invested in us and our relationship. I'm not sure I want more hormonally charged opinions on my love life being thrown in my face unsolicited while I'm trying to teach watercolor techniques.

As if he could read my mind, Noah knocks on my classroom door. "Hi there, Ms. Edwards, I was hoping you could help me with a boy problem," he calls in with his typical "student" voice.

"No help for that here. You're on your own," I call back.

Noah comes in already laughing. "Please, I need to talk about it, it's urgent."

"You know, I know a counselor that would love to talk about it with you." Winking at him, I trail off before taking a sip of my coffee. With my literal running late today, there was no time for Bobbi's and I cringe at the taste of the sludge in my hand.

"Actually, it's you specifically I need to talk to." Noah's voice is back to normal, his eyes wide, and eyebrows inquisitively raised toward the fluorescent ceiling. "How was the run? I've been dying for the details all weekend."

"It was good, but Sunday night was even better," I say smugly, hiding my face behind some newsprint I'm folding for a project. Noah bats it down at the same time the first bell rings. "Thanks for stopping by, his office is down the hall."

"You are cruel, Poppy Edwards. Cruel." He starts out of the room as the first kids come in. "Your teacher is messing with my emotions this morning, children, watch out."

A few of the kids give him a concerned look before looking back at me and shrugging. "Don't worry, he can handle it."

CHAPTER FORTY

Owen

My phone continues to buzz in my pocket. I'd answer it if it weren't for the four boxes of cat toys, including a new cat tower, balancing in my arms as I unlock my apartment without them toppling down the stairwell.

After work, I took a little trip to the pet store and found several promising options to bring out when Samson needs something to distract him from Poppy being in my room. I'm quite happy with the options too. He'll probably curl up in the boxes instead of playing with the toys for the first day or so.

"Hey bud," I say, opening the door and craning my neck to see around the boxes so I'm not accidentally stepping on him. The boxes aren't heavy, they're just big and I feel like I'm about to drop them since they're all different sizes.

His body flashes in and out of my limited vision as he circles my feet. "I'm trying to get to the table so I can open these for you, so if you trip me, you're going to have smashed toys that you can't use."

He ignores my warning and continues to make my short journey treacherous, but the toys and I survive. Setting the stack on the table, I grab my phone and walk back to shut the door as my mom's face fills the screen.

"Owen, is everything alright?" she asks, moving her head around like she might be able to see past me even though she's on the phone.

"I was going to ask you the same thing," I say, feeling confused over her back-to-back-to-back calls.

"I was worried when you didn't pick up on the first call since you usually do in the afternoon."

The door clicks behind me and I kneel down to remove my sneakers with one hand. "I'm good, Mom. I was just coming home with some new toys for Samson, so I couldn't get to my phone."

"What's wrong with his old toys?"

I'm not about to explain the real reason behind these new options even though my mother and I are close, so I settle on saying, "I figured he could use something new since school has been back in session for a bit."

She nods knowingly. "Well, that's sweet of you."

"Thanks." Samson comes in front of the camera to rub his face against my chin. "How's Dad feeling?"

"Good, he's still at the store for another hour. He promised me he wouldn't stay until closing and that he'd let Marty handle training the new guy."

"Is he using the scooter?" I ask, feeling guilty, once again, that I'm not there to stop by and see how he's doing.

"Yes, and that's helping keep the swelling low since he refuses to rest longer now that his stitches are out." She waves a dismissive hand at my stubborn father's need to be hands-on. He took over the flower shop that gave him his first job as a teen. The owner retired fifteen years ago and had made him a manager when he was in his mid-twenties so it wasn't surprising that she made an offer for him to take over. He's poured himself into that little shop, making sure it's just as loved by the neighborhood as when it opened.

If I was there, I could have still taught and helped run the store after school so he would rest longer. Another thing that I feel guilty about even though he always encouraged me to do what I was passionate about. "Enough about your father, I want to hear more about your weekend. Mae said you went for a run? I could hardly believe my ears."

Of course my aunt heard about the run after I told my cousins. "It wasn't as terrible as I expected."

My mother's facial expression falls flat and she blinks a few times. "You've always hated running. I wasn't born yesterday, Owen. What got you out?"

"Oh, so Aunt Mae didn't have all the details?" I tease.

"If she did, I would have already been asking you about the person, so," she pauses and makes a circling gesture with her hand for me to start talking.

"My friend, Noah, from school, suggested a few of us go for a sunrise run. He's the counselor, you'll have to meet him when you're here this winter."

"And, someone joined you…" she says, fishing.

Brandon or James must have hinted that I might be seeing someone. Not that I'm hiding what's happening with Poppy, well, except at work.

"Actually," I say, ripping the Band-Aid off even though I'm not sure if we have a label yet. "Andi, Brandon's wife, has a friend who I teach with and she's the other person who was invited on the run. Her name is Poppy and she's the art teacher at my school, but we met at the wedding."

"Is she the reason you left the reception early?"

"Where did you hear that?" My cheeks must be beet red right now.

"That's a yes, then," she says, smiling. "So it was Poppy who got you out for that run."

Chuckling, I shake my head at myself for being surprised she already had a hunch. "Yes, mom. And Noah didn't even show up, we think he planned it all on purpose. But, we spent some more time together over the weekend and we're seeing each other now."

"I knew something had shifted for you. Call it a mother's intuition." She taps her temple. "So tell me about her."

"Do you want to tell me what you already know?" I joke as I sit with my back against the door and let Samson curl up in my lap, purring.

"I just had a few details, nothing major. I know Mae thinks she's a very nice gal."

"Well, she was traveling last semester, doing some photography work, so I didn't meet her until the day of the wedding. We hit it off and we had this little thing where we were "just Poppy" and "just Owen" which was nice. I didn't need to explain to her that we were *almost* coworkers when I hadn't even told Brandon I didn't get the job, and she was enjoying one more night of her time away." Thankfully, my mom doesn't ask for more details about Poppy's request for anonymity. That's not something I feel comfortable sharing for her. "We didn't exchange details or anything, but I was planning to move back to the city. Then I got the call and, as you know, had to scramble to unpack and get ready for the start of the year."

"So have you been seeing this Poppy since the school year started?" She raises her eyebrow and gives me that look only my mother can give. The one where I'm potentially in trouble.

"No, Mom," I say. "Yesterday was our first date, actually. So I promise I haven't been keeping a relationship a secret from you."

"Okay, I was worried something had happened that made you feel like you needed to hide it."

"Absolutely not," I reassure her. "In fact, we first needed to navigate suddenly being coworkers, and then, through a little help from Noah, who I think was playing matchmaker, we started hanging out."

"And running," she adds.

"And running, which would have likely been a disaster if we had run the full route. Thankfully, we stopped at the jetty to the lighthouse and then walked back. I'm sure she was going easy on me, but I kept up with her."

"You look happy," she says after a moment.
"I am."

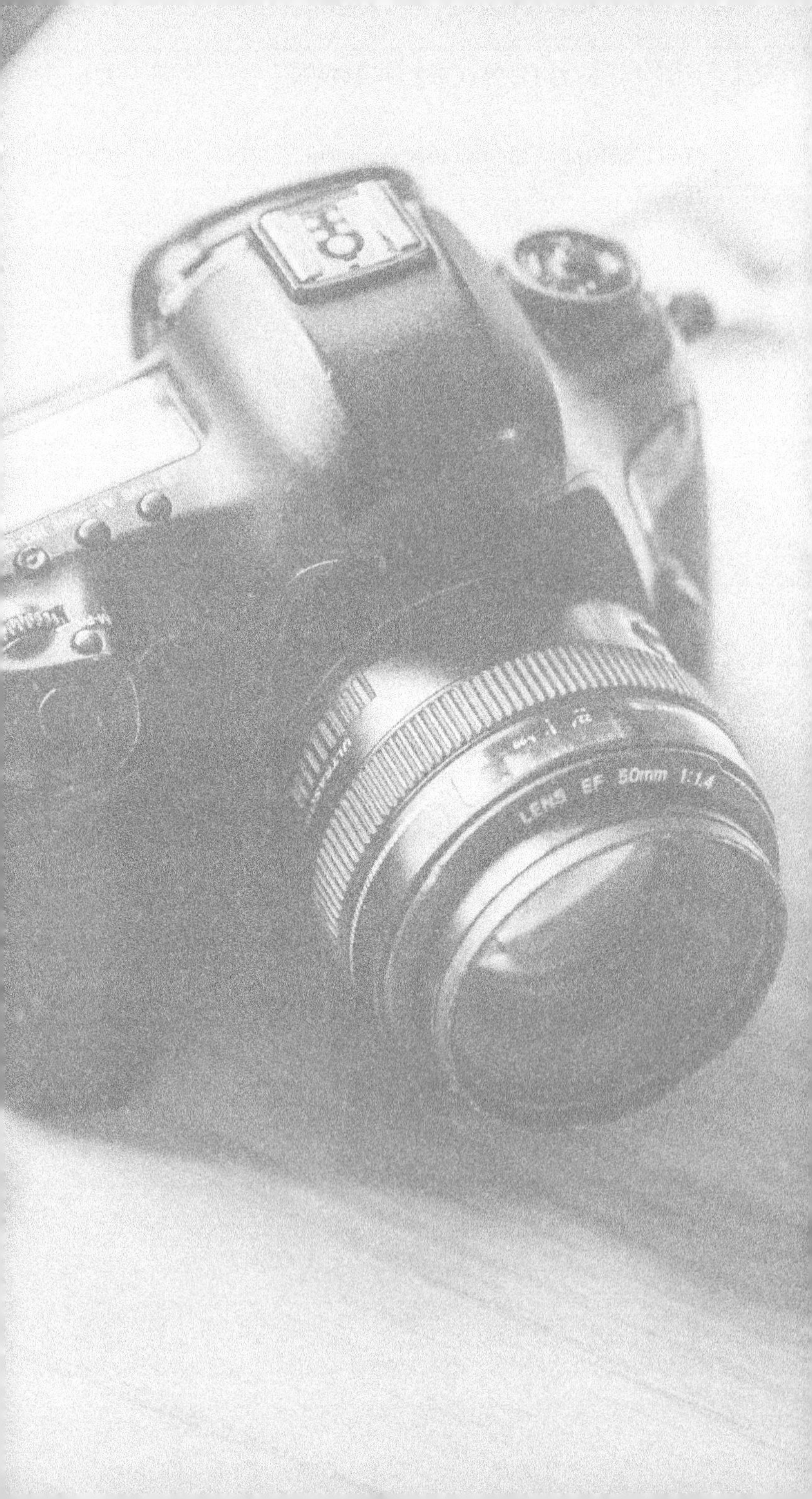
LENS EF 50mm 1:1.4

CHAPTER FORTY-ONE

Poppy

Late October

Click. Looking through the camera lens, I take a few more shots of the bay before glancing over my shoulder at Owen. He's looking handsome, as always, with wind off the water tousling his hair around—it's slightly longer than when we first met and I really like it. Waving, he turns back toward the boardwalk and heads off to get us a refill on our drinks. The air off the water is bitterly cold, despite it not even being past Halloween yet.

My attention goes back to my camera and the fall colors of the trees, trying to get the focus just right. A few adjustments to the white balance should hopefully get the colors the way I'm hoping. *Click.* Seeing the vibrant colors and the way they contrast over the open water, I like it, but want another shot. I decide to try some different settings before calling it a day. A few aperture adjustments and a couple lens changes later, I finally get the shot I was hoping for.

Walking across the wet sand towards where Owen sits, my mind brightens at the promise of a warm drink and a cozy blanket to snuggle with him under. He shoots me a warm smile, looking back to the book he's been absorbed in while I've been off taking pictures. I tried shooting with Steven once and I felt myself constantly worried that he was bored or annoyed with me. And he usually was. Owen is more simple and perfectly happy to sit, reading on the beach while I take as long as I need. Even encouraging me to take my time.

I'm not sure when I'll finally get used to how kind and affirming he is.

Slouching down on the blanket, he hands me a warm to-go cup. I chatter out, "Thank you." I didn't realize how cold I had gotten by being closer to the water.

"You're welcome," he says as he leans down to kiss against my hair. "Clara was shocked you wanted something other than coffee, but I promised her I was only doing as you asked."

"It is rare, but I do drink other things."

"How is it going?" He gestures to my camera.

"Great." I click through the pictures to show him the shot.

"That's beautiful." He leans over my shoulder to watch the pictures as I click through them all. I always take a million shots in hopes of getting that one perfect one and he seems content to sit through them all.

"Thanks, I've been trying to get a similar shot the past few years, but this year the trees and the weather finally cooperated for me. How's your book?" I can't help but smile looking at the shot. It's perfect and I can hardly wait to edit it and see how it looks printed.

"That's great. Book is good, also just enjoying this view. I'm not sure I'll ever get tired of it." He looks out towards the water, taking in the spray and surf as it dances around in the fall sunlight.

"If Honey Cove had a tourism department, that picture would be perfect," he adds before taking a sip of his own drink.

Sally, my friend from my hotel in Toronto, had called me last month and asked if she could purchase some of the photos I had emailed her after my trip for use by her hotel. I didn't realize she's also the owner. I was definitely surprised, but excited by the idea of anyone other than me enjoying the photos. *My photos.* It was quite flattering and I have been happily basking in the glow of that and everything with Owen ever since.

"Oh, perhaps I'll email them." We laugh. Just as I'd hoped, he wraps us both in a blanket and pulls me close to him. After packing up my camera, I return the snuggle and lean in, savoring the extra warmth and break from the wind.

"Can you believe it's almost winter? Winter is a lot worse here than in New York. Did you bring your parka?"

He rolls his eyes, but shoots back, "I'll be fine. I have a very cozy girlfriend to keep me warm." He leans down, pulling my face softly towards his and kissing me with the smallest hint of pressure that makes me question if it even happened. When he pulls away, his eyes are looking straight into mine and my heart races at the closeness.

I remind myself that he's been here before, often visiting relatives for the holidays. He should be well prepared for the cold that is coming. While I know all of his relatives, our paths never crossed before this due to breaks, traveling, and other things. "Hey, Owen," I whisper.

He turns towards me, chin brushing over my head before he leans down to meet my eyes. "Yeah?"

"This is nice."

CHAPTER FORTY-TWO

Owen

"I think 'nice' might be putting it mildly," I say, leaning in for another kiss. Her lips feel right against mine. Just like this day.

She gives me an extra peck on the cheek and shifts so she's tucked against me with my arm around her once more. Letting out a contented sigh she says, "You might be right about that."

I smile. Something I do a lot around this amazing woman.

We watch the water for a bit longer, content to take in the view with our drinks and I think about her photos and how beautiful they are. And how I can tell when she scrolls through and finds that she got *the* shot. It's not just her eyes widening or her face lighting up. No, her whole body seems to radiate with pride.

"Can I ask you something?"

She rests her head against my shoulder. "Of course."

I try to phrase my question the right way. "Is there a reason you don't have any of your photos up in your house?"

"I think Andi might be the only other person to ask me that," she says, amusement tickling her voice for a moment.

"You have an observant best friend," I comment.

"And an observant boyfriend," she says, playfully nudging my side with her elbow. I kiss the top of her head and then rest my cheek there, feeling the same fluttering sensation whenever she calls me her boyfriend.

"The only photos I've taken that are framed or displayed are at my parents' house," she explains.

"You never put your own up?" I ask, looking down at her.

She shakes her head slightly and her nose scrunches up adorably. "I didn't feel that keen on filling the walls with my art in case I was going to be moving in with my ex at some point. It seemed, I don't know, presumptuous maybe, that he'd want a bunch of my photos up."

My mouth opens to say what I want to say... *Why wouldn't he already have your photos up after being together for over five years?* But I close it, take a breath in through my nose and settle on saying, "Well, he was a fool for not already having one up on every wall."

I lean down to kiss the tip of her nose. "On a completely unrelated note, can I get some of the photos from today?"

She snorts out a laugh. "Completely unrelated, huh?"

"Absolutely," I say, cupping her cheek in my hand and kissing her until her mouth opens and I can taste her. Pulling away so we're not making out like teenagers on the beach, I rest my forehead against hers. "I was going to ask you that before I knew why you didn't have your photographs displayed. I want reminders of you all around my apartment besides the handful of things you've left."

"I suppose that could be arranged, Mr. Wright."

Immediately straightening up, I look around us for a student or one of their parents.

"What on earth was that about?" she asks.

"You only call me Mr. Wright at school and I thought you might have seen someone," I explain.

"Owen, you do know that people have seen us together outside of school, right? That's part of life in a small town."

"You're okay with it? If a student sees us together?" I ask.

"Well, I don't need to grab your ass in front of any young, impressionable minds, but I wouldn't have a problem with your arm around me or holding your hand." My body relaxes with her response, we really hadn't covered what to do when we run into a student or their parent. She gets that little wrinkle between her brows as her expression turns thoughtful. "Are you okay with that?"

"I like that I don't have to hide anything about how I feel about you," I explain, trying to get my thoughts in order. "I mean, we're not kissing at school or anything, but that's where we work and that wouldn't be appropriate, even if it would cause Noah to do a happy dance to see us holding hands walking down the hallway."

"Oh, he definitely would," she laughs.

"But I like what we have. A lot."

"I do too," she says, leaning against me once more and looking out over the water that's still catching the last of the sunset's colors. After a few minutes of quiet, she starts to shiver a little.

"Okay, time to go inside," I say, giving her waist a squeeze.

"But it's so pretty." She pouts adorably.

"I know it is, so why don't you unpack your camera for a few last shots while I get the sand out of the blanket?"

"I get to take pictures while you clean up?"

I nod.

"How can I say no to that?" She gives me a quick kiss on the cheek and enthusiastically gets her camera out, picking out just one lens.

As I bring the blankets away from our books and drinks, I turn back and watch her for a moment. She's completely engrossed in the views and capturing the fading light. And she's absolutely stunning. Her bangs are blowing this way and that, while her hands are steady and sure.

I know she's freezing again, so I only fold up the blanket we sat on and drop it over my book. As I approach her from behind so I don't disturb her frame, I feel calmer and more alive. She's both grounding for me and filled with endless possibilities. It hasn't taken long for me to figure out that I'm already falling for this incredible woman.

"Let me know when I can put the blanket over your shoulders so you don't start shivering again," I say quietly so I don't startle her and ruin her shot.

"It's like you read my mind," she says, her shutter clicking a few more times before lowering the camera. My hands rub her arms to add warmth after draping the blanket on her. "Just a few more?"

"Take your time, Poppy. I'm not going anywhere."

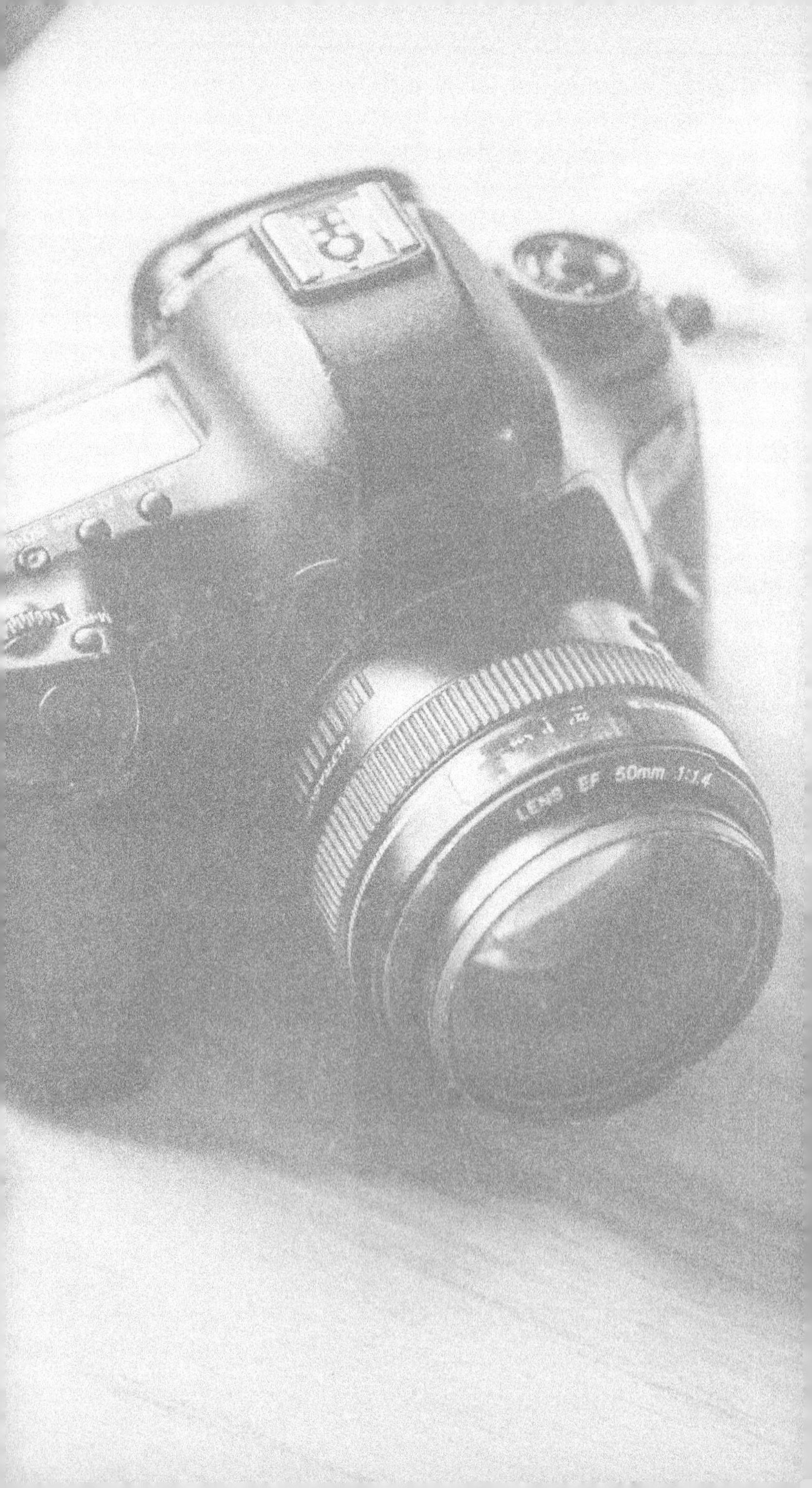
LENS EF 50mm 1:1.4

CHAPTER FORTY-THREE

Poppy

I don't know how he does it. In the span of one sentence, he makes me feel more secure in our relationship than I have with any other partner. *I'm not going anywhere.*

One sentence and my mind is racing, jumping to the future when it's only been a short time together. *Calm down, Poppy.* My hands shake with shivers as I try to focus on another picture, this one down the shoreline, catching the waves as they crash over rocks and send salty spray onto the shore. Despite my best efforts, my heart continues its thumping, making it hard to concentrate.

Owen's warm hands run down my arms as I look at the screen to see if I've captured the shot the way I wanted. I love that he doesn't rush and isn't afraid to just stand here with me while I take pictures. "That one is gorgeous," his deep voice whispers in my ear. Another shiver runs down my arms but this time for an entirely different reason.

"Thanks, I think that's good for today." Turning around in his arms, I meet his gaze and I find myself wishing we could have more time together today.

"Head home?"

"Yeah, it's so cold and I have some grading I need to get done before Andi comes over." His face flashes with a quick sadness but it's quickly replaced with a grin.

"I'm glad you'll get to see Andi. I'm afraid I've been monopolizing all of your time lately. It will be good for you two to talk."

"You haven't been monopolizing me. I've just been *enthusiastic* about our time together." Leaning into him, our lips meeting halfway. A flush works its way up my neck and I feel both so at home and so alive in the moment. "Besides, I think she's been busy being a newlywed too."

Breaking away, I crouch to put my camera away before the trek back to the boardwalk and home. Our kiss goodbye is long and drawn out, making me wish there were more hours in the day.

"Coming!" I shout as Andi continues to knock on the door. The afternoon got away from me and as I run down the stairs, hair sopping wet from my shower, I can see Andi's green eyes peeping through the window.

"What are you doing? Did you forget about me?" Her slightly annoyed voice echoes through the closed door.

"I could never," I say, opening the door. "I'm so sorry, the day has just gone by so quickly."

Her eyes widen. "Oh, did Owen hang out here for a little too long?" She narrows her gaze suspiciously, taking in my disheveled look and wet hair.

"Hey now," I give her shoulder a playful slap. "Nothing like that. I've been grading all afternoon." Gesturing at my piles of papers and artwork on the table, I open the door wider for her to make her way inside.

"Okay, okay. You two have just been...*intense.*"

"In a bad way?"

"No, not at all. Just like very into each other in an adorable way." She pulls two beers out of one of the bags she brought and hands me one before we both collapse on the couch.

"It has been intense."

"How are you feeling about it all?"

"Good, he's so sweet and mature in a way. I feel like I'm actually dating a man," I laugh. I've thought this for a while now, but never voiced it before. "Every other guy I've been with, which was mostly Steven, has always seemed like they've been in it for them, you know? But with Owen, it feels like we're both wanting to make each other's lives better."

"That's great. You deserve to be with someone like that." She takes a long sip before adding, "Are you wanting to run or are you handling it okay?"

This makes me pause. I've been blissfully happy in my time with Owen and it's just like my best friend to bring out all the hard, no bullshit questions within five minutes of walking in the door. "I don't want to run. But it does feel strange, like I'm not entirely sure what to do with myself or how to just be content."

She is quiet, letting me think.

"Today, for the first time, I thought about the future with him in it. We were just on the beach, I was taking pictures, and somehow it just felt good and right to be with him." Our slow day of doing everyday, normal things was my favorite day we've spent together. Thinking back about even our first official date, we've always been able to enjoy our time together no matter how mundane the activity.

"I don't think it's strange, but I can understand why that might feel odd given your last relationship." She smiles at me over her drink.

"Ah, I forgot, I have snacks!" I jump up and race over to the kitchen to pull out the guac and chips, but can't seem to let go of the comfort I feel in Andi's reassurances and encouragement. It means a lot that she supports me and sees this relationship as a positive one. Stopping, I turn towards her, I'm sure assessing if I'm deflecting or ignoring what she's saying. "Thanks, Andi. I needed to hear that."

"You're welcome, now bring on the guac."

CHAPTER FORTY-FOUR

Owen

I shouldn't be surprised when Brandon sends a group message that we should hang out tonight. It's something that tends to happen when Poppy and Andi spend the evening together, so I invite my cousins over.

"No blue-eyed date tonight?" I ask Graham, the first to arrive, since he's been lighter than usual on details in our messages.

He gives Samson a few head scratches while getting out of his shoes and then flops on the couch with a groan. "No."

"This seems to call for a beer," I say, marching to the kitchen to get four, knowing the other two are almost here. Graham now has his arm draped over his eyes dramatically. "Maybe I should give you mine, too, you look like you could use a few."

"I think I fucked up," he mumbles, not moving.

"Do you want to talk about it now or wait for the others?"

"Might as well wait." He sits up and holds out his hand for a bottle when the buzzer sounds.

"You don't have to wait long, at least," I say, leaving him for a moment to buzz the brothers up. A gray ball of fur trots over to the door, purring, which makes me suspect he thinks Poppy might be coming up.

After a moment, the brothers are inside and Samson jumps into his cat tree after getting a few pets, clearly minimally interested in my guests.

"We need a schedule that doesn't revolve around when Andi and Poppy are having girls' night," James says.

"Did we interrupt something for you?" his brother asks.

James shakes his head. "It's not about if something was interrupted, it's about the four of us having our own thing." Then he gives Graham an assessing look. "Why do you look miserable?"

"Likely because I feel that way," he replies, rubbing the stubble on his chin.

We all give him time to speak. Even though he's clearly distressed, there's something that I love at this moment. We're all comfortable. There's not a question if Graham is going to share. There's not a question if we may or may not be interested in listening. We're all just *here*.

"So, you know that I've been seeing someone?" he asks.

"The mystery someone with blue eyes?" Brandon asks. "The person you've given us no more hints about?"

Graham gives me a look like I can give them details and I shrug saying, "I just saw him at the wedding."

"My wedding?"

Both Brandon and James look back and forth between Graham and me.

"What did I miss at the wedding?" James asks.

"Nothing, really," Graham says. "I danced with him once and we talked for a while."

"Oh my god, I'm going to lose my marbles over here if you don't tell us the name of the guy you met at my wedding, or what we shall now refer to as the match-making event of the year."

"Casey, his mom and Andi's mom are friends from college, and they live in Marietta." He picks at the label on his bottle which is half full now and takes a deep breath. "I don't know where else to start, so here we go. His grandmother lives with them and needs round-the-clock care. Casey has been taking night shifts for years so his parents can keep working their regular jobs. Insurance covers day nurses, but the modifications for the house have been a lot so hiring someone isn't really an option if his parents want to retire in the next decade, or four. But they make sure he always has weekends free."

He takes a deep swig of his beer. "I'm telling you this because it's not easy for us to see each other and we try to make the most of that time. Anyway, we've been together since shortly after the wedding and the other day we went to a movie and out for dinner. Everything was going great. Then Brad came in with his girlfriend and stopped at the table for a moment, being friendly. And I introduced Casey as my friend."

Graham drops his face into his hand, making a sound of frustration.

"Damn," Brandon says, patting Graham on the shoulder.

"I know, it was a stupid-ass thing to say," he says. "The rest of the night he was withdrawn, and instead of coming back to my place, or even kissing me, he gave me a fist bump, got in his car, and went back to Marietta. I've called and messaged a dozen times and he finally responded yesterday with, 'we're good, buddy.'"

"Ouch," James says, wincing. "I'm sorry, Graham. Even I can see he's not taking it well and we all know how terrible I am with relationships."

Over the years, I definitely noticed that James was usually single whenever my family visited, so I'm not surprised to hear his admission now.

"So, in short, with one very poorly-chosen word, I seem to have screwed everything up." He runs his free hand through his surfer-length hair and sighs.

"Well, you just have to see him and talk." Brandon makes it sound so simple. "When I screw up, I need to see Andi, preferably with daisies, and then I can get my thoughts in order and calm down to apologize. Otherwise, my thoughts spiral with all the ways she might hate me."

Graham shakes his head. "I don't think Casey would appreciate me showing up on his family's doorstep, even if I had a bouquet of flowers for him."

"He might just need some time. And you might need some time, too, so you can be clear with what you hope to have with him," I say. "I don't mean you need to declare your undying love for him and ask him to marry you or anything like that. But you might want to know what you want him to be to you. Do you want him to be someone you introduce as your boyfriend or partner?"

He nods. "It felt wrong to introduce him as just a friend. Neither of us are seeing other people and we've been really fucking happy."

"So tell him that." We all look at James. "It doesn't have to be complicated. Apologize first, and then tell him that it felt wrong and you shouldn't have said it."

"I tried."

I think about the space Poppy needed. That we both needed, really, just so we could wrap our heads around what we had experienced at the wedding through becoming coworkers. "Time might not be easy to give him, but maybe it'll help both of you."

"Yeah, you might be right." Another frustrated sigh before he sits up and slaps a hand on his thigh. "Okay, time to talk about something else so I have a break from obsessing and kicking myself for being stupid."

"Cards?" I offer.

Three enthusiastic yeses sound and we spend the rest of the evening playing poker and using pretzels to place our bets.

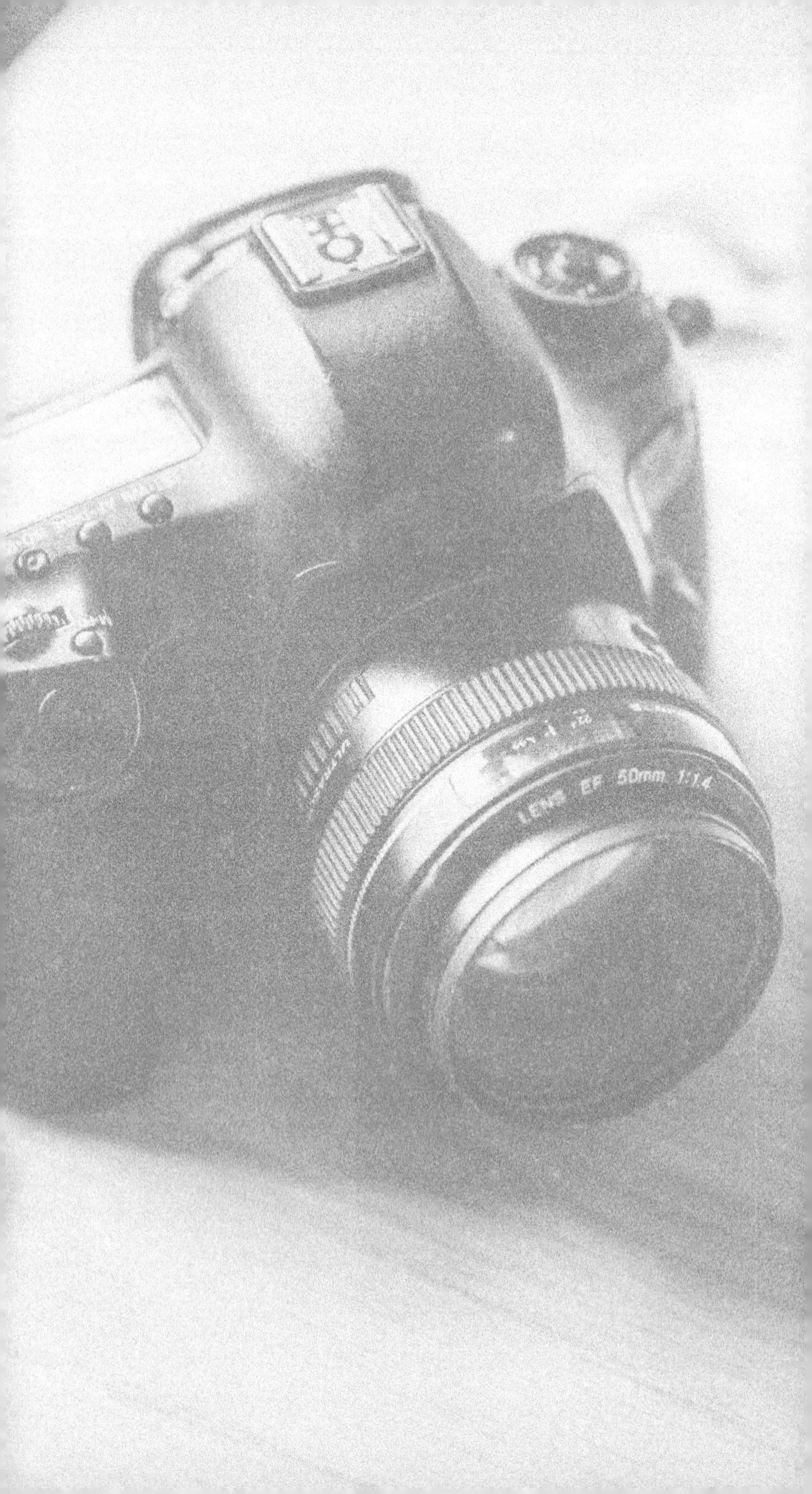
LENS EF 50mm 1:1.4

CHAPTER FORTY-FIVE

Poppy

Early November

"Did you grab the mums for my mom?" We're rushing out the door and I can't help but catch how adorable Owen is as he carries a million things: my water, his own bag from staying over last night, and other things for the dinner. I lock the door behind us before walking down the steps to his car.

"Yeah, I have them. Where are we meeting them again?" Both sliding into the car, I bristle as the freezing seat hits my back, luckily, he has heated seats so it will soon be a forgotten memory.

"Calico Cafe." I rub my mittens together and blow into my hands. It isn't even December yet but the air has a crisp, cold feel and it's been below freezing the past few nights.

"Oh yeah, that's right. I can get that IPA I love." A smile spreads across his face. One of my favorite things about him is his ability to get excited about little things. It could be a fresh cup of coffee, a snuggle from Samson, getting to help me with something, or an IPA, but he brings a lightness to my life that I didn't even realize I was in search of.

"What?" he asks, turning the car on and pulling out of the driveway.

"I just like you." Leaning over, I peck a kiss onto his cheek and bask in his summer, cedar scent that has come to feel so comforting.

It's only a few minutes drive down the beach to the Cafe, so there isn't much time for chit chat, but I'm looking forward to seeing my parents. I message with my mom most days, but with how much time

Owen and I have been spending together, I haven't been able to see them quite as much as I'd like.

As we pass by the bookstore, I ask, "Did Grace get in that book you were looking for?"

"Not yet. She said she'd call when it came in."

The cafe is one of the only places that has an actual parking lot on the boardwalk, which tonight I'm thankful for as it looks fairly busy. Getting out of the car, we wave to a fellow teacher, and Grace herself actually is walking in at the same time. *Looks like this is the place to be tonight.*

As we pass through the front doors, the owner calls out to us and I see my mom frantically waving at me from a booth towards the back.

"There they are," I call out over the many voices echoing in the small restaurant. Owen follows me, holding onto my hand as we weave through the tables getting to my parents.

"Hi! I'm glad you found us, it's crazy in here tonight," Mom says, pointing us to the hooks for our coats along a back wall. Pulling off my scarf and setting my bag down in the booth I take in the room again, spotting Cicely and her family as well. She waves with a big smile on her face and I wonder if she's seen Owen as well.

"Yeah, do you know why?" We both get settled across from my parents and I start to look over the menu even though I've been here so often I have it memorized. Owen and my parents have spent time together, but this all still feels new and the familiar butterflies give my stomach a fluttery feel.

"Robert thinks everyone is wanting to get out with the cold moving in," my dad chimes in. Looking towards Owen, he adds, "How are things going with school, kids treating you alright?"

"Yeah, for sure. I think it helps they know me from last year, so I'm not a brand new face in the building. A little trust has been built there." He pores over the menu as well, even though I know he chose what he wanted when we were still at my house. *Must be a little nervous too.*

Too quickly, my mom adds, "That's good. Are you thinking you'll stay?"

"Mom!" I stare at her over my water, almost spitting out my sip.

"What? I think it's a fair question." She holds up her hands and gives me a look like I should know her better than this. *Of course she would want to get involved.*

"That's the plan. I am loving being closer to my cousins and of course, spending time with other people." He reaches for my hand under the table and I feel heat rise to my face.

"Well, we like to hear that." My dad gives my mother a similar disapproving look before smirking towards me. "We're buying, so get whatever you'd like." *Such a fatherly thing to say.* I'm a grown woman, but my parents still like to treat me when we go out.

A waiter steps up to the table, clearly flustered and out of breath. I recognize him as a student from a few years back, but can't place his name. "What can I get you all?"

CHAPTER FORTY-SIX

Owen

I pretend to study the menu some more and wait for everyone else to order. As I suspected, Walter gets apps for the table.

"And what can I get for you?" It's a new waiter who I don't recognize and he seems stressed and a little sweaty.

"I'll have the IPA on tap and a taco salad," I say, handing him my menu.

"Great, I'll have your drinks out in a minute."

Walter thanks him and brings the conversation back to me. "Tell us more about your cousins. We know Brandon pretty well by now, but not the other two as much."

"Well, Brandon's brother James is the oldest. He's in IT and lives in Maple Springs. Graham is the youngest who lives between Honey Cove and Maple Springs."

"Graham has longer hair, correct?"

I catch Poppy sending me a sympathetic look as I get peppered with questions, but really, I don't mind talking about my family.

"Yep, he's a bartender who surfs when there are waves nearby. It's been really nice being able to see them regularly." I pause as our drinks are delivered and take a sip of mine, which is delicious as usual. "Poppy has shared a little with me, but I'd love to hear about how you two started dating."

Her mom blushes. "Oh, that old story?"

"Oh come on, Mom, it's adorable," Poppy chimes in, slipping her hand in mine under the table.

Michelle begins the tale of how Walter accidentally bumped into her outside of the high school, dumping her papers right into a muddy puddle. He promised to help her redo all the work and met her at her locker at the end of the day to walk to the old malt shop.

It really is a cute story, and being able to sneak glances at Poppy while her mom tells it feels pretty perfect. She has a soft smile during most of it and laughs when her dad interjects with details her mom claims to be irrelevant, like how Michelle refused his help all day because she was so distraught and that he was waiting at her locker at the end of the day so she couldn't avoid him.

"The rest is history," Michelle says, looking at her husband and putting her hand on his arm.

He covers her hand with his. "And it's been a pretty phenomenal time since I did that."

"Did you know each other well before that?" I ask.

"Not really," she answers.

"She was in the advanced classes along with choir and band. I was a bit of a jock at that time, if you can believe it. So we almost never had classes together."

"What sports did you play?" I ask as Poppy's thumb caresses mine and I flash her a smile.

"Football and baseball. I was a wide receiver and outfielder."

"We'll have to pull out the team photos the next time we visit so you can see his long hair," Poppy says excitedly. "I haven't seen those in a while."

"We should do that soon," Michelle says warmly.

"Absolutely," I reply.

It's not much longer until our food arrives. Conversation flows fairly naturally and I let myself relax more. I realize that I haven't been at this point in a relationship in quite some time. I'm trying to remember the last time I met someone's parents back in New York and I think it was at least three years ago. The last time I saw a girlfriend's parents several times was even longer.

Wow.

Was I just disconnected in New York? I don't think so. Poppy makes me feel more than I ever have this early in a relationship. We've already had a few bumps along the way, but I wouldn't trade any of it for anything else.

Even with the rocky start, I'd like to think she feels the same.

They continue to tell stories of Poppy growing up over the years. Early piano lessons, art projects, and even a summer as a lifeguard. But I notice the stories all take place before she would have started seeing her ex. Did he hit it off with her parents?

I don't feel like I have to show him up or anything like that. But I do want them to see that I'm not him. They've been so open and welcoming so far. Her mom has been pretty direct with her questions about my intentions for staying in Honey Cove and they seem to be happy with my honesty.

If the school would like to keep me on, I'd really like to stay. The longer I'm here, the more connected I feel to this community and the harder it would be to go back to New York. My relationships with my cousins have all grown and I think we'd stay in touch better, but it would be different. It would be like it used to be. Those three seeing each other regularly and me visiting a few times each year.

"Is everything okay?" Poppy leans in to ask.

"Sorry, I was just thinking about how much has changed since I moved here."

"Good changes?"

"Only the best."

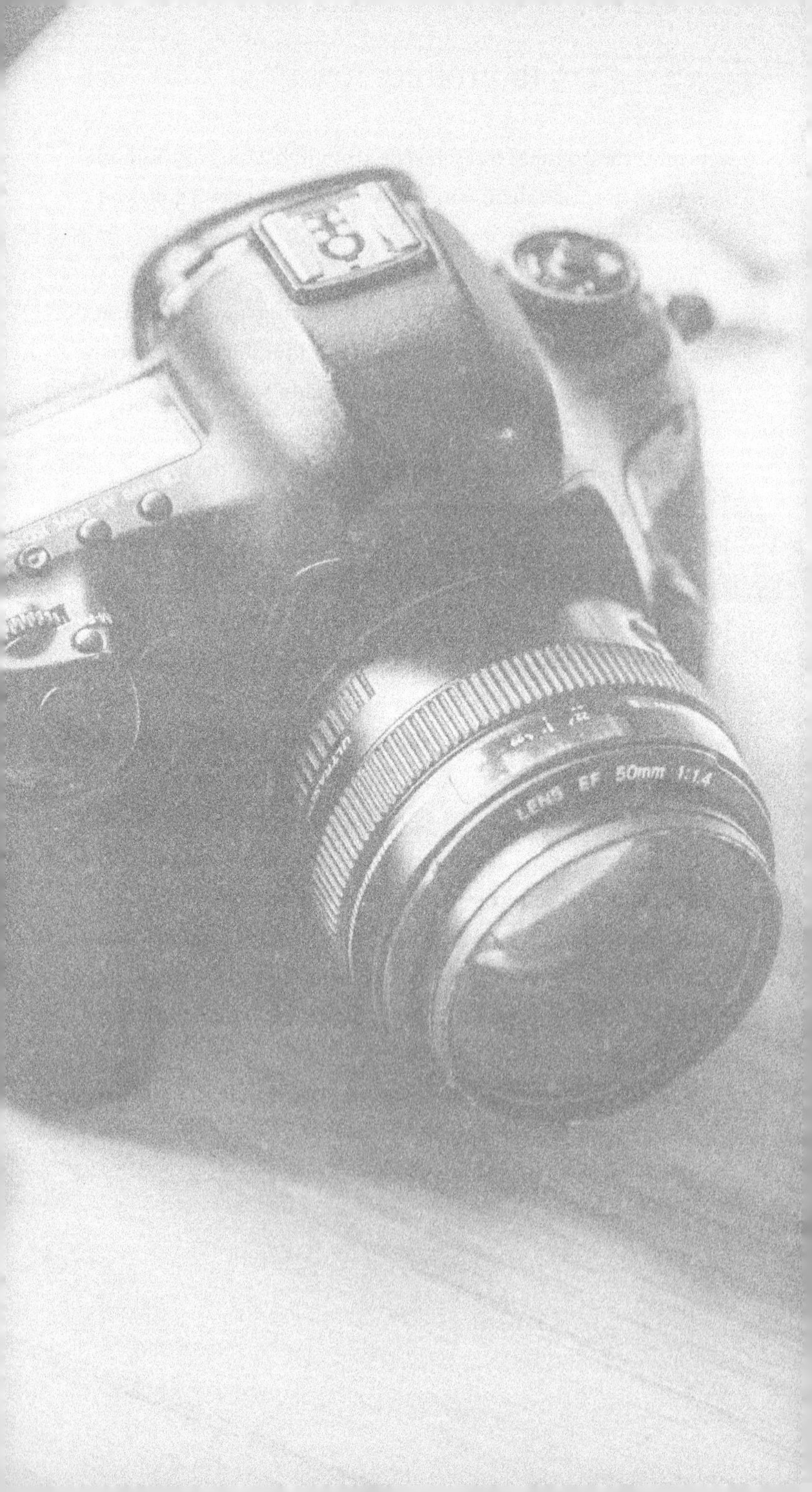
LENS EF 50mm 1:1.4

CHAPTER FORTY-SEVEN

Poppy

Mid December

The bell rings. The *final* bell.

"Okay, make sure to work on your research project over break and have a good time off," I yell, suddenly out of breath. "And, be safe." *Oh, please be safe.* With winter finally here, the roads are snowy, icy, and bound to create some terrible conditions. Along with the multitude of poor choices high schoolers can make in this town...I should know.

Waving as the last student bounds out of my classroom, I rush down the stairs to join the other teachers at the front doors to see the kids off. Standing next to Noah, he leans over to whisper, "So, excited to meet the fam this week?"

"Shush!" My eyes dart around quickly, scanning the entryway. While not everything is a secret here anymore, Owen and I have somehow kept it fairly quiet from students that we're together. I haven't had one of them mention it to me and I'd like to keep it that way.

Before I get a chance to admonish him even more, my eyes catch with Owen's across the busy hallway. He smiles and his eyebrows lift in a way that I've come to adore. It's something in between surprise to see me and excitement, but I'll take it. My heart flutters from the attention and I attempt to turn it back to sending students out for break and into the snow.

I am still slightly in shock that I'll be meeting his parents in a few days. Like everything with him, things have been fast and crazy, but lovely. I'm sure meeting his parents will be more of the same, but it hasn't stopped my nerves from wreaking havoc on my composure about the situation.

After the last student is ushered out into the snowflake filled air, teacher small talk ensues and I attempt to make a beeline back to my classroom to pack up. I'm stopped by Ms. Neemeyer, who asks for my opinion on an outfit for a Christmas party she's attending with some coworkers. I wonder if Mr. Grube will be there.

After helping her decide and telling her how beautiful she will look, I'm safely back in my room and start packing up all of the grading I need to catch up on. Grabbing my laptop, papers, and a print I had developed for Owen's present, I begin putting them into my bag. Before I can finish getting everything safely hidden inside, I hear, "What's that?"

"What's what?" I innocently ask, recognizing his voice instantly and maneuvering my body to hide the print as quickly as I can.

"That, there in your bag."

"Oh nothing, just my computer and some grading." Turning towards him, I smile and try to plaster on my most innocent looking face, but know I am terrible at lying.

"Mmhm, okay." He wraps his arms around me before tilting my chin up to meet his in a sweet kiss. "You're so sneaky. You ready?"

"Yeah, I'm ready." We agreed to spend tonight at my place since his is already spotless for his parents' arrival, order in food after the craziness of the last few days before break, and watch my favorite Christmas movie.

Taking one last glance at my classroom, I turn out the lights and head out into the snowy wonderland that has become Honey Cove. It's hard to imagine being gone from here for two entire weeks, but the break is much needed and I am looking forward to the time with Owen and both our families. Despite these pesky nerves.

"How'd you like the pizza?" I say, my mouth still half full of my own slice. Owen finished a few minutes ago while I continued to scarf down more.

"It's good. I like the pepper flakes they put on it."

The movie ended a bit ago, but we're still lounging on the couch, finishing our food and talking.

"How are you feeling about this week?" I've been secretly wondering if he is as nervous as I am about spending time with each other's families. He's met my parents a few times, so it isn't anything new for him, but I would guess it's still somewhat nerve wracking. Turning, I set my feet next to him on the couch.

"I'm really excited to have my parents here. They know the town of course, but it will be great to show them my own space and let them into my world here." Nodding, he runs his hand up my calf.

"That makes sense. Are you feeling okay about spending more time with my parents?"

"Of course," he shoots back, rather quickly. "I don't get nervous around them anymore. They're really nice people."

I know that should make me happy, and I'd never want him to suffer, but how is he so calm? "I'm feeling a bit nervous."

"I know, you've been biting your lip for the past week. I think it might be permanently marked."

"So funny, silly guy." I move to reposition myself away from him, but before I can, he grabs my leg again. This time using his hand to make his way up from my foot, rubbing slower, gentle rhythmic circles until reaching my thigh.

"You have nothing to be nervous about. They'll love you," he whispers. Moving his body next to mine on the couch, he pulls me in for a kiss. He looks at me intensely, setting my body on fire before adding, "I promise, they will. How could they not?"

My nerves are temporarily forgotten as I wrap my arms around him and quickly forget about the rest of the pizza I was planning on eating and decide on an entirely different type of dessert.

CHAPTER FORTY-EIGHT

Owen

"Owen, honey, can you help your father up the steps so he doesn't break something?" my mom says loud enough for Dad to hear while she reaches for the enormous floral arrangement he put together for the party.

"Of course, Mom." I hand it over, making sure she has a good grip since she's wearing gloves. "You be careful, too, we don't want anyone to have a broken bone tonight."

"I grew up with this ice, I know what I'm doing. It's you city boys I worry about."

My dad closes the trunk, several bags on each arm while mumbling something about New York getting plenty of snow and ice.

"Dad, let me take some of those." I know he'd be a little offended if I took them all. He'd likely say something about not needing to be fussed over and that he's all healed, which is mostly true.

"Did your mother put you up to this?" His eyebrow raises in suspicion.

"No, I just don't want to be the only one walking in empty-handed."

He smiles at my reply, obviously knowing that I want to help him, and letting me take some of the bags. We walk up the sidewalk to Brandon and Andi's home, which is already bustling with people. A few icicles hang from the edge of the roof, sparkling with the light of the setting sun.

Poppy would take a beautiful picture of them.

Looking away from the house, I shift the bags to one hand so I'm ready to assist my father in case he slips. Thankfully, he brought his grippiest boots for this visit and we all make it inside the house without incident.

"Uncle Daniel! We're so happy you made it," Brandon exclaims, stepping out of my mom's hug and coming in to hug my dad.

Andi stands just outside the crowded entryway with the arrangement in her arms. "It's so lovely to see you again, Mr. Wright, I'm just going to put these gorgeous flowers on the table, thank you so much. Please come in and we can take your coats to the office."

Aunt Mae comes around the corner waving to me and tugging my parents with her. I think back on the number of times we've had family get-togethers and how much my mom loves to be with her siblings.

"Your girlfriend is in the kitchen so my wife can greet people," Brandon says, slinging his arm around my shoulders and accepting my parents' coats with the other. "I've been kicked out for being 'too exuberant' apparently, so they might need another set of hands, if you happen to be interested."

"Well, I wouldn't want to leave them short-handed."

"No, we wouldn't want that." Mirth dances in his eyes and he gives me a playful shove toward the kitchen.

Andi grabs my jacket before I can bring it to their office myself, startling me with how fast she returned. "Sounds like you have someplace to be while I handle these."

"Are you two conspiring to give us alone time since my parents are here?"

She purses her lips at me. "Are you complaining?"

"Never."

"Then shoo," she says, flicking her hand toward the kitchen.

Poppy is poking dough with her fingertips with her back to me. Keeping my steps quiet, I slip behind her and grab her hips, pulling her against me.

She gives a little squeak of surprise at the contact, but relaxes into me almost immediately. "I wasn't sure when you were going to be here."

"How did you know it was me?" My lips kiss just behind her ear.

"No one has hands that grip me like that." She rests her back against me. "Plus, it would be highly inappropriate for someone else to hold me like this."

"I won't argue with that," I say, turning her around in my arms.

"But the bread," she protests feebly, already tugging me closer.

"I'm quite confident that the bread can wait for fifteen seconds while I greet my girlfriend."

She quickly looks at the two entrances to the kitchen to see if anyone is coming.

"They're all busy catching up and saying hello."

"You're sure?" she asks, looking once more.

"Aunt Mae took my parents into the living room, so all the commotion we can hear is them being fully absorbed in their own world. Do you think I can kiss my girlfriend now?"

A small smile appears. "I suppose you can."

Raising up on her toes as I lean down, she kisses me. We take our time, our lips confident and sure. When a little sound of pleasure leaves her, I wind my fingers through her hair and tip her head back, deepening our connection. Our mouths part and when our tongues touch, I can feel it all the way to my toes.

I can't get enough of this woman.

Laughter from the next room breaks us apart, reminding us that someone could walk in at any moment. A light flush rises on her cheeks—something I always love to see when she's kissed me.

"Oh no," she whispers frantically, using her arms to turn me around awkwardly. "I had a little oil on my hands from the bread and I think it's in your hair."

"At least you didn't grab my butt." I can't help but laugh at the situation as I spin around for her.

"You're lucky I didn't because I really like your butt." She uses her forearms to push on my shoulders. "You have to kneel so I can fully assess the damage."

Obediently, I do as she asks, sinking to my knees in the middle of the kitchen. She makes a few sounds of displeasure.

"Just run your hands through my hair a few times," I suggest. "It'll look like I used some product to look nice for the party."

"It's olive oil," she deadpans.

"My grandmother on my dad's side is half Italian, we'll pretend it's the latest trend if anyone notices."

"Oh my god, I can't believe I'm going to purposefully rub oily hands through my boyfriend's hair at a party where our parents are meeting." She's still hesitating.

"Need I remind you that you're a skilled art teacher and can likely turn this into something beautiful?"

"Nothing about this is anywhere close to what I teach," she says, her voice worried.

Tipping my head back, until I can see her hovering over my hair, I get her attention and say, "I trust you."

She lets out a little huff of air and gets a determined look on her face before nodding once, and putting her fingers into my hair to tilt my head the way she wants it. Using confident motions, she distributes the oil throughout my hair.

"I'm going to let you do this any time you want, just so you know," I murmur.

She gives my hair a little pull, forcing my face back up and swoops down for a quick kiss and then smiles at me. "You can stand now. It's hardly noticeable now that it's distributed."

Running my hand through it, I'm surprised that it doesn't feel weighed down. "Maybe this will be part of my hair routine from now on."

She rolls her eyes and washes her hands. "Yeah, right."

I follow her and wash up next before she puts me to work chopping olives for the focaccia she was preparing. As I'm chopping away, Andi comes into the kitchen with a stack of sheet pans covered in foil with a dusting of snow.

"These were sitting outside to stay cold since the fridge is packed," she explains when seeing my confused expression. She pauses and looks at me for a moment. "Did you do something different with your hair tonight? I don't know how I missed it when you came in."

Poppy and I exchange a glance, both of us trying to not smile.

"Just trying a little product in my hair, that's all."

"Well, it looks great. Kind of tousled."

Poppy has to cover her giggle with a pretend cough and I manage to thank Andi without bursting out laughing myself.

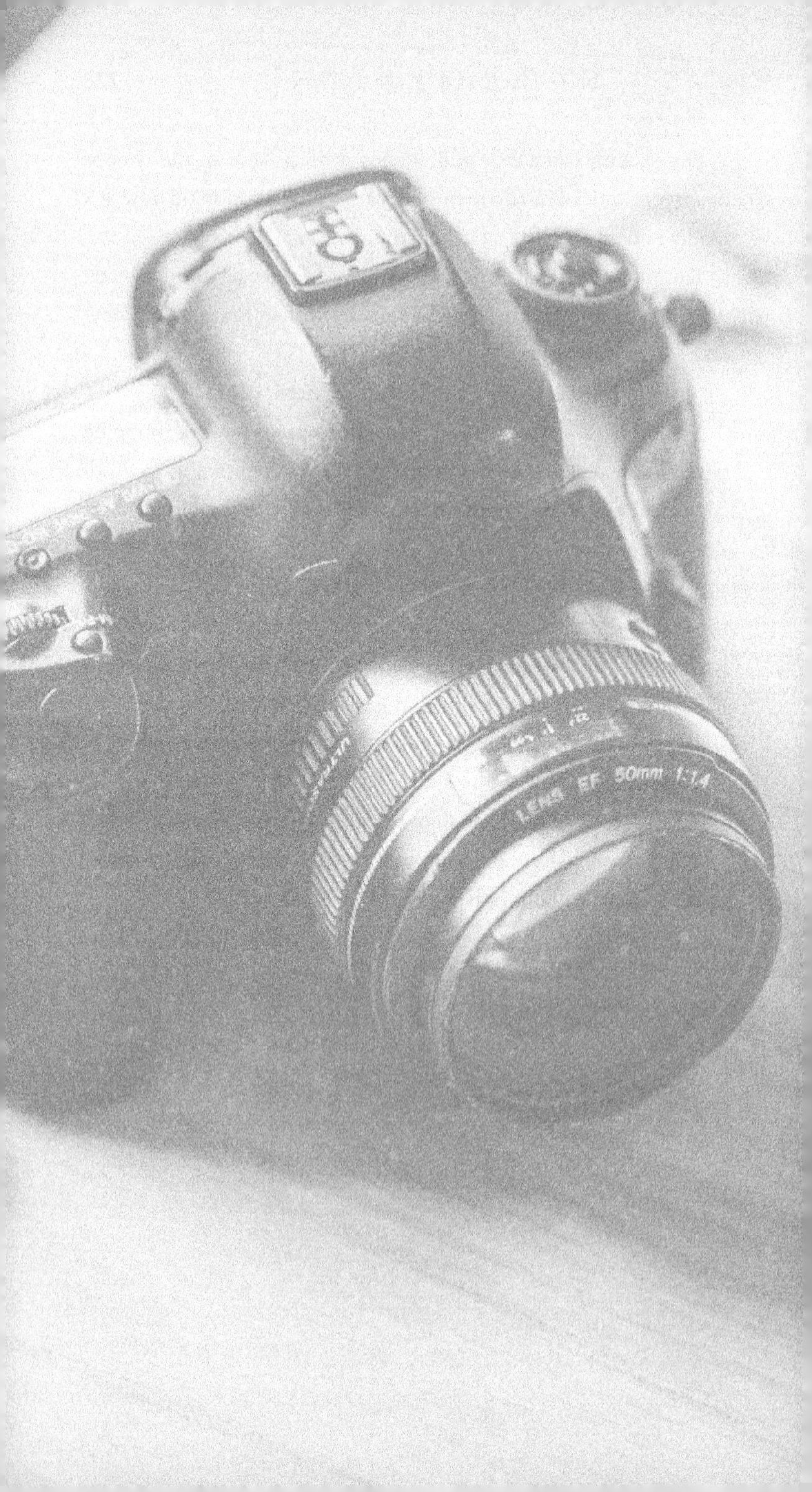
LENS EF 50mm 1:1.4

CHAPTER FORTY-NINE

Poppy

Andi's house is somehow more packed than the day of her wedding, which is saying something. Between all of Brandon's extended family, her parents, and my own, there is little room left to move around. Despite the cramped space around the many tables our parents have cobbled together, no one seems to mind. Everyone is happy, enjoying good food, drinks, and the best company.

Looking around and feeling Owen's hand move to my knee under the table, I can't help but think about what a difference a year makes. This time last year I would have been packing up for the holiday party at Steven's parents. The irony isn't lost on me as I think about how different I already feel given my short time with someone new. *I wonder if the others see it too?*

He leans over to whisper in my ear, "Are you okay, babe?" His hand squeezing my leg slightly. He knew I was nervous about today and I appreciate the subtle encouragement from him.

"Yeah, my head was somewhere else for a minute. I'm good though."

"I think they like you. My dad keeps asking me when he can see more of your photos." He nods towards his dad across the table from me. "Also, your mom and my mom have not stopped chatting for the past twenty minutes. They could be conspiring about something, but I'm going to assume it's a good sign." His breath feels warm against my neck and I lean my head over to his shoulder for a moment.

I'm struck by the fact that despite everything that's changed and everything I've been through this year, that I'm blissfully happy. I don't feel any longing or regret anymore. If anything, my time with Owen has shown me how much I deserved more and how Steven could never have given that to me no matter how things ended up between us.

"Thank you," I say softly back to Owen. My eyes glistening slightly.

"For what?" He looks back at me, his concern and confusion evident.

"Just for being you. I feel really happy."

He slides his arm around the back of my chair, angling his body closer to mine, his face suddenly serious. "I do too. I have a lot more I'd like to say and...I'd like to show you." He smiles, a devilish look in his eyes. "But my parents are here and I am not sure they'd appreciate it as much as you will."

"How about a kiss instead?"

Leaning down, he brushes his lips against mine and I revel in the way it warms me. He looks down at me for one last heated moment before we turn our attention back to the table and I'm snapped out of my daze.

"Everyone ready for a game of extreme spoons?" Brandon yells out. I've heard of the epic battles of the Taylor family for years from Andi, but didn't imagine I'd be part of them someday.

Owen laughs and shouts, "I'm in! And I know Poppy's been just waiting to play."

I give him a shocked look, before turning to everyone else and adding, "If you're ready to lose."

Amidst a chorus of, "ohhhs," another heated look passes between Owen and me. I lift my eyebrows in a flirty response.

"I know you're not all leaving me with the cleaning. Everyone helps clear first!" Andi has a crazed look on her face as she grabs a bowl of leftover salad and heads to the kitchen. We all know enough to listen and start bringing bowls and plates into the kitchen, dividing up jobs and before we know it, the food is put away, plates are clean, and all the parents are sitting around the kitchen table while the rest of us make our way to the living room with a fresh round of drinks.

"For those that haven't played before, the point of the game is to get four matches, then grab a spoon. If you see someone else grab a spoon, you can grab a spoon. Basically, you don't want to be left without a spoon. And the spoons have been placed outside in the snow by my beloved, Andi, who will not be playing this round for fairness. Thank you, sweetie." Brandon blows her a kiss as she settles herself on a couch, waiting for her turn in the next match.

My heart beats a little faster as the cards are dealt. *In the snow? I don't even have shoes on.* But before I can think too much about how unprepared I am, Brandon is yelling to start and I'm flipping cards like my life depends on it. Before I've even matched one card though Brandon has taken off through the doorway, whooping loudly, his four matching fives laid out on the ground. There's a split second where we all look at one another before bounding after him.

The snow is colder than I thought on my feet as I push through the others, all of us digging through the white powder frantically. I find one and can't believe my luck, but before my fingers curl around the handle, Owen has me around the waist, pulling me out of the way. Without thinking, I grab a handful of snow and toss it at him. He pauses long enough for me to grab my own spoon and shriek in victory.

"Ha!" I yell out, but before the words can get completely past my lips, he tackles me into the snow and we all start laughing. I turn and see our parents watching from the living room window, shaking their heads in disapproval, which for some reason makes me laugh all the more. I'm cold and wet, but my heart is full.

CHAPTER FIFTY

Owen

Being here with all of our families reminds me of Brandon and Andi's wedding. So much has changed since that day. I was waiting another day to tell my cousins that I'd be moving back to New York so it didn't take away from the celebrations. And I met the incredible woman who just rolled around in the snow with me, crowing her well-earned victory. Something about her caught my attention from the moment she walked into this house and subsequently turned my life into something *better*.

After we've shaken the snow from our clothes, we go back to the table and pass the spoons off to James who decided he was done with "snow wrestling."

"Owen, I'm surprised you're the one who lost that round," Graham says above the chatter.

"I might have been a little distracted by *someone* pelting me with snow." I tug Poppy closer to my side, only making her laugh.

"Yeah, it was definitely just the snow that distracted you," Andi teases.

"You got me there." I give the top of Poppy's head a peck, her hair damp from the snow. My heart swells when she looks up to kiss me. It's not the first time we've kissed in front of everyone. Hell, it's not the first time we even kissed at this table tonight. But the way we're both able to share our affection around our loved ones feels incredible, especially since she was feeling nervous.

Part of me wants to take this moment to finally speak the words that reflect what I'm feeling. But those words, especially the first time I say them, are only for Poppy.

James returns and Andi points at me. "You're back in since I'm playing," she says. "We'll call that the warm up round."

Brandon begins to protest and with one look from Andi, he stops and looks ready to take us all down. We start the game, and Brandon complains every few seconds about how long he has to wait for the cards to make it through all of us to get to him, since he's on the wrong side of his wife to get her discards. As I pick up cards, I notice Poppy tensing to my left, excitement almost radiating off of her and I'm sure she's getting close to a four-of-a-kind.

Instead of worrying about what I might be trying to find or missing something, I change tactics and wait for someone to leave the table first.

Sure enough, Poppy lets out a little squeal of disbelief, throws her four sevens face-up on the table and almost knocks her chair over in her rush to get outside. Of course I'm hot on her trail and by the time she slows to open the front door, I'm caught up.

The others are closing in, their laughter pouring out into the cold evening. From what I can hear, Andi must be on Brandon's back trying to slow him down with Graham blocking their path. I quickly scan the snow, looking for footprints away from what we all churned up last round and, sure enough, there are some leading to the right. Two spoons stand upright in the snow just a few feet apart from each other. Poppy, mere inches from me, sees them, too, and we both dive for the same one.

"You're going down, again," she says, her eyes glued to her target. That simple challenge switches my focus from the spoon to her.

My arm snakes around her waist mid-air and I pull her against me and roll both of us away from the first spoon. The second spoon is just above my head, but when I reach for it, She wriggles out of my grip, straddles my chest, and tickles my sides. My arms automatically drop to guard my ticklish spots and she quickly pins them in place. Before I know it, she has the spoon in hand and she turns her head at the sound of everyone else barreling towards us with Brandon in the lead even though Andi is clinging to his back trying to slow him down. Part of me thinks Poppy is going to try to keep me pinned, but she scrambles off my chest, throwing herself into the powder.

"Catch!"

The spoon she dove for flies through the air to me and I snatch it before it falls in the snow. Brandon tries to slow down, but with Andi on him, he loses his balance and they both end up next to Poppy who has a wild smile on her face.

Time seems to pause for that moment. The picture in front of me juxtaposes with the woman I met on that wedding day. The one whom Andi was so protective of. Andi is still just as protective of her, but this Poppy is free of all that weighed her down last summer. I want to be here with her through all of her transformations and growth.

There's no question how hard I've fallen for her. It's high time I tell her, too, and as I stand and help her up, I begin thinking of ways to do just that. Her brown eyes sparkle with delight when they meet mine. The sounds of Graham's victory and Brandon and Andi's struggle to get the final spoon fade away. I cup her cheeks as her hands grip my waist. Our lips brush once, the chill from the snow surprising us, before sinking against each other. The kisses are so natural and easy, yet each one sends a jolt of desire through me. She has quickly taken over my world and I can't get enough of her.

Andi's shriek of victory pulls us out of our bubble and we turn to see Brandon fall into the snow in a dramatic heap of defeat.

"You kids are going to catch a cold if you keep doing that," Aunt Mae calls from the doorway. "I started warming some cider and it'll be ready soon, so come in and dry off before you're all soaked through."

There's a silence before she turns around and we all laugh and move towards the house.

Brandon pats Graham's shoulder then mine with his free hand, his other tucked into Andi's. "Just like old times, right?"

"Exactly," I agree.

"We're just missing James's declarations that he wasn't going to be cold because he's wearing wool socks," Graham adds.

"Wanna place a bet if he's wearing some tonight?" Brandon asks.

"Oh, we all know he is," Graham says. "There's snow on the ground, how could he not?"

"Too true."

Poppy gives me a little squeeze just before we reach the door. "You seem happier than usual."

"That's because I just might be the luckiest guy to have all of this." I gesture to everyone inside before wrapping her in a full hug. "I couldn't ask for anything more."

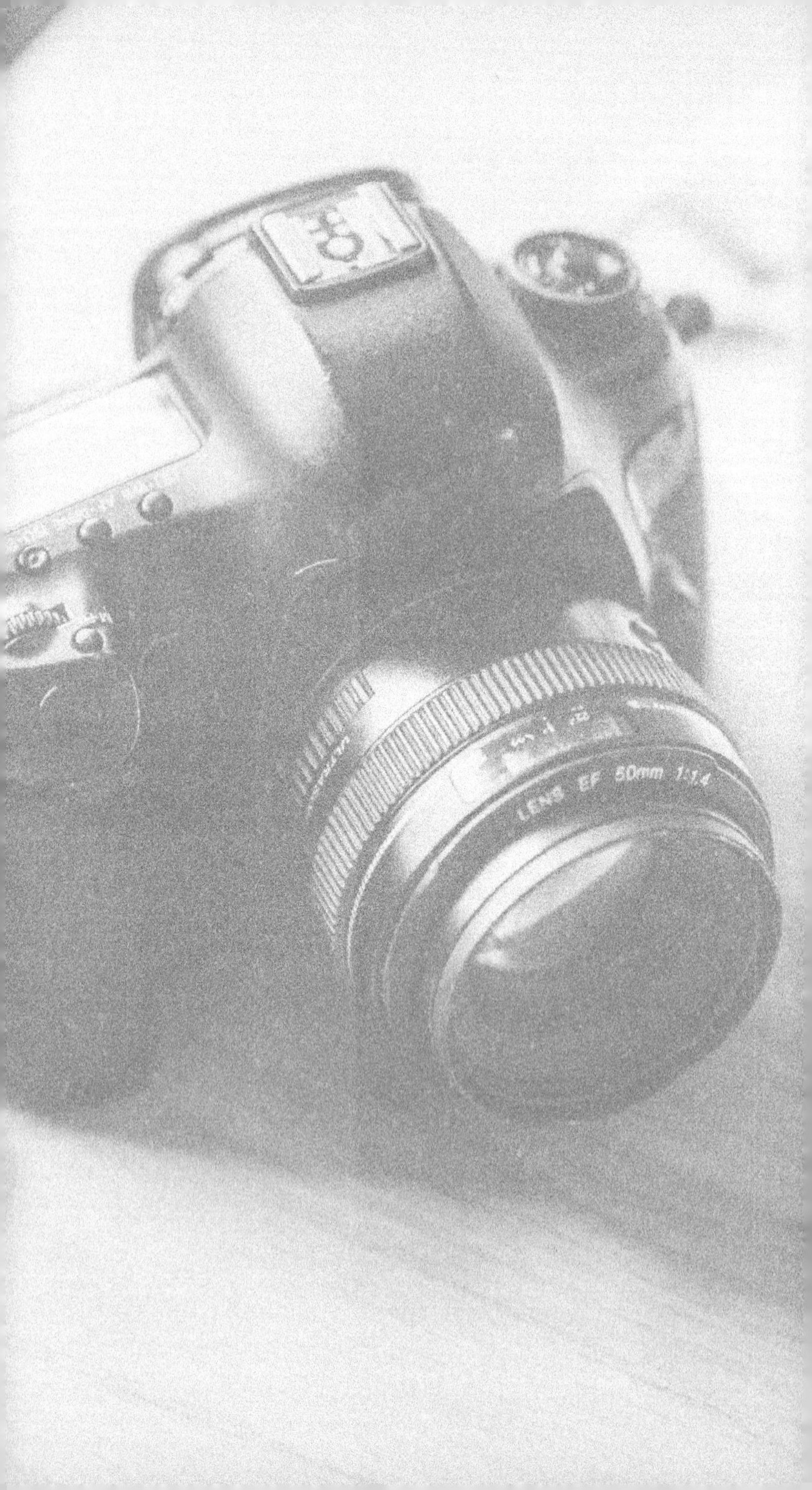
LENS EF 50mm 1:1.4

CHAPTER FIFTY-ONE

Poppy

"I like him," my mom whispers to me over her steaming mug of eggnog.

"You've told me before. And I'm glad." I smile back at her as the lights from my parents' Christmas tree catch my eye. "Mom, I thought we agreed that specific ornament would *not* be put out anymore."

My mom looks confused for a second before realizing what I'm referring to. "Oh my God, I forgot, sweetie. Let me grab it." It's too late though, Owen heard both of our loud surprised exclamations and walks mischievously over to the tree.

"I am guessing you're referring to this one?" He points to the ornament in question. "I noticed it earlier and wanted to say something but kept it to myself." He glances back at it once more and I can't help but run over and snatch it from under his handsome gaze.

"That's private," I stammer before laughing and looking down at it myself. Inside a small frame, a two year old version of me stands next to a tree in this very same room, tinsel decorating my hair and in my very exposed diaper. Apparently I thought I'd look pretty that way. I still love tinsel.

"A private ornament. Well, I shall respect your wishes." He turns the ornament upside down in my palm, closing my hand over it as he leans to brush his lips against my cheek in a soft kiss before moving to the couch to sit by his parents. "But, know that I love it."

"So, Walter, how long have you lived here?" His father chimes in from the couch, sipping on his own steaming mug of eggnog.

"Oh, we've been in this house since before Poppy was born. We loved the location, being a little ways out of town, but still close enough to drive in when we need something. I don't know how you can do it in New York. All those people and buildings." My dad shakes his head. He's always been a small town guy and has never liked too much busyness or large crowds.

"There's something quite lovely about it actually. Especially during the holidays. Who knows, maybe next year we could have you out to our place for Christmas." Owen's mom has been so open and welcoming to me and my family. It's been great seeing him with them. I can definitely see where he gets his handsome looks and kind heart from.

"That would be wonderful." My mom perks up. I'm sure she's loving the idea of us still being together this time next year and planning that far ahead. She has always been supportive, but I know she wants to make sure I'm happy and supported by someone too. "I'd love to see your shop."

"It's amazing everything they've done with the place over the years. It's become a real staple in the neighborhood." Owen glows talking about his family's flower shop. The pride and joy he has for what they've accomplished is clearly evident.

"That's amazing. I'd love to hear more about how you started it."

"Michelle, there will be lots of time for that later. Let's open presents." My dad has always loved presents and giving gifts to people has become one of his specialties. Moving towards the tree, he grabs one for Owen's parents. A gift basket with a bunch of things from Honey Cove—coffee from Bobbi's, honey from the farm up the road, a book about the history of the town, toffee from the sweetshop on the boardwalk, among other things.

They seem to like it from their excited squeals and "thank yous." Before I know it, only the gifts between Owen and I are left. I bring my large package over to him and nervously hand it to him. I hadn't thought much about it until this moment, but I suddenly feel worried he won't like it and wish I had given it to him privately earlier.

His mouth drops open as he rips the paper off. "Poppy, I love it," he says, his voice soft and quiet.

"What is it?" his mom asks.

"It's a photo I took one day when we were out together. He had said he liked it, so I had it framed."

My mom coughs a little into her mug, choking on her eggnog. "You gave him one of your art pieces?"

"Well, yeah. To go next to all his photos of New York."

"I don't think you've ever done that before. Even the photos we have, we had to ask you for the digital file and that took months of negotiation."

It's too quiet in the room. And I'm not sure what to say. I didn't even think anything of giving him the photo.

"Well, I love it." Owen turns and looks at me with something hidden in his warm look.

"Would you all be alright if I stole Poppy for a quick walk? It's so nice out now."

Everyone echoes their agreement and as we get our boots, coats, and other winter gear on, we hear the sounds of a rousing game of Rummikub starting from the dining table, a family favorite.

"It's really nice that they get along so well," I whisper to him. He wraps his arm around me and smiles back.

"It is. Are you all bundled up?" He reaches down to tug my fur lined hood tightly around my face. "I want to make sure you're warm."

I can't resist the cheesy response, "Oh, I'll be plenty warm with you there." We both laugh as we head out into the snowy wonderland.

CHAPTER FIFTY-TWO

Owen

We leave the house to find a gentle snow falling. The light from the street lamps add a little sparkle as they descend giving us our own little winter wonderland. She wraps her hand around my arm and we walk down the slightly icy sidewalk in a relaxed silence for the rest of their block.

"It's so pretty tonight," she whispers.

"Are you thinking of ways you could capture this with your camera?"

She looks up at me and lets out a little huff. "I am now."

Before she can tilt her head down again, I catch her chin with my gloved hand and nudge her nose with mine, chuckling. "I guess I'm starting to see things differently now that we're together."

"What do you mean?" She pulls back just a little so she can see me better.

"Every now and then, something catches my eye and I think about the fact that you could capture it. The snow tonight is a good example, but the other night at Brandon and Andi's house, I had the same thought when I saw their icicles."

"I noticed them too. They were so lovely." Her eyes light up just remembering them. "And they made you think of me?"

"Anything beautiful makes me think of you."

She shakes her head slightly but can't hide the blush from my words. I duck down enough to kiss her and she gives a little sound of surprise before it morphs into a contented sigh. Her lips feel so damn perfect against mine.

My hand moves to the back of her hood so I can deepen the kiss. We've kissed in front of our families and friends a few times and even stole a few deeper kisses when we had a moment to ourselves these past few days. But I've been dying to be alone with her. I crave her touch when we're apart and the harder I fall for her, the more it hurts to be away from her.

We might be outside, but no one else is walking or driving around here right now, so I let myself relax and savor this connection. My tongue touches her lips and they part instantly. Her slick tongue glides against mine, eliciting a groan from me. When she hears that, she tries to clasp her hands behind my neck, finding it harder to grasp them with her big mittens on. Even bundled up in all of her layers, I can still smell her sweet perfume and it makes me yearn for the privacy of one of our bedrooms so I can properly show her everything I'm feeling.

I want *this*.

I want *her*.

Our puffy jackets do nothing to take the edge off the desire that's been growing between us as we try to press closer together. I tighten my arm around her waist, bringing her as flush against me as our outerwear allows, feeling perilously close to unzipping our jackets just to feel how her body molds itself to mine. To let my fingers roam under her clothes in all the places that make her gasp and shiver. I put all of those wants into these kisses, devouring each little sound she makes.

Suddenly, I can't keep putting it off, waiting for that right moment. Wrenching my lips away from hers, I whisper her name like a prayer. Our heavy breaths are visible in the cold air even as my body feels more alive than ever. Her gaze is heavy with emotion while she looks up at me.

"I know we've seen each other every day since break, but I miss you." My forehead rests on hers as I close my eyes and feel her here with me. "I miss holding you at night, and kissing you first thing when we wake up."

"I have terrible morning breath," she whispers.

"Oh, I'm well aware of that and it's still what I want." Pulling off my gloves, I cup her cheeks, needing her to feel this connection that has hit me like a freight train since we met last summer. To know how real this is for me. "Poppy, I love you."

A smile so beautiful and bright appears as a tear falls down her cheek.

"I hope it's not too much of a surprise or just…too much to say," I add.

"Not too much," she whispers, her words choked up with emotion. She shakes her mittens in adorably frantic motions, which make me smile, until they fall off and she can place her hands on my cheeks.

"Owen," she begins, her eyes searching mine. "I love you too."

My heart somehow feels like it's doubled in size hearing her say those words to me. She's absolutely perfect.

Rising up on her toes, she kisses me softly. When we pull apart, we're fighting against smiles that we can't seem to hold back until we're both laughing.

"Please tell me you're staying over tomorrow night after my parents leave."

She nods and a coy smirk appears. "Be sure to have extra treats for Samson's toys because I plan to have your bedroom door shut for a while."

"How can I say no to that?"

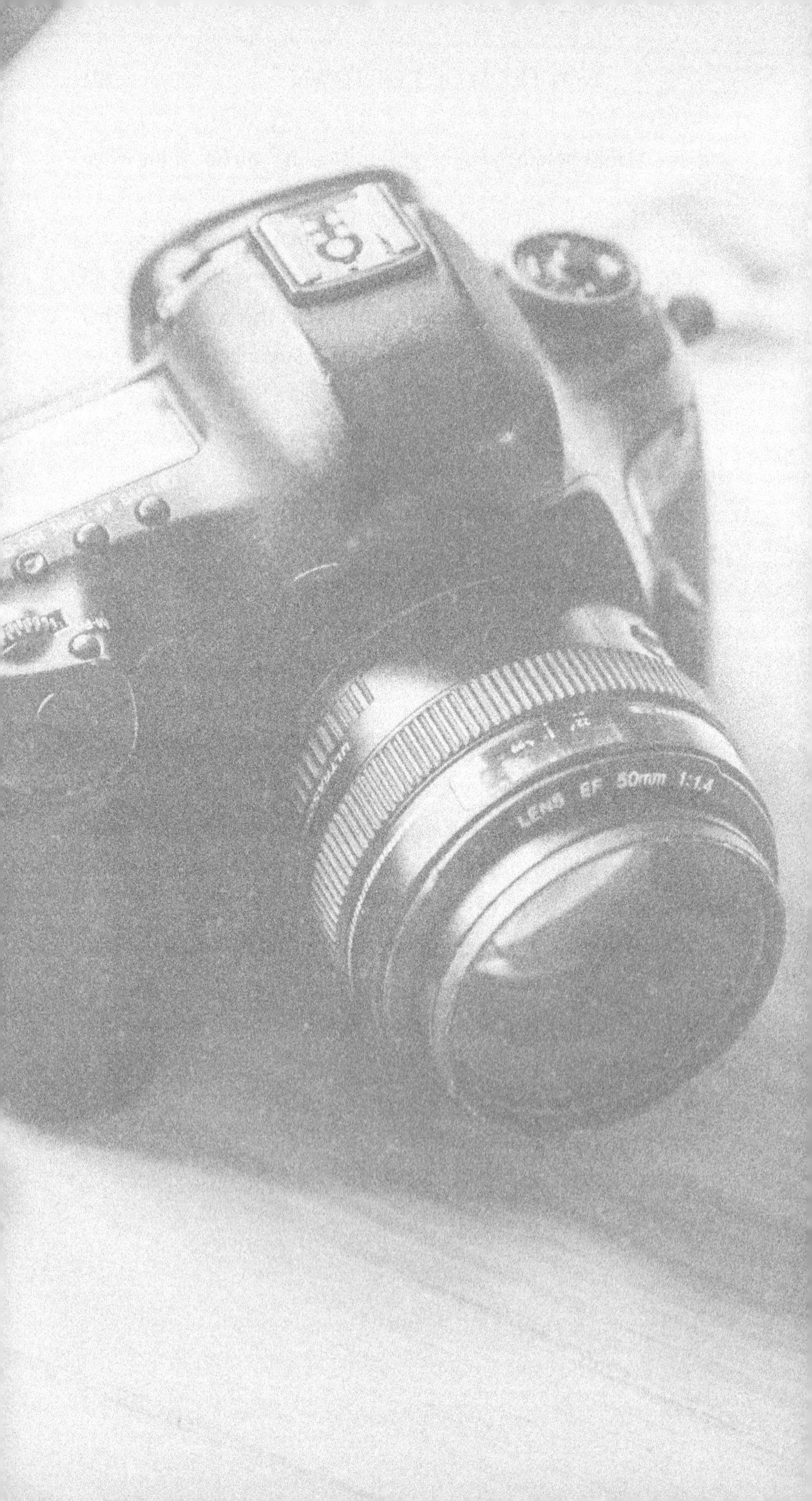
LENS EF 50mm 1:1.4

CHAPTER FIFTY-THREE

Poppy

My heart is already beating with anticipation of seeing Owen again. His parents left this morning and while we've been together or seen each other almost every day of break, we haven't had any time alone. It's been all stolen kisses and hand holding and while that is wonderful, I've been wanting something a little...more. Especially after his unexpected admission yesterday.

I've known I was falling in love with him for a while, but hearing him say the words brought everything together for me. He is the kindest, most thoughtful man I think I've ever met and it is hard for me to imagine what my life was like before him. Seeing our parents together and navigating the holidays this year really brought everything home for me. The way he supports and encourages me is something I never want to be without.

Owen brings a joy and simple lightheartedness to my life that I find to be so refreshing. I feel so much gratitude towards him for what he brings into my life and can't wait for the chance to show him how I've been feeling.

The drive over takes less than five minutes, but it feels like forever. I have on my sexiest black underwear and bra. I'm wearing a new dress. I shaved my legs. I have a bottle of our favorite wine in my bag. I am ready for whatever the night may bring.

The roads are surprisingly fine after yesterday's impromptu snow shower, but I know better than to speed over. Breathing deeply, I try to calm my already ramped up body. *You'll be there and in his arms soon enough.*

Pulling up to his apartment building, I thank the boardwalk gods for blessing me with a close parking spot and am able to scoot my car right in. Looking up towards the window I know is his, I can see Samson looking down at me and think I even see his mouth open in a precious, "mew," before I jump out of the car and head inside.

Taking the stairs two at a time, I remind myself that Owen might want to talk or have something he wants to discuss after the holiday get-togethers. *There's also dinner and the wine.* But I can't ignore that I just want *him. Now.*

When I get to his landing, I see the door is already flung open. He is standing in the doorway, looking at me with the same hunger in his eyes that I'm feeling. I barely get out the words, "I brought wine," before his hands are tangled in my hair, his mouth on mine in a passionate kiss. All my thoughts of talking are gone.

He shuts the door as I drop my bags, being sure to not break the wine bottle, and we move quickly towards his bedroom, our bodies pressed against one another in a desperate attempt for more contact.

He feels so damn good. *This is exactly what I wanted.*

"Samson?" I breathe out. My entire body tingling with desire.

"I gave him treats and a new toy," He whispers against my mouth, simultaneously pulling at the zipper on the back of my dress. I step away to pull it down and off my body as he takes me in, sitting down on the bed. "Damn, you look gorgeous."

He looks at me like I'm what's been missing in his life and I step back towards him, his hands softly making their way from my thighs up to my waist and arms before our eyes meet. "I love you." I feel my body light up at hearing him say it a second time, warmth hitting me like a freight train in my core.

"I love you too." Then I'm in his arms again and we tumble onto the bed. I work on the buttons of his shirt, every movement frantic. *Nothing is happening fast enough.*

Somehow in all our haste, we manage to remove each other's clothes without ripping them. Thankfully, I chose my lace bra as well as the underwear—the latter of which is now somewhere on Owen's floor—I move over him until I'm straddling him, enjoying the full view this position gives me.

It's hard to resist staring at him like this. He's so sexy and while I'd love to tease him more, I need him *now*. Rocking against the entire length of him almost sends me right over the edge. Taking a deep breath, I let myself calm down for a moment, reveling in the kisses he presses up the side of my neck and to that spot behind my ear. A shiver runs through my body in response to his touch.

"Let me taste you."

My breath catches and I turn to roll off him, giving him better access, but before I can he grabs my hips to hold me in place, sliding farther underneath me. I'm momentarily caught off guard at his forwardness.

"Are you sure?" He's always been giving in this department, but this is something new we haven't tried before and I'm a little nervous.

He looks to the headboard and then back at me. "Hold on tight."

CHAPTER FIFTY-FOUR

Owen

Shifting so she can tuck her feet beneath my shoulders, she gets into position as my mouth waters. Her hands grip my headboard and she hovers as I lift my head up and take one long lick.

"Babe, what are you doing?" I whisper against her sensitive skin.

"I'm sitting on your face. What does it look like?" A little uncertainty creeps into her voice.

"The headboard is to steady yourself, not to hold yourself up and away from my mouth." My fingers dig into her ass and I pull her down.

Fuck. I'm not sure whose groan is louder now that she's right where I need her and my tongue circles her clit. One hand stays on her glorious ass, massaging her flesh and tipping her hips so I can drive my fingers deep into her. They pump a few times, coating them so they're slick. The first time I hit that rough patch, she whimpers and clenches around my fingers.

I do my best to ignore the precum leaking from me already. She's so all-consumingly intoxicating and I can't believe I'm lucky enough to have her. The urge to be seated deep inside of her is growing harder to ignore.

But being able to have her grinding down on my face as she's climbing fast for her first orgasm tonight? It's so fucking perfect.

She draws out my name into a long moan as my fingers work faster. My tongue could cramp up and I wouldn't be able to stop. Not when she's so damn close. Her mouth falls open as she pants and tenses.

"Oh my god," she cries out and presses down everywhere. She's clamped around my fingers so tight, they almost slide out of her. The rush of her desire slips down into my palm. Her thighs tremble against my face while she rides out each wave I'm able to draw out with her clit between my lips and my tongue pressing against it. This time, when she hovers, I let her.

"Holy cow, I need a second," she says as she falls in a heap across the pillows.

She covers her eyes with her arm and laughs when I lick my fingers clean, but that laughter turns into a sigh when I kiss my way up to her, starting with her ankle. I take my time, savoring that we're finally alone again and have the privacy to do this. When my lips are working their way up her thigh, she runs her fingers through my hair and I pause, looking up at her.

"I'd like you to stay."

"I can stay tonight," she says, trying to tug me up so she can kiss me.

Grabbing her waist, I reposition us on the bed so we're in the center of it and keep my face an inch from hers, my gaze dropping to her soft lips. "What about more than just tonight?"

"I will need to go home at some point before school is back in session." Her arms drape around my neck and she gives me a peck.

"That's highly unfortunate."

Those pecks quickly build into something deeper and we both seem to be diving into round two. Soon, she's whimpering as I remove her bra and lavish her breasts with attention. She reaches for the drawer in my bedside table without needing to look since we've done this plenty of times before and I trace my tongue around her pebbled nipple one final time as she rips open the packaging.

My eyes feel like they're rolling to the back of my head in pleasure while my lips brush hers as she rolls the condom onto my length. God, even something so routine as this has me almost seeing stars, which feels a little ridiculous at the same time as making perfect sense.

Tossing her legs around my waist, I line myself up to her core. I knew she was ready for me, but I'm surprised how fucking easy it is to slide deep inside in just one, hard thrust. This sense of rightness is almost overwhelming right now.

"I love you so damn much."

"I love you so much too," she says, our hips finding a steadily faster rhythm. "You feel so good."

I prop myself up on my forearms and kiss her again and again while a beautiful ache builds deep inside of me with each thrust. Our connection feels more intense, maybe because we've put words to our feelings, or maybe because we've spent more time physically apart than usual. But it's like something has been removed between us and there's no holding back. No questions about where we might stand. Our families click and we seem to fit together everywhere. My damn cat is even crazy about her.

Not once in this move did I think I'd find a person who complimented me so perfectly. She came out of nowhere when I wasn't even interested in dating. God, I even tried to only see her as a friend. But this is Poppy, my Poppy.

That tingling sensation hits me and I reach between us, rubbing her clit as her back arches off the mattress. She cries out my name, almost sending me over the edge just with that sound. Her fingernails press into my back and she tightens around me. I can feel her legs slip down my back with each frantic thrust as she whimpers that she's close.

My fingers circle her clit and she writhes under me. I come with a moan while pistoning into her and watching her come undone once more.

"You're so damn gorgeous," I pant, while her breathing evens out and she pulls me flush against her.

"Oh yeah," she jokes, her eyes rolling. "I'm sure I look ready for a night out."

"This look isn't for anyone else to see, just me." I wink at her as she laughs and I capture her lips with mine, relishing in her afterglow.

Which is perfect because it's not long before my cat demands our attention.

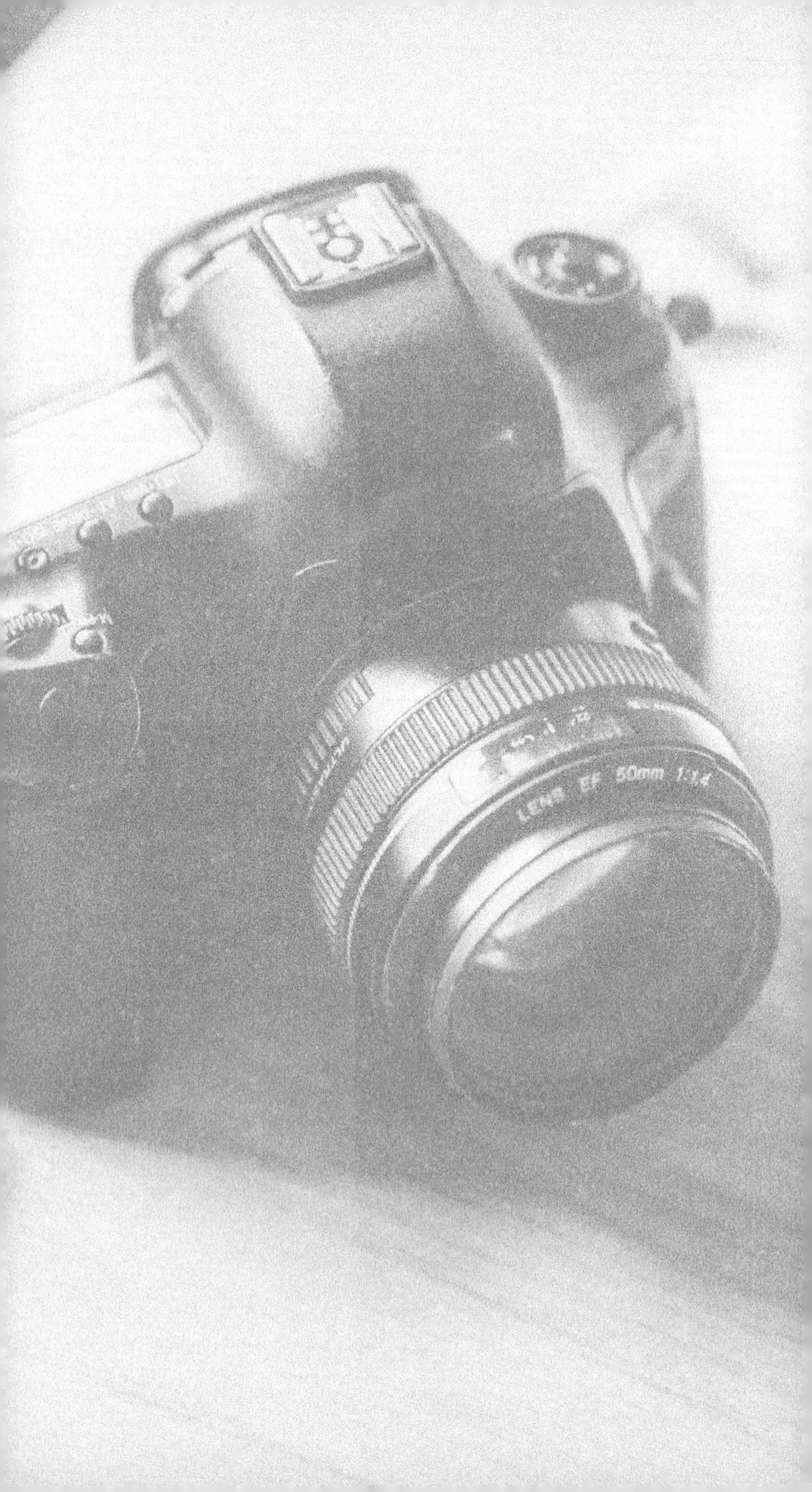
LENS EF 50mm 1:1.4

CHAPTER FIFTY-FIVE

Poppy

Blinking my eyes open, I find Samson curled up next to me purring like a motorboat with warm sunlight peeking through the blinds. Owen snores softly next to me and I feel too cozy under his overstuffed comforter to get up just yet. Reaching out, I stroke Samson's soft fur, his purrs growing louder exponentially with the attention.

I quietly shush him as Owen starts to stir. Not wanting to wake him yet, Samson and I pad to the bathroom together. It must have snowed more last night, a fresh dusting coats the window ledges and the cove has a fog hanging over it. My body shivers, goosebumps working their way up and down my arms. I let the cat circle my feet while I brush and wash my face and wrap a blanket around my shoulders once we're back in the living room.

I know I told him I needed to leave at some point today, but I'm already rethinking that decision. With the coldness of the morning, the allure of hunkering down in his apartment for a quiet day is strong. It would be nice to relax here with him and Samson, maybe order in some lunch or make dinner together. If we feel like venturing out into the snowy day, maybe another trip to the bookstore he loves after a chai from Bobbi's.

I love this quiet normalcy that he and I have fallen into. It feels comfortable and homey and my heart swells with the happiness of wondering if I've found my person. After enjoying the view of the gray, snow blanketed cove for a few more minutes, I decide it's time to start some breakfast.

Heading out to the kitchen I pull out the French press before glancing at my phone. I see a missed call from a number I don't recognize. The area code is Toronto though, which is strange. I click through to listen to it, sliding down onto the bench at the table.

"Hi, Poppy. This is Sally from the White Pine Inn. I know this is so odd of me to call you again, but your photos did so well for our ads. Some of our guests even commented about how much they loved them. Anyways, we're hiring for a marketing position and I thought that you might be a good fit. Now I know this is crazy. You don't live here. You're a teacher. But if you have any interest, give me a call. I'm really open to making the position what you'd want it to be if you'd like it, I just had a feeling that you're the right person for the job. I hope you're doing well and that everything with that wedding went okay. Miss you. Bye."

I sit in stunned silence for at least five minutes before noticing Samson playfully batting at my hand desperately trying to get my attention. I curl him up into my lap. *Sally wants to hire me? To take photos?* I never thought that art could be a way for me to make money, which is why I pursued being an art teacher. It felt more stable and consistent, but that dream has always been there.

A back and forth starts unfolding in my head. A fight between loving trying new things and the love I have for my life, *here*. When I was in Toronto, the focus was on finding *me*, my independence, my *new* life. But now, I have those things and more. I'm not sure I'm ready to upend everything all over again.

Owen starts to stir in the bedroom and I feel a bit frantic. *Owen.* I couldn't leave him and he loves Honey Cove so much. He wants to settle down, put down roots, not move again. Before I can even realize what is happening, tears spring to my eyes. How can I be this upset over something I didn't even know existed ten minutes ago?

Warm hands wrap themselves around my shoulders and he leans down to kiss my cheek, his stubble lightly scratching my face. "You okay?" he yawns. "Want some coffee?"

"Oh, sorry." I jump up to start grinding the beans. "Yes. I got distracted."

"It snowed." He looks thoughtfully out the window, taking it in. "Are you sure you can't stay? I could make us omelets and hash browns." Turning back towards me, he has a different look in his gaze. "Or we could stay in bed for a while."

Forcing a smile, I add, "I can stay for a bit." He moves closer to me, scrutinizing my face. His gaze roves over my body and the room trying to make sense of my strange demeanor.

"What is it? Something is up. Did something happen last night? Was I too rough?"

"No, it's not that." He takes me into his arms as my hands awkwardly go to my hair. "Do you remember when I was in Toronto? Before coming back for Andi's wedding?"

"Yeah," he says nervously, trying to figure out where I'm going with this. He holds my hands, seemingly knowing I need a little grounding right now.

"Well, I got close with the woman who owns the inn, Sally. And she just called me."

"To...catch up?"

"No, she had purchased a few of my prints from when I was there to use in their marketing and on their website." Pausing, it's my turn to look up into his eyes and decide how to handle this. I choose to quickly rip the Band-Aid off. "Apparently they've worked so well she wants to offer me a job."

"A job? In Toronto?" His eyes widen. Understanding.

"Yes, well, I'm actually not sure. It was a short message and it didn't have details."

"And you want it?" He backs away from me. Just a step, but it's enough to feel like my walls are crashing down.

Stepping towards him, closing the gap, I take his hands in mine again. "I want to get more information." Raising his fingers to my lips, I kiss them slowly before flicking my gaze back to his face. "Nothing has been decided here."

"Okay." He leans down to kiss me, but it's reserved and colder than before. I know I haven't made any decisions, but even my admission of interest seems like it's cracked the tether between us.

He moves away and starts to grind beans for our coffee. Without thinking I launch my body towards him and grab him in a bear hug, needing to reconnect and feel that closeness from last night again.

"I love you."

CHAPTER FIFTY-SIX

Owen

"I love you too," I say against her hair, loud enough for her to hear over the grinding coffee. "Do you want to start the water?"

"Of course." She tightens her arms once and steps away, filling the kettle.

God, all of this feels so damn normal and *natural*. Samson meows at us, rubbing against our legs as he walks around. He's likely trying to guess who is going to feed him this morning. Poppy started doing it when she's the first to wake up after I walked her through what he needs in the mornings. But how much longer will that happen?

She might move.

Trying to be a good boyfriend, I kiss her on the cheek and mutter that I'll be right back on my way to the bathroom. Once the door is closed, I give myself a moment to just stand there, trying to absorb my shock. I can't wrap my head around the possibility of her being in Toronto.

She'd really leave?

Her parents are here. Her best friend is here. Her students are here.

I'm here.

And she knows that *this* is where I plan to stay. Where I hope to stay.

Shaking myself out of this stupor, I take care of business. As I'm brushing my teeth, I think back on every time I've watched her with a camera. She has always had a specific demeanor when she's looking at the world through a lens. Confident and relaxed. Excited and at home.

I can't be surprised that her photos have been great for marketing. She's amazingly talented. It's just...a lot.

Splashing cold water on my face helps to reset my mind. She didn't seem too keen on diving into a conversation about this since she doesn't have a lot of information and I can wait while she gets what she needs.

Receiving an offer doesn't mean she's gone. I can't ask her to stay just for me. She needs to be able to process this and decide what she wants. Even if my heart feels like it's growing more and more numb.

When I'm back in the kitchen, Samson is sitting at her feet, his eyes glued to the can of food in her hand. He hasn't figured out how to easily perch on her shoulder like he does for me. And he might not need to figure it out since she might be moving.

God, I have to just focus on what we have. We can talk about what we want later. I think.

What if she has to give them an answer soon?

"What kind of cheese would you like?" I blurt, needing to do something normal so I can stop obsessing over something she doesn't have details about.

"Whatever you're having is good," she says brightly. Almost too brightly.

She usually requests either the block of mozzarella or whatever shredded blend I have on-hand. I usually like fresh mozzarella or sharp cheddar.

"Are you sure?"

"What can I say? I'm feeling adventurous this morning." Her tone is light and playful, but then her eyes widen a fraction while watching me. Shit, I didn't even realize I took a step away from her.

Moving to Toronto would be an adventure for her and apparently all I can do right now is see how I'm going to lose her. I have to get it together right now so I can wrap my head around this logically and not be such an asshole.

I can hear when she grabs my favorite pan for cooking omelets while I get the rest of the ingredients from the fridge, trying to make a mental list of things I'm out of to grab at the store later. She's already getting the cutting board out and my heart gives a painful squeeze because we've built something here.

But does it have to only work *here*?

"Want to put some butter in the pan and turn it to medium heat?" I ask, leaning down to kiss the top of her head. There's this strange mix of feelings of needing to reassure her that I'm not freaked out by this job prospect while giving myself a little space so I don't get more hurt than necessary if she takes it.

She looks up at me and stands on her toes for a quick kiss. Something that's normal for us, but there's a worried strain in her expression that helps shake me out of my mini spiral of doom. Gently grabbing her chin before she can turn back to the stove, I hold her gaze a moment. I can't make her any promises and it wouldn't be fair for me to ask any of her, so I repeat the words that are at the center of everything for us.

"I love you."

Her eyes get a little misty as she nods. "I know. I love you too."

"I know." Leaning down, we kiss, letting ourselves relax a little, to just be in this moment. When we break away, I smile and say, "You're lucky you wanted the same kind of cheese as me this morning."

"Why is that?"

"My parents must have snacked on what was left and I've been a little too distracted to go to the store with my girlfriend coming over."

She smiles, just like she does every time I call her my girlfriend. "Well, it's a good thing my boyfriend has excellent taste, isn't it?"

"Absolutely." I rinse the tomatoes and peppers while she finishes prepping the pan.

"Should I start a list for groceries?" she asks, grabbing the notebook I keep in the kitchen for that purpose.

"Yeah, that would be great." My mind goes to doing this simple thing with her each week. Heading to the grocery store together. I try to picture what it would be like in Toronto and feel a little...cold.

I know what it's like for me to live in a big city. The only reason I stayed as long as I did was because my parents lived there. Could I potentially move for Poppy without one day resenting that choice?

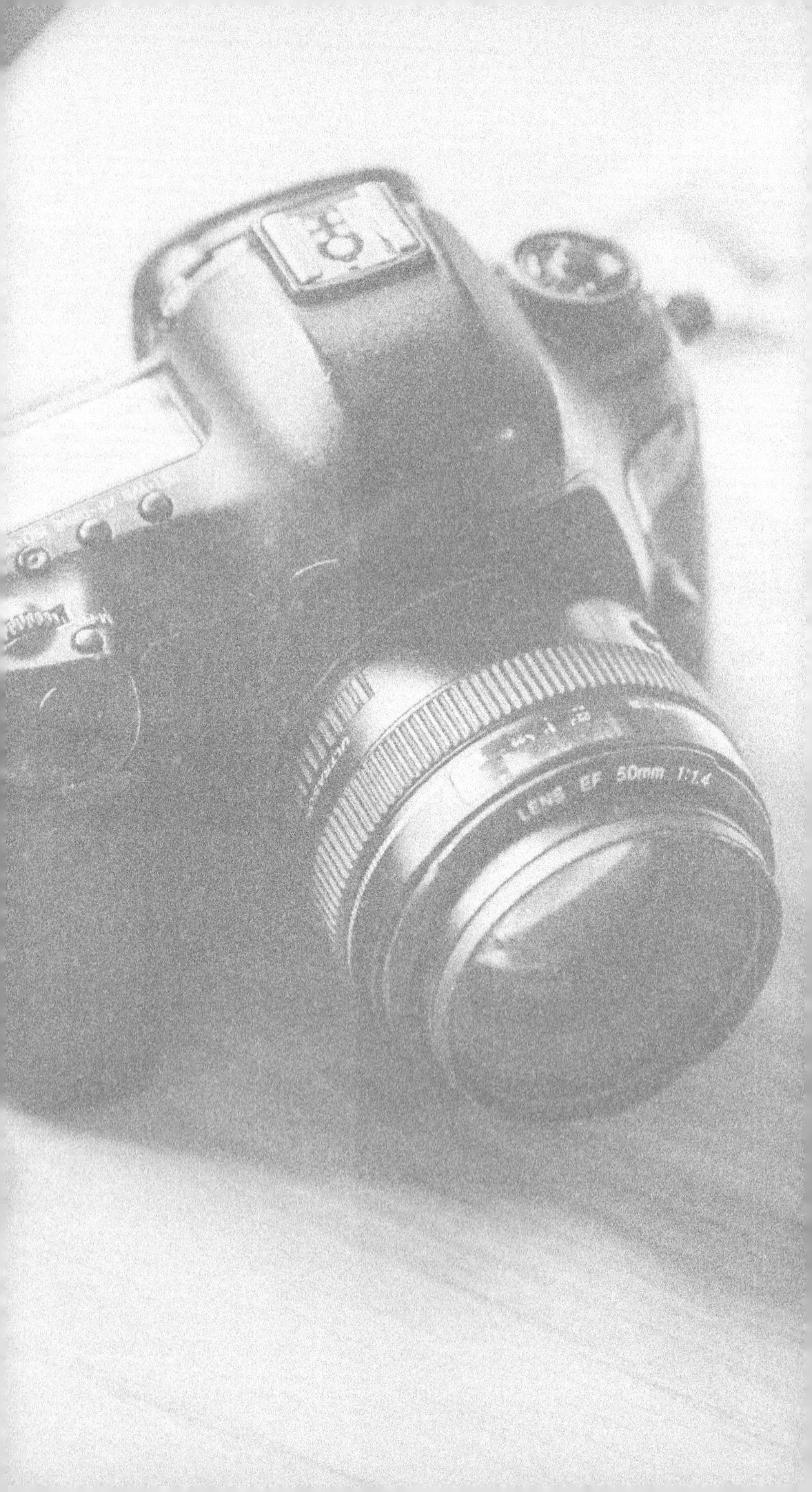
LENS EF 50mm 1:1.4

CHAPTER FIFTY-SEVEN

Poppy

The phone has been ringing for five seconds and my heart feels like it is doing somersaults in my chest. *Am I really doing this? Am I actually considering it?*

"Hi, this is the White Pine Inn, how can we help you?" The voice is one I don't recognize. I know they sometimes had others working the front desk, but somehow I am surprised Sally isn't there. Maybe they are expanding and she's delegating more. *That would be good for her.*

"Hi, I'm returning a call to Sally. Is she available?"

"One moment."

Elevator music rings through my phone as I try to wait as patiently as possible. In the span of fifteen seconds, I've talked myself into and out of the job at least twenty times. Taking a deep breath, I try to calm my racing pulse.

You're just getting information. A call is not a commitment.

"This is Sally." She sounds a little exasperated and I wonder if her nephew is causing issues again or maybe it's another one of the million issues I know she has to deal with at the inn.

"Hi Sally, it's Poppy. I got your message," I say cheerily, hoping my call will brighten her mood.

"Oh, great! I'm so glad to hear from you. How are you?" The change in her demeanor is instantaneous and I'm so thankful. I don't think she'd offer me a job if she didn't like me, but it's good to have the confirmation just the same.

"I'm good, I'm eager to hear more about the job and see if it could be a good fit." My voice cracks slightly at the end and while my heart is calming now talking to her, I only see Owen's face in my head and how off things were between us after I told him about her message yesterday.

He's understandably upset that I'm considering the job when we really haven't talked about our future or our individual plans yet. I definitely see him in mine, but also want to give myself the space to explore this opportunity if I want to. When I was with Steven, everything was about him and what he wanted. With Owen, everything has been different and I don't want to fall back into old patterns unwittingly. This is giving me the chance to really think through my own ambitions and dreams for my own life.

"I left a few details on the message, but can definitely give you some more info." She pauses and I hear papers shuffling in the background, then a slurp of a beverage before she continues. "Sorry, wanted to grab my notes. We're looking for someone to be in charge of our marketing photos, so the main duties of the position is to take photos of our property, restaurant, venue, etc. We'd also like to have a photographer on hand during our busy wedding season for couples to hire in-house. If there are other things you're interested in like social media, management, concierge services since you were on that side of things, or anything else, I'm happy to work with you on making sure it's a good fit. Does that make sense?"

"Yeah it does. So the position is permanent in Toronto?" I know her answer, but feel like I need to ask it anyways.

"Yes, I'm sorry if that wasn't clear. The position would be here and we'd like the photographer to be on site during those busy times or available to meet with anyone who is looking to book our venue."

"How many hours per week?"

"During the busy times it would be full time, on the off season it would likely be less, but we're open to pairing it with something else on site if that's something you're interested in. We're really focused on finding the perfect person for the job, so we're open to working with you if that's something you want."

I breathe in a shaky breath. The job sounds like so much fun and like something I would actually be good at. But could I leave my friends and family? My students and Honey Cove? I never have considered living elsewhere. "Can I have some time to think about it?"

"Of course. Let me grab your email and I'll send over all the logistical info, salary, that sort of thing. We'd like to have someone hired prior to the summer, but I don't mind waiting to post it if you need some time. I know it would be a big change for you."

"Yeah, it would. I loved my time in Toronto and at your inn. It's a lot to think over." *So much to think over.* And talk over with Owen. I have no idea what he's going to think about this. I'd be asking him to leave his family that he just moved to Honey Cove for. Or asking him to do long distance which I'm not even sure he's open to.

"I'll send you the details and just let me know if you have any other questions or things you're wondering about. I really think you're the woman for the job, so I'm willing to work with you if there are parts of the job you'd like to focus on or things you'd like to explore."

"That means so much, thank you. I'll let you know as soon as I decide."

We talk for a few minutes more, but my mind is a blur trying to take in what she's just told me. The flexibility in making the job something I'm interested in is a little shocking. Not only would I get to use my own artwork as my career, but I'd be given real agency in my own development and interests. Burying my face in my hands, I let out a long sigh.

How in the world am I going to make a decision?

CHAPTER FIFTY-EIGHT

Owen

The apartment is quiet.

Too quiet now that Poppy left so she can get ready for drinks with Andi. My cat even sat at the door for fifteen minutes after she left, clearly hoping she'd be right back.

"Hey, thanks for picking up," I say, switching to speakerphone so I don't upset Samson who is curled up on my lap getting a pet.

"Any time," Brandon says. "What's going on?"

A slightly dramatic sigh escapes me as I look out at the cove from my window. "Okay, you know how the plan has been to stay in Honey Cove?"

"Yeah, you already filled things out to keep your position, right?"

"I did."

Samson gives me a little growl and I realize I stopped petting him for a moment. "Sorry, bud," I whisper to him and resume.

"I feel like there's a 'but' coming. Did something happen where your info didn't get submitted or something and you have to apply differently?"

"Sorry, Samson distracted me," I explain. "No, all of that is good. I still have to wait to hear their decision."

I groan. God, this is hard. Once I tell him, it's going to be that much more real.

But it's time to get over the first hurdle and open up to someone about it.

"Poppy got a killer job offer in Toronto." The words spill out of me and even though I needed to say them, I don't feel any better.

"Toronto?"

"Yes."

"As in, Canada?"

"That very one."

"You sure it's not a new bar or something that's going to open?"

"What?"

"Sorry," he says. "I'm just trying to wrap my head around this and I was hoping I was mistaken somehow."

"You and me, both."

"Damn," he says softly.

"I know."

"What's she thinking?"

"That might be the hardest part for me because I have no idea." I run my hand down my face, somehow forgetting that I've been petting my longhair and sputter as I keep fur from getting into my mouth.

"You okay over there?"

"Samson," I say in explanation for the sounds he just heard.

"It sounded like you ate something that turned out to be rotten."

"No, just got fur all over my face."

"I wish I had some response to that, but I'm so lost." He laughs and that makes things feel a little less heavy inside me. "So, Poppy?"

"I'm guessing Andi is going to get all the details when they meet up, but don't tell her so she can hear it from Poppy."

"Of course."

One more sigh before I dive in and tell him the details I know.

My cousin whistles long and low when I finish.

"And Poppy is calling the owner today to learn more?" he asks.

"She did."

"What'd she learn?"

"Ah, I'm not sure. She looked a little overwhelmed and said she had a lot to process. Then she asked if we could watch something for a bit, so that's what we did."

"Well, that's a good thing, right? She can't make a decision without having the actual details."

I definitely appreciate that he's trying to help me feel better, that's for sure.

"Is it weird that she didn't ask me to be in the room during the conversation?" I ask.

"Did you offer to be there?"

My mouth opens and nothing comes out for a moment. "I guess I didn't."

My cat shifts so he can start kneading my stomach and purring loudly as I scratch his back as I continue. "The whole thing seemed to come out of left field for both of us and I suppose I didn't want my weird energy messing things up."

"Messing things up for her?"

"Or messing us up, too. I don't know, I'm really getting in my head for some reason."

"Look, Owen, it's not 'for some reason' that you're in your head," he says, calm but sure. "You chose this place and this life. The decision to leave New York City wasn't some whim. It had been building for a while, hadn't it?"

"It took a bit for everything to come together with the job, but no, it wasn't a whim. Once I talked to my parents, it started to feel possible and that was amazing."

"So now, your girlfriend was offered what could be a dream job in a big city. And the only reason you stayed in New York as long as you did, was because your parents live there. Toronto wouldn't have that, so you'd be moving for Poppy."

"Damn, you summarized that better than I could have."

"You're an English teacher, you literally work with words, so you would have gotten there." He pauses for a moment. "You just need to give yourself, and her, some time. This isn't something she applied for or sought out, so she's just as surprised as you. Plus, there's a lot at stake with talking to you about it."

"What do you mean?" My hands stop as Samson walks in a complete circle before curling up in a ball again.

"I'm guessing that she's feeling additional pressure talking to you about it because it really affects your relationship, but she'll be seeing my wife tonight, and they can talk without it feeling as big."

"When did you get so wise?" I ask him.

"When I married Andi," he says, laughing.

"Fair enough."

"You're going to be okay. It's all new and you'll both process it."

"Thanks, Brandon. I needed to hear that."

"No problem, really," he says. "We just got you here and you know we want you to stay. But it has to be right for you. I've seen you two together and know this isn't a fling. So whatever you decide, we're still here for you, okay?"

My throat tightens a little at his words. "Okay."

"We'll see you soon?"

"Of course, thanks, again."

"Alright, sounds good, bye."

Hanging up, I feel so different. Not like I have everything figured out, but a little more settled.

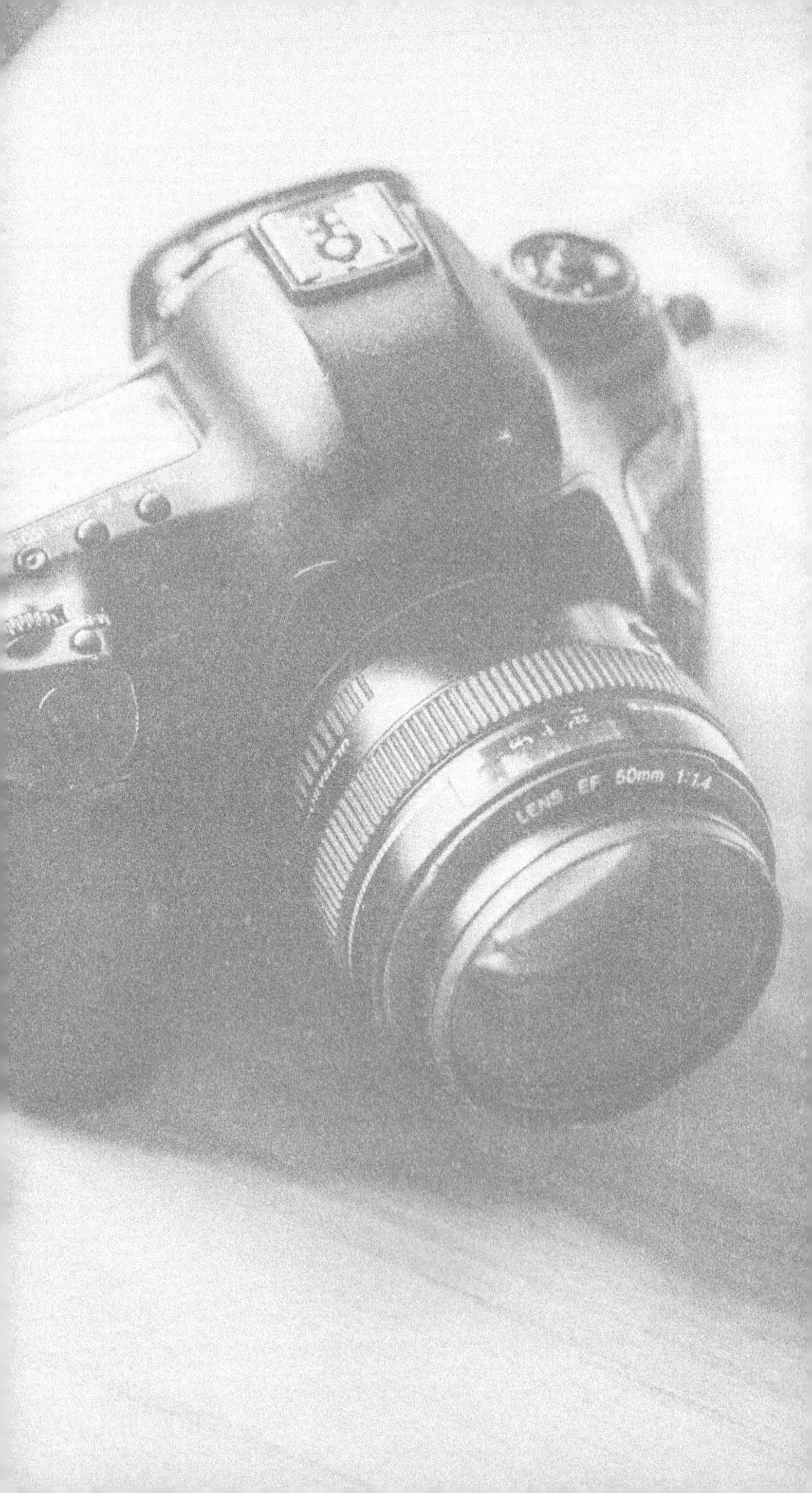
LENS EF 50mm 1:1.4

CHAPTER FIFTY-NINE

Poppy

"You talked to Sally?"

Andi stares from across the table at me as we both polish off our second round of margaritas. This conversation feels like it will need a bit of tequila. For both of us.

"Yes."

"Tell me." She's waiting for the blow of what she thinks I'm going to tell her, but the truth is I haven't decided anything and am not anywhere near a decision. All I know is that I'm interested.

Having a job where I can use my art, *my actual art*, to make a living is a dream. I love what I do at the school. Teaching is a passion of mine, too, and the students are amazing. But how can I pass up an opportunity like this? Toronto was also beautiful and it could be a new adventure.

I decide to just dive right in. "Well, she is open to making the job what I am looking for," I say, tentatively. "It could focus on material for marketing, taking photos, or social media, that sort of thing. She also wants my input on their concierge service for guests since I have experience being on the other side of that."

She nods, taking everything in. Andi and I haven't been apart for more than a day or two, aside from her honeymoon and when I was gone, so a move this big would be an immense change for us. My heart drops a little considering yet another facet of what a move this big would mean.

"But it would be *there*, you'd have to move?" Her foot kicks the table as she fiddles nervously. I can see her wringing her napkin within an inch of its life.

"Yes. The job is there."

Her eyes glisten just the slightest bit, but she shakes her head and adds, "Of course I support you. But I would miss you so much. Have you decided anything? Talked to Owen?"

"No. We are apparently ignoring what is happening." Absentmindedly, I check my phone to see if I've missed any messages from him. Nothing since his last gif of a cat seemingly drinking a margarita.

"You haven't talked about it at all?"

"Not in detail. He has always wanted to settle down in a small town near his family. That was his dream in moving to Honey Cove. A move somewhere else, and a *big* city, no less, really puts a damper on that."

He has been quiet about everything, but I can tell it's bothering him. He is still sweet and affectionate, but I see the way his eyes linger on me and the sadness that's behind them. He doesn't want to move, and I think we're both too terrified to actually have the conversation.

"Have you decided anything?"

"No. How can I? It's choosing between two impossible things. I love Owen. And I love photography. I love Honey Cove and I love seeing new places." Burying my face in my hands, I take a deep breath to keep myself from bursting into tears. I can't imagine leaving him, but I also can't imagine passing up an amazing opportunity like this.

"You don't think he'd move with you?" She stirs her now empty glass, eyes darting around looking for our waiter before deciding on another bite of her burrito.

Shaking my head, I answer, "I don't think I can ask him to do that and I want his dream of living in a small town to come true for him, you know? He talks all the time about how happy he is to be near his family now. I can't take that from him right after he's just gotten it."

"I'm sorry, honey." She reaches out and touches my hand, giving it a squeeze. "I can see why this is feeling so hard for you."

"And before you say it," I add, holding up my hand. "I *know* I need to just talk to him. I feel like this is eating me up without his input and it also feels like I can't talk to him because I already know what he wants."

She nods. "Yeah, but you never *really* know until you talk with him."

"I think I just want to live in this bubble together for a while. Things have been amazing since Christmas and the time with our families. It's been so nice."

"Oh yes, the amazing post parental exit sex." She raises her eyebrows and gives me a joking seductive stare before continuing, "Talk to him. It might help you figure out where your head is at with everything too."

"You're right, you're right. Well, on the bright side, if I do take the job, you'd have a free hotel to stay in whenever you come to visit." I know that goading her isn't a kind thing to do with such a big decision, but I can't resist the chance to tease her a little.

Andi gives me a shocked look before a loud, appalled scoff. "How dare you." She turns her eyes up at me. "I need another fucking margarita!"

CHAPTER SIXTY

Owen

Per usual, Grace has the new young adult releases I ordered waiting in a bag behind the counter for me.

"I'm assuming you'll browse the other new titles, but I wanted to let you know that I was able to request an extra signed copy from a couple of authors and made sure to get those in your order." She points to the "Local Authors" display. "We also have copies left from last night's signing. Several of your students said how much you talked about the event beforehand, so the author and I thank you for the turnout."

"That's fantastic they made it," I tell her, feeling warm inside that my students are connecting with authors and their stories. "And thank you, as always, for tossing in the signed copies when you can. Sometimes that's what gets them to try a new genre."

The "Local Authors" section now takes over an entire bookshelf instead of just the top half. I grab a couple of the adult titles for myself and two more for the classroom.

My phone chimes while I'm reading the back of a horror story a couple of students mentioned the other day. I set the small stack of books I've accumulated already down and fish my phone out of my pocket.

Brandon:

> *I won't tell you the details of their conversation, don't worry, but Andi told me about the job. I hope it's okay that I said you talked to me about it.*

It feels more real now that Andi also told Brandon. I appreciate that he remembered my request to not know any details Andi got. I want to make sure that Poppy and Andi have their confidentiality while not having him feel like he's in any way obligated to fill me in about what his wife then tells him. He's always wanting everyone to be happy. But Poppy and I will, hopefully, talk some more soon.

> *Thanks. It's totally fine that you told her we talked about it.*

Brandon:

> *We're hoping you two can figure this out. You've both been so much more smiley since you got together.*

A quiet snort escapes me. No one calls me a gump or anything, but I didn't know someone would describe me as "smiley" at any point.

> *I hope we can too.*

> *As much as I want to be here, I can't ask her to give up this opportunity.*

Brandon:

> *And you need to be honest with yourself if moving to another big city is really what you want.*

> *Exactly. Especially one that's so far away from you guys and my parents.*

Brandon:
> *And we are pretty phenomenal to live near.*

> *No question.*

Brandon:
> *Just let me know if you want to get a drink or something, okay?*

> *Probably soon.*

Brandon:
> *Deal. Just say the word and we can have James and Graham there too.*

Poppy doesn't seem to have been given any sort of timeline for telling Sally her decision, but that doesn't mean we have months to talk this through. My gut twists a little because I just don't see how this would work well. At some point, it seems like I'll have to choose between this little life in Honey Cove near my extended family I'm growing closer to while not being too far from my parents and going to Toronto with Poppy. I quickly set a reminder in my phone to look up requirements for teachers in Canada and if any pieces of my license might transfer over because I assume I'll need to take at least some coursework to teach there. It feels wrong to not have my options researched.

She hasn't explicitly asked me to move with her if she takes the job though. But maybe she hasn't asked because she's afraid I'd need to say no? That I don't want to be in another big city.

Realizing I've been standing here, staring at my phone, I like Brandon's last message, shove my phone back into my pocket, and take my books to the counter. All I want to do right now is to hang out with Samson while learning about requirements for being a licensed teacher in Toronto. Honestly, it's already stressing me out to think about going through the process for another license and now I'm worrying about how long it would take to get a license just so I could be qualified for a potential job there.

"I wanted to mention that young adult audiobook purchases have increased dramatically recently and I have even gotten phone calls from parents requesting titles for their kids. A few have mentioned your name, so that's just another thing I have to thank you for." Grace puts the additional books into the bags she set aside for me as I pay.

"Can I share that with the school admin team?"

She gives me a confused look.

"I was able to pilot an audiobook program this year," I explain. "I know that we can't lend those through you, but I would love to be able to include how there might be a direct correlation between the school providing access to the required reading on audio and continued enjoyment."

"Oh, absolutely," she says. "If it might help in any way to keep the program going, I can send you sales data, no customer information of course."

"That would be really fascinating, actually. I could definitely use it in my write-up at the end of the school year discussing the impact it's having." My thoughts are already churning for making the case to expand the program to the district sooner than planned if the data is compelling enough. "Are you finding that narrators are playing a role in what people are purchasing, or is it more about a specific genre within young adult?"

"A mix, really, within young adult fiction. I can get some of that data broken down easily for you. I already do that for reporting for best seller lists. But, there has been an increase in non-fiction, too, particularly audiobooks on mindfulness, and a few related to the college admissions process written for teens."

"I'll have to let Noah know about that."

Grace blushes. I don't think I've ever mentioned him before and now I'm wondering if I've missed something with my good friend. He hasn't mentioned anyone lately and he's been more open about trying to date a little more. I don't know Grace well enough to try to arrange something like Noah did with Poppy and me, but I'm definitely curious how that might go.

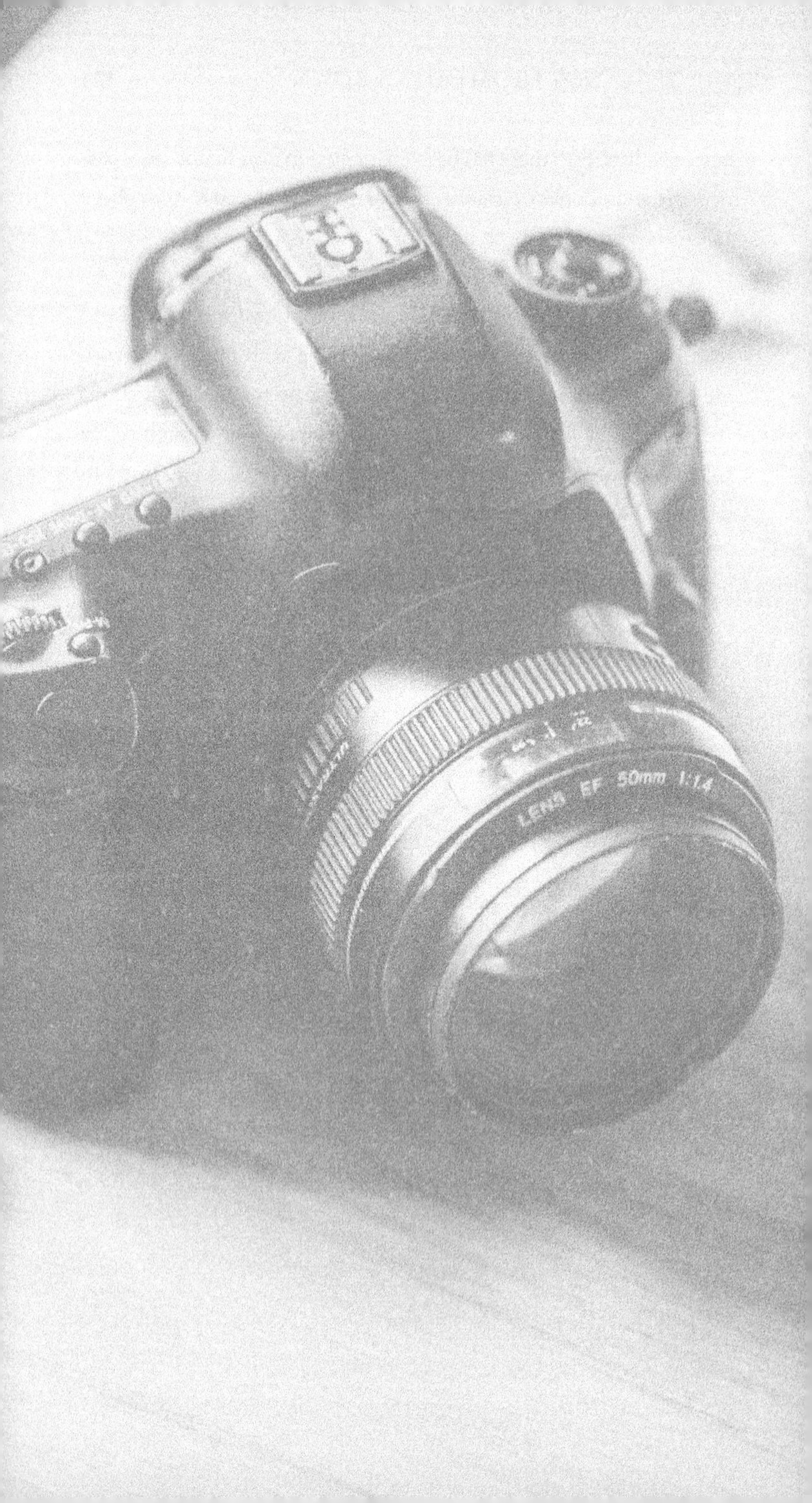
LENS EF 50mm 1:1.4

CHAPTER SIXTY-ONE

Poppy

Mid January

Snow lightly falls, making my lashes stick together as Owen and I walk up the path to my parents' house. Closing my eyes, I breathe in the cool air and try to let go of the tension I feel growing between him and me. This afternoon was rushed and I was hoping to talk more with him about where my head is at, but students stayed late to finish a test in his classroom and then we needed to head straight to this dinner with my family.

I haven't made a decision yet and I know it is hurting him. It will hurt us more in the long run though if I side step this choice before I actually have figured out where my heart is on it. My heart sinks wondering if I'm dooming our relationship with taking my time to decide. *You have to do this for you.*

I am feeling stuck in this no-win situation. If I don't take my time and figure this out on my own, I'll always wonder if I was doing this for Owen or for myself. But with how things are going with me taking my time, it seems to be alienating Owen anyways.

My mom throws open the front door before we're even to the stoop, making me jump a little in surprise. Instinctively, Owen reaches out to steady me, his hand on the small of my back to keep me upright. "Thank you," I say, catching his other hand in my own. He gives it a squeeze before moving in front of me with a terse tensing of his face. *This could be a rough dinner.*

"Welcome," my mom calls out to us, stepping to the side as we pass through. Walking into my childhood home is always a comforting feeling. The smells and the feel of being in the space always make me reminisce a bit. "Everything okay?" my mom whispers into my ear as I give her a hug.

"We're good, just a little off." I leave it at that, I don't feel ready to talk about the job with her and want to make sure they also don't sway my feelings either way. When the time is right, I'll clue them in too.

My mom gives me another reassuring hug before ushering me into the living room. "Hi sweetie," my dad calls from the table in the kitchen. "Just in here putting my finishing touches on our charcuterie board." His smiling face greets me as I round the corner. "Did I say that right?"

"I think you got it. Looks yummy."

Owen leans against the doorframe to the kitchen, silently watching as my dad takes his time placing the final olives and cheeses on the wooden board, his arms crossed stoically in front of his chest.

"What do you think?" Dad holds the board up proudly. He's actually done a great job.

"Perfect," my mom smiles, rubbing her hand in circles on his back. "Why don't we dig in and I'll grab some wine for all of us." Looking over at Owen, he nods slightly before moving to the couch and seemingly reluctantly digging into the appetizer.

Maybe he was just hungry. His mood seems to improve slightly with the food and wine, making small talk and sharing about the craziness that seems to always happen at school after winter break.

I try to venture an innocuous question, hoping to connect with him a little more. "Have you heard from your parents about when they'll visit next? It was so much fun having them here."

"No, they haven't decided yet." He has a definite tone and I pull back the hand I had placed on his back. My mom's eyes flick between me and my dad. I can't help but feel a little embarrassed. He had seemed so on board for giving me space and I don't understand why he's had a sudden change.

"Why don't you help me in the kitchen with dinner," my mom says, pulling my dad along with her as they head out of the room. Once they're out of earshot, I look over at Owen who stares ahead, lets out a long sigh, then runs his hands down his face.

"What is wrong?" I whisper, reaching my hand out to touch his knee. Our connection feeling even more fractured at the moment.

"I'm just having a harder time than I thought I would with giving you space. You haven't even told your parents, Poppy." I rake in a breath, unsure of how to respond. *Where is this coming from?*

"Should we just go? I can tell them I'm not feeling well."

"No, let's stay. I'll work on it. I'm sorry." He turns towards me and brushes my hair behind my ear. "It's my own thing. I got some news today and it's been making me think about everything again."

Before I can find out what this news is though, we hear, "Dinner is ready."

"News?" I ask frantically. What is he not telling me?

Before I get an answer, he stands up and heads to the dining room to join my parents, leaving me confused and alone on the couch.

CHAPTER SIXTY-TWO

Owen

My head is all over the place tonight and I need to get my shit together.

"It looks amazing," I tell Poppy's parents as I take in the homemade pizzas with olives, artichoke hearts, sun-dried tomatoes, and pepperoncini.

Poppy comes in after me, subdued because I know I'm being a jerk. Any ounce of frustration that I've been able to let go of the past two weeks has come out with a vengeance today and I feel like I can't just enjoy this evening.

Instead, I'm pouting and being cranky. It's like I can see it happening and can't stop it.

Maybe I should leave so they can have a nice family dinner without me ruining it.

It's not fair for Poppy to make up an excuse for us both to duck out.

I look back at her and I feel like an ass for even thinking of excusing myself. I can have a shitty day at school without wearing my emotions on my sleeve, so I can absolutely get it together enough to be pleasant for dinner.

Instead of going to my usual place, I pull out Poppy's chair and kiss her cheek before she sits down. Her hand slides into mine so easily and I give it a little squeeze, loving the way it feels.

"What news did you get?" she asks, tugging lightly on my hand so I stay put for a moment.

If only everything felt easy right now, especially answering that question.

"Oh, we'd love to hear," her mom says.

God, I shouldn't have let anything slip out because now I have to tell everyone while pretending it's great news and I have no reason to be pessimistic about it.

Looking down at Poppy, I give her a sad smile before I walk around to my place across from her.

"Of course." My voice is a little hoarse and I clear my throat as I take my seat. "It's not final yet, the plan is to have the paperwork ready on Monday, but I was offered a position for next year at Honey Cove in the English department."

"Owen, that's so exciting," Michelle exclaims while Walter congratulates me and raises his beer for a toast.

I say something thanking them, but I can't look away from Poppy as emotions quickly flick across her face. She gives me a bright smile while sadness creeps into her eyes and she says, "That's huge, congratulations."

"To Owen and him staying in Honey Cove," her dad says and we all clink our glasses and take a drink.

"Thank you." My voice is thicker than I'd like so I take another sip.

"Here, please start the pizza," Michelle says, handing me a serving plate with slices from different pizzas. "Will you be teaching the same courses?"

I accept the plate and grab a few pieces. "I'll find out later what the needs are, but it sounds like I might have the option to keep these same classes."

That wasn't a lie, at least.

A little guilt stirs in my gut because I know I'm choosing my words carefully so I don't force Poppy to tell her parents about the offer before she's ready. It doesn't matter what I think, she needs to be able to decide when and how they have that discussion.

"What did your parents say?" her dad asks.

"Ah, they don't know yet," I say. "I just found out and will call them tonight or tomorrow."

"I'm sure they'll be so proud of you," Michelle says, putting her hand on my arm in a motherly gesture that makes my guilt swirl even more. But I manage a genuine smile because she's right.

Not only am I pretending to know that I'm staying here in Honey Cove versus possibly going out of the country with their daughter, but I'm telling the Edwards family before my own parents.

For the next few minutes, I ask about everyone's plans for the next few weeks to keep the topics neutral and I avoid looking directly across the table as much as I can. It's childish because she had no idea what my news was about. It was my own damn fault for saying something about it earlier and I don't want her to feel like she made me share before I wanted to. I only brought it up to help her understand that I was in a messed up headspace having just heard my dream of living in Honey Cove just got one step closer to being real.

Now, who knows what's going to happen?

I know this is a *huge* offer that she really does need to take her time considering. When I privately vented to Brandon the other day, he mentioned that her ex pretty much made decisions for the two of them in ways that made her think she had a say, but she basically didn't.

Hearing that broke my heart and I've been even more determined to be patient for her because this is the first big decision we're facing as a couple and it sounds like she was pretty much bull-dozed over and was told whatever he wanted was what was best for her and that was it.

I know I'm not that guy. She knows I'm not that guy. But she does deserve to weigh something as life-changing as this properly so she's confident she understands what *she* truly wants.

This is just so much harder now that I got my offer. It has me questioning whether or not I should sign the damn contract.

Thankfully, it's not due until everyone's contracts are renewed, so I have more than a month to finalize everything on my end if I indicate I'm planning to officially accept.

As we finish off the final slices, I mention how great dinner was and soon enough, Poppy and I are bringing our dessert dishes to the kitchen.

"You two don't have to do any of these, we have it covered," her mom says, shooing us away.

"Mom, we should actually get going. Both of us gave tests today and have a mountain of work to get through this weekend."

"Of course, we knew tonight wouldn't be too late but are happy you two made it," Walter says, already elbow-deep in dishwater and scrubbing pans from tonight.

"Thanks so much for having us, it was a great evening. We'll have to do it again soon," I say, being especially mindful to keep a warm smile on my face while I give her mom a hug and her dad a soapy handshake.

Once we're bundled up and outside, I pull her to a stop on the sidewalk so we're facing each other.

"I'm sorry." There aren't other words to say. She doesn't need me to list each instance of my being an ass.

"I'm sorry, too. I know this is hard on you and with your news–"

"It's nothing to worry about right now." I lean forward to kiss her forehead. "Do what you need to do."

"I love you," she says, her voice tinged with sadness.

"I know, and I love you."

We stand there, small snowflakes falling all around, and kiss. Her lips feel like home against mine and the way we fit perfectly together gives me hope. Even if things seem a bit desperate right now.

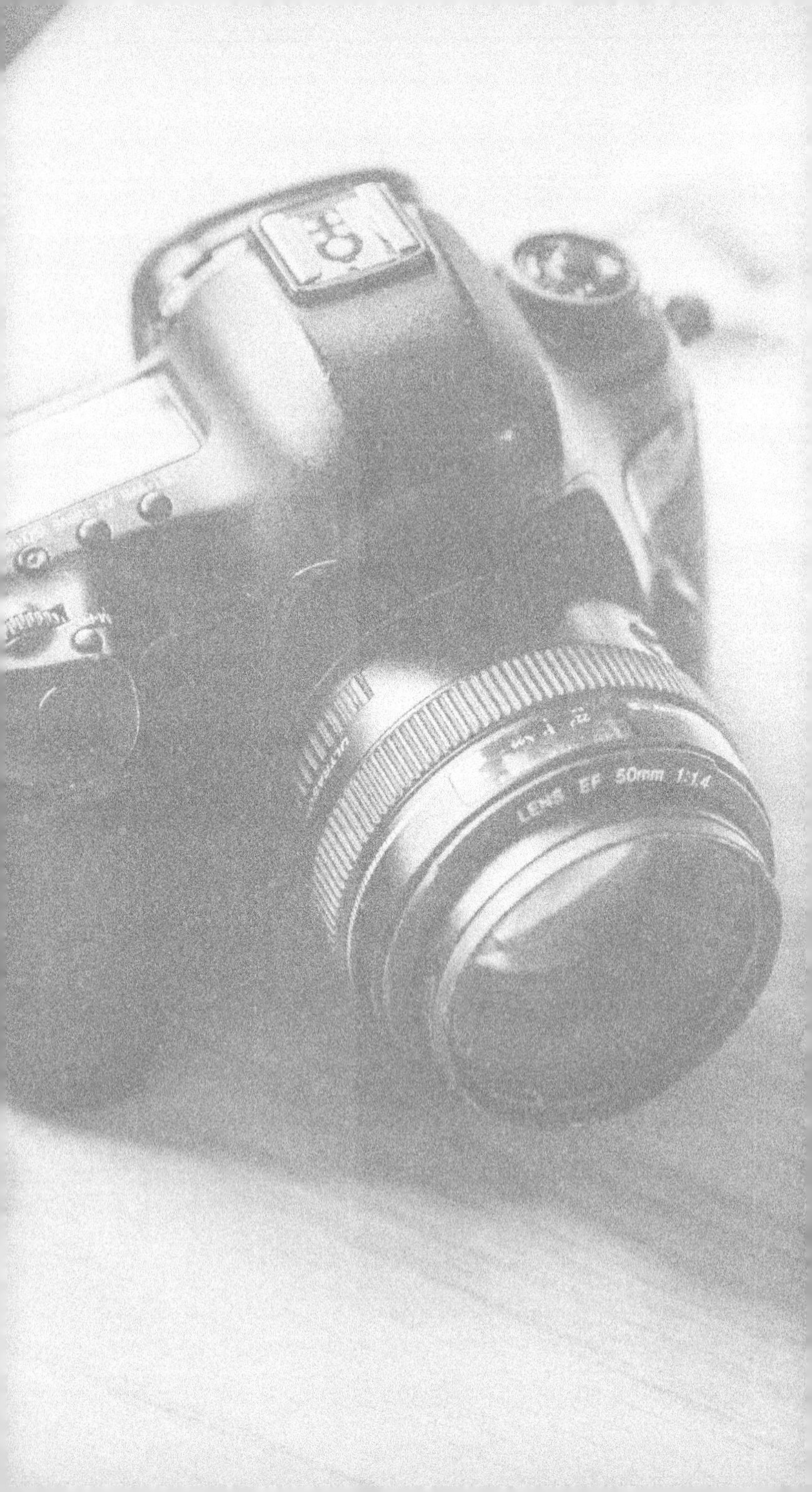
LENS EF 50mm 1:1.4

CHAPTER SIXTY-THREE

Poppy

Oh. My. God.

Looking at the pile of grading in front of me brings a few tears to my eyes. I know it isn't hard, but there's just so much of it. *How did I get so behind?*

Between everything with this potential job, Owen's contract for next year, and school, my brain has just not had the space or time to focus on any one thing enough these past few weeks. Every night I come home and collapse into bed. A heap of stress and indecision.

Owen and I attempted to talk about things the other day, but were promptly interrupted by his neighbor who needed help moving her new couch. Afterwards, I think we were both too tired to even attempt to discuss the situation.

Running my hands through my hair, I look at the test in front of me that I've been staring at for the past five minutes, but not actually grading. *Why don't you know what you want?* It *should* be Owen and Honey Cove, right? But after my last relationship, I told myself I wouldn't let a guy be the center of my universe anymore. I need to be a whole, happier person on my own, regardless of who I'm with.

Would I be happy with a life here in Honey Cove without Owen? I'd have my family. My friends. Most of my friends are getting married, settling down. What if I became the odd one out, the person without *their* person? Would that be okay? An image of "Auntie Poppy" comes to mind. Sitting at a party while my friends' children run around me and they chase after them.

But, is that even likely? Owen is amazing and wonderful and everything I've dreamed of in a guy, even after my breakup. He's been so understanding of everything and thoughtful on how we handled our relationship. I could see us being together long term. A new image flashes in my mind of us, together, older, living in a small home near my family. Owen roasting his own coffee beans in the barn. Me, painting and reading the newest autobiography Owen brought me on our front porch.

Both images don't feel quite right, and I can't shake this fear that I'm at some sort of crossroads in my life. I don't want to lose him. But I also want to be true to who I am.

Back at square one, I guess. Turning my attention back to my student's test on composition, I try once again to focus, only to be startled by my phone ringing.

"Hi, Mom," I say, a little breathless as I answer her video call, quickly smoothing down my hair and making sure I don't have any outward signs of my inward mental anguish. Composing myself, I set the phone up against a vase of flowers Owen had brought me the other day.

"Hi, sweetie. Your father's here too." She moves the phone so I can wave at both of them. I personally love that they act like it's been a month since they've seen me, every time they see me. Reality is, I saw them just a couple days ago for dinner with Owen.

"Hi, Dad. What are you two up to?"

"Oh, just watching that new Gordon Ramsey show. It got your mom thinking that she should whip up a roast this weekend though. Would you be able to come by?"

"I'm not sure. I need to check with Owen."

"Is everything okay there? You two seemed a little, not tense, but maybe not at ease at dinner the other night," my mom chimes in. *She's always so perceptive.*

"What do you know?" She looks from my dad and back to me a little too frantically.

"I heard from Andi's mom about a job offer. Why didn't you tell us?"

"I'm so sorry." Dragging my hands down my face, I temporarily hide behind them. That is not how I wanted them to find out, but I totally forgot to ask Andi to keep it quiet. "I haven't made any decisions, but I have a job offer I'm considering."

"In Toronto?" My dad's voice sounds quiet and sad, verging on heartbroken.

"Yes, it would be in Toronto. But it would be using my photography for marketing a large inn. The same one I stayed at when I was traveling. They have weddings there, too, that I could be available to photograph, parties, that sort of thing. And it's beautiful there—" I am rambling in hopes of making the situation better, but it isn't helping.

"We were just surprised and wanted to talk to you about it. But you haven't decided? What does Owen think?"

"We haven't discussed it fully. I'm not sure what I want. I love Owen, and I love being near you two of course, but I also love photography and the chance to expand that would be amazing."

"It is a tough decision." My mom is holding it together so well. I can see even through the small screen, the tiniest of tears tugging at the corner of her eye. I love that they're doing their best to be supportive of me even if it might be something they wouldn't like.

"I will let you two know as soon as I decide. I promise. You won't hear about it from Andi's mom."

CHAPTER SIXTY-FOUR

Owen

February

Since I have our pizza and apps order piled in my hands, I ring Poppy's doorbell instead of letting myself in. Without hearing her words, I can tell she's giving Noah some sort of instruction. He simply replies to her with an exasperated "fine" just before he opens the door.

"Hey Noah," I say, peering into the house to try to see what the commotion was. Things have been a little strained between Poppy and me. We've started talking a couple of times, but we keep getting interrupted or one of us changes the subject.

I know we have to sit down and really talk about everything, but each time we get close, all I can think about is her leaving and I clam up. She's shared the details Sally mentioned and I told her to send her the photos she took that day on the beach when the sun was setting.

Then I changed the subject and asked her about the upcoming senior art show. I'm a complete coward who keeps putting off this conversation because once it happens, it'll be official that the right thing for her will be to take this job. We just need to sit down and *talk*.

"That already smells amazing," he says, taking the stack from me so I can remove my winter gear. "Poppy is in the kitchen where I've been banned from."

"What happened?"

"She won't let me clean up the mess I made when I dropped the half-full bottle of wine." He takes the food to the dining room table and I see the Christmas gift I got her hanging on the wall: a framed photo she took that day on the beach. "She has also banned you from the space so you don't step on any glass."

"You're both okay though, right?" My sock slips off my foot while I step out of my taller boots. We just got another wave of snow earlier today, so I pulled out my "serious" winter boots that I wear when I shovel Poppy's driveway and sidewalk.

"Completely fine," he says, waving away my concerns as I walk to the kitchen.

"Don't come in," she yelps. "I'm doing the final sweep to get the remaining glass."

She looks adorably frazzled and I want to just step into the kitchen to work side by side with her. I know that she has this covered and my joining would only make her worry.

"What *can* I do?" I ask.

"Why don't you and Noah start setting up whatever game he brought? I'll be done in a minute and will bring in the dishes for our snack."

"There isn't really much set up."

"What do we need to do before playing?" I ask.

"Nothing, really." He shrugs, walking to a black bag by the front door that I hadn't noticed until now.

"What kind of game—" I begin before seeing what Noah brought. "That's not a game."

"A puzzle is a form of entertainment and is therefore a game." He turns and looks toward the kitchen, calling out, "Aren't I right, Poppy?"

"Right about what?" She comes into the dining room with plates, silverware, and napkins, setting them down on the table.

"Noah brought a puzzle," I explain.

"But it's game night," she says with a slight frown.

"A puzzle is a game," he says, still sounding sure.

"There aren't turns to take," she argues.

"And there's no strategy," I add.

"There's plenty of strategy. You could sort out all of the edge pieces first, *or* you could sort by color." He's definitely grasping at straws to make his case.

"It's still not a game," she says laughing and putting her arms around my waist as I engulf her in a hug. "But we can do the puzzle, right babe?"

"Of course." My lips brush over hers twice, those familiar sparks always present when we kiss. "Can I get you two something to drink?"

"I'm hosting, I should be asking you that."

I shrug. "You sit down and get the first pick from the apps. After all, you cleaned up all the glass."

"There's another bottle of red in the kitchen if you wanted to open that."

"That sounds great," Noah says.

"Consider it done." I kiss Poppy once more and go to the next room. She keeps her unopened wine bottles in the highest cupboard and I pick out one that she's been enjoying lately. Moving around her kitchen with ease, I uncork the bottle and pour three glasses.

It's hard to ignore the push and pull that seems to be my constant companion lately. The pull to be with her. To allow myself to continue dreaming of what life might be like here together.

The push to guard myself for her possible move. A move she hasn't asked me to join her on. But if she did, would I want to live in Toronto? I could visit regularly, but long-distance would be hard. My heart aches at just the thought of not being able to hold her every day.

Noah's laughter brings me back to this moment. Gathering the glasses, I join them again. We pass the pizza boxes around so everyone can fill their plate. If I didn't move with her, I'd be missing out on simple dinners and game nights with her new coworkers and friends in Toronto.

God, I need to refocus.

"How's the senior art show prep coming along?" I ask as Poppy takes a big bite of pizza.

"It's looking fantastic," Noah says. "We don't move the pieces to the room until the Friday before the show, so the students have other projects to discuss."

She nods along. "They have worked so hard and it shows. I can't believe the level of talent this graduating class has."

"Agreed. Owen, can you pass me the wings?" I hand the box to him and it's not long until we shift all of the to-go containers to the end of the table.

Noah opens the puzzle box and dumps the pieces out of the bag smiling like a kid in a candy store. "Who is taking the edges with me?"

I raise my hand tentatively as Poppy says, "I'm better at sorting the pieces by color and putting the puzzle together that way."

"Race to see who's done first?" he asks, rubbing his hands together gleefully.

"Do you mean, me, one person, tackling everything but the edge competing against the two of you who are only putting together the border?" she deadpans.

"Fair point," he says, frowning.

I look at the cover of the box. "How about we do the border and you do the fishing boat?"

Competition sparkles in her eyes. "You're on."

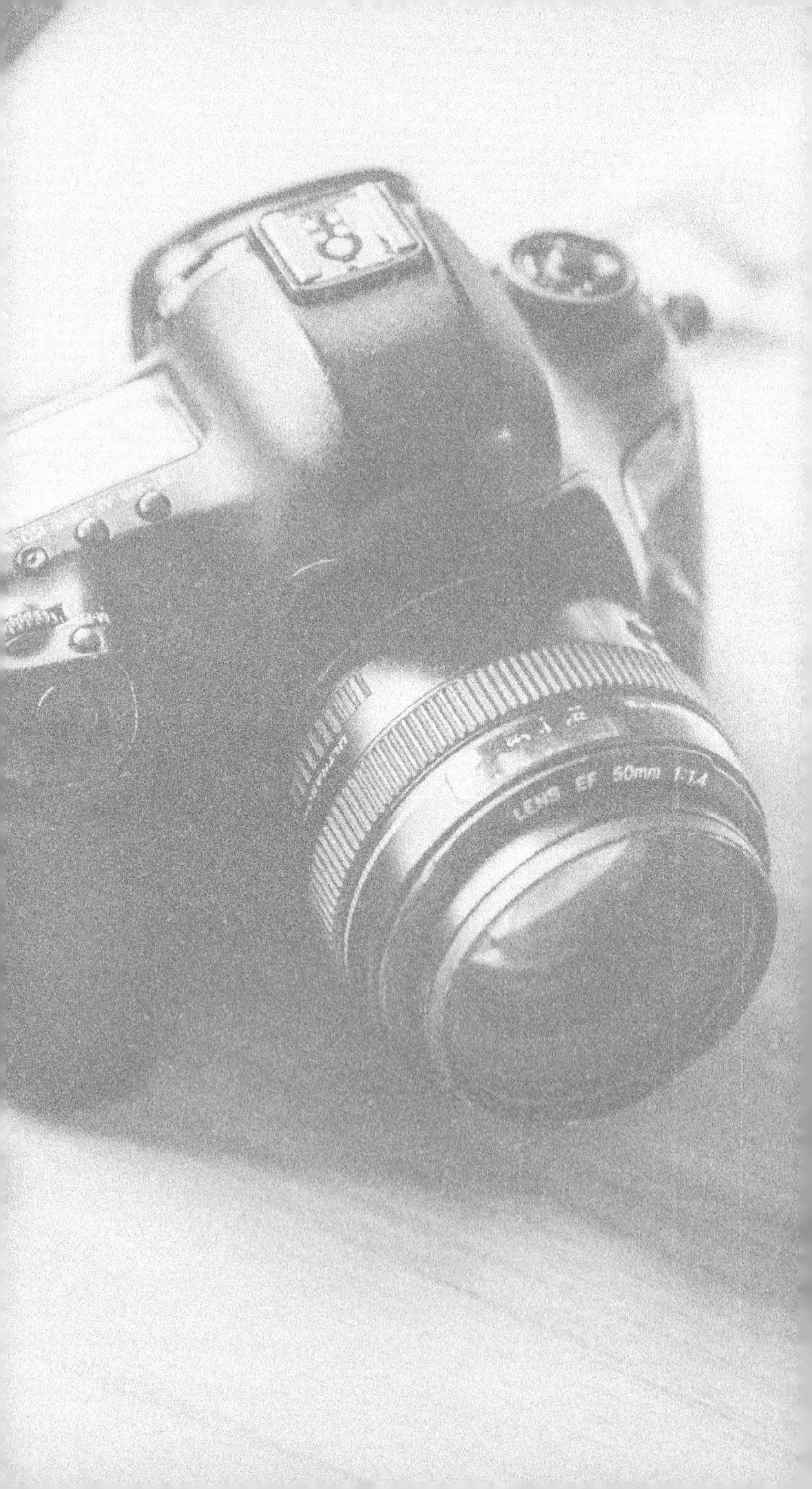
LENS EF 50mm 1:1.4

CHAPTER SIXTY-FIVE

Poppy

I don't think I've ever tried to put a puzzle together quite as fast as I am right now. I allow myself some short breaks to grab a bite of pizza or another wing before diving right back in again. The guys are quick, but I think I'll be faster once I find all these illusive boat pieces.

Despite my best intentions, my attention feels pulled from the puzzle back to Owen. I know that we need to talk and this game night was probably a bad idea given how the tension has been between us. Seeing how this is affecting him makes me feel selfish, but I can't help that I like to be around him even when there are unspoken things between us.

Noah looks at me and nods towards Owen. He thought this would help the issue between us, but I know that nothing will really fix this until we figure out what our plan is moving forward. Everything is a big question mark right now and even I struggle with not knowing what comes next. Owen is a planner, and I can't even imagine what this must be doing to him.

Not feeling quite ready to bridge the divide yet, I opt for tactical choice. "Did you see Cicely's final piece? She dropped it off yesterday and it took my breath away."

Noah looks up at me again momentarily, squinting his eyes before his gaze returns to the puzzle. "I'm not going to fall for your distraction trickery."

"Distraction trickery?" I scoff, knowing he's right. Owen lets out a small chuckle before eating a few more fries.

After another ten minutes of searching, it's become apparent that I cannot win this race. Noah and Owen are almost finished with the outline and I have barely half of the boat completed. Sighing, I dramatically stand up. "I concede, gentlemen, this is too hard and I have decided I'm getting more wine instead."

Taking the two steps to the kitchen, I turn back and see both men are looking up at me and the energy of the room has changed dramatically.

"You gave up so easily," Owen says quietly, shrugging his shoulders and running his hand down his glass before finishing off his drink.

"I wasn't going to win and the wine sounds better at the moment." Trying to lighten the mood, I add, "Anyone want popcorn?"

"So you just gave up and left?"

I freeze in my tracks because suddenly it doesn't feel like we're talking about the puzzle anymore. Noah fidgets nervously in his chair before announcing he needs to go to the bathroom. Owen and I look at each other. Then his gaze lands squarely on a piece of puzzle in front of him, he turns it with his finger, fiddling to avoid the inevitable.

Waiting until Noah is safely in the bathroom, I ask, "What do you want to say?"

"How can you not know what you want?" His voice is desperate, sad.

Taking a deep breath, I consider how to respond. I've been waiting for this conversation for over a month now but still don't feel wholly prepared for it despite how many times I've gone over it in my head. "Because *you're* here and you want to stay here."

"You never even asked me what I wanted." Crossing his arms over his chest, I push down the urge to run over to him. To sit on his lap and kiss his lips and to keep pretending that none of this exists.

"Since even before we were together you've talked about how you want to be with your family, how that's the most important thing to you. How could I ever pull you away from that?" Tears threaten to fall down my cheeks. He's talking like I don't care about him and never considered him, but that *is* exactly what I am trying to do.

"Sounds like you've already decided what you want to do."

"No, Owen—" But before I can even get the words out, Noah has returned from the bathroom, looking even more uncomfortable than he did previously.

We all stay in an awkward silence for a moment before Noah breaks it. "I think something with the pizza didn't sit right for me, I'm going to head out. You can just bring the puzzle to school and I'll get it from you there."

We both nod at Noah, I walk him to the door and whisper, "Sorry," as he leaves. He reaches up and wipes a now fallen tear off my cheek before giving a knowing smile and heading off into the night.

Closing the door and turning back towards the living room, my eyes lock with Owen's once more and my heart skips a beat. My love for him has continually grown over the past six months and I can see how much this is hurting him, which hurts me. I don't know how to approach this conversation without one of us being hurt more.

"I haven't decided *anything*. I feel like I can't decide. There is no right answer." I hold up my hands as a peace offering, moving to sit next to him at the table. I try to reach out a hand to his knee, but he moves away in one swift move, which hurts even more than I thought it would.

"Poppy, I—" He leans forward and kisses me before he can finish the words. We both fall into a tangle of emotion and passion and sadness, kissing one another with everything we have before everything changes.

CHAPTER SIXTY-SIX

Owen

I shouldn't be kissing her. I know this.

I should be talking to her, or trying to.

But the need to feel that our connection is still there overwhelms me. To know we're still as strong as ever, even when things feel like they're so tenuous.

Holding her is like being home.

I've never felt like this before. This amorphous limbo that causes me to lose sleep.

"Please talk to me," I say, breaking off our desperate kisses. "Tell me what you want."

It's like a punch to the gut seeing tears form from my plea.

"Owen, I *want* to talk to you about all of this. God, I want to know what you want. But if I don't give myself the independence to really weigh this possibility, I'm going to question how I made my final decision and if I, once again, let someone else's wants overpower my own before I've really considered them." Her hands hold my face so our foreheads are touching, like she can feel how easily this could slip away depending on her choice. "I know it's unfair of me to take this much space, but when I think about what this could mean. I never thought my photos were good enough for anything remotely close to this opportunity and I just feel...frozen."

Something about what she says feels like a slap in the face.

"And you think I'd ask you to *not* consider accepting this?" I ask, pulling back so I can try to read her expression and her hands fall to her lap as she looks shocked.

Am I such an asshole like her ex that she thinks I wouldn't be supportive of her dreams?

"What? Why would you think that?"

"What am I supposed to think, Poppy?" I stand because everything feels like it's crowding in around me. Or maybe that they're crashing down is more accurate. "I've been stewing for weeks while trying to focus on work, the students, and gathering the data needed for the English initiatives. All I can think about is you and *guess* what you're planning. Without me."

"I've never said anything about not being with you."

"True," I say, letting out a rueful chuckle. "But you also haven't said anything to even hint that you're considering me in the equation."

"What am I supposed to say to you right now?" her voice hitches and she wraps her arms around herself as my heart breaks and my own pain grows. "Each time I think about the possibility of truly moving away, my stomach is in knots. And that's only when I think about leaving my parents and Andi."

I wait.

And wait.

Finally, I nod and walk to the door only taking the time to slip into my boots and grab my jacket. I don't even care enough to put the damn thing on. The pain of hearing her not even say she'd miss me making me go numb.

"Well," I say as I walk out the door, unable to fully look back. "When you know what you want, you know how to find me."

And I leave.

Samson rubs my face with his and stretches on the pillow next to mine, pulling me out from my restless sleep.

God, why didn't I say something else last night? *Anything* else? Now I just need to wait to see if her decision is to rip my heart out and have her dream job, or stay here with me while knowing that she could've done something amazing with her photography, but that she gave it up for me.

I think about how she simply might not want me to move with her and maybe that's why she hasn't asked.

Fuck, if nothing else is a clear sign of where her head's at, that should be a good one. She's simply not interested in me going with her. Even if her reasons are about why I chose to move here, it's not what I want.

I want her.

Part of me is dying to tell her. Part of me is trying to relax, remembering that her last relationship had her life revolving around Steven and his wants. I have to give her the space to think about what *she* truly wants because she's even busier than me with the senior art show coming up and she's balancing so much.

The other part of me needs to be reassured that we're in this together. That she wants to hear my thoughts about what could be and plan a future for *us*.

Samson hops out of bed and stands in the doorway, looking back at me until I throw the covers off of me. "Okay, buddy, if you're up, it can't be too early in the morning."

Grabbing my phone, I check the time and it's not quite seven. I might as well get a workout in. There are a few messages on my phone though, so I scroll through them.

Brandon:
> Hey man, call me if you need anything.

Well, I can only assume that Poppy and Andi talked last night. I start typing a note that says that I'm okay, but delete that and just send one thanking him. We've gotten too close for me to start lying to him now.

I read the next message several times, looking for any clues about what she's thinking, but finding none.

Poppy:
> I'm going for a run in a minute. I didn't want you to message and think I was ignoring you or anything like that. I love you so much.

> I love you, too, babe. Have a great run.

An impatient meow gets my attention. "Alright, Samson, time for breakfast."

He hops into my arms and I place him on my shoulder on the way into the kitchen, purring happily. He watches intently while I prepare his food, occasionally kneading my shoulder with his front paws. When I place his dish on the ground, he starts scarfing his food down as noisily as ever.

After going to the bathroom and washing my face, I go back to my bedroom and grab my pull-up bar from where I store it behind the door. I stare at it for a moment, thinking about how long it hung in the doorway before Poppy came along and how I've been taking it down daily because she might come over.

"Stop throwing yourself a pity party," I mumble, putting the bar into place. The first pull-up is never quite right and I make a few minor adjustments then start my reps. Today, I work in some different leg lifts and twists while hanging and push myself further than usual, breaking out into a sweat while I'm still using the bar.

When I drop, I leave the bar in place and pull out my mat and go right into my usual sequences. Then I repeat them, doubling my regular workout and letting my mind focus on the burn.

A fluffy gray and black face peeks over the top of his cat tree in the sun room every now and then, but this morning, Samson leaves me to my workout. He must be able to sense that I need to burn off some of this mounting frustration.

My muscles are aching when I fall back on the mat, finally feeling spent. One thought is on my mind:

I wish I could tell her.

That's the core of all of my frustration. I can't tell her that I'd move to Toronto with her. She deserves to figure out exactly what she wants to do without having a guy weigh in, no matter how good his intentions may be. She spent five years thinking of Steven and what he wanted.

She'll ask when she's ready. I just need to be patient.

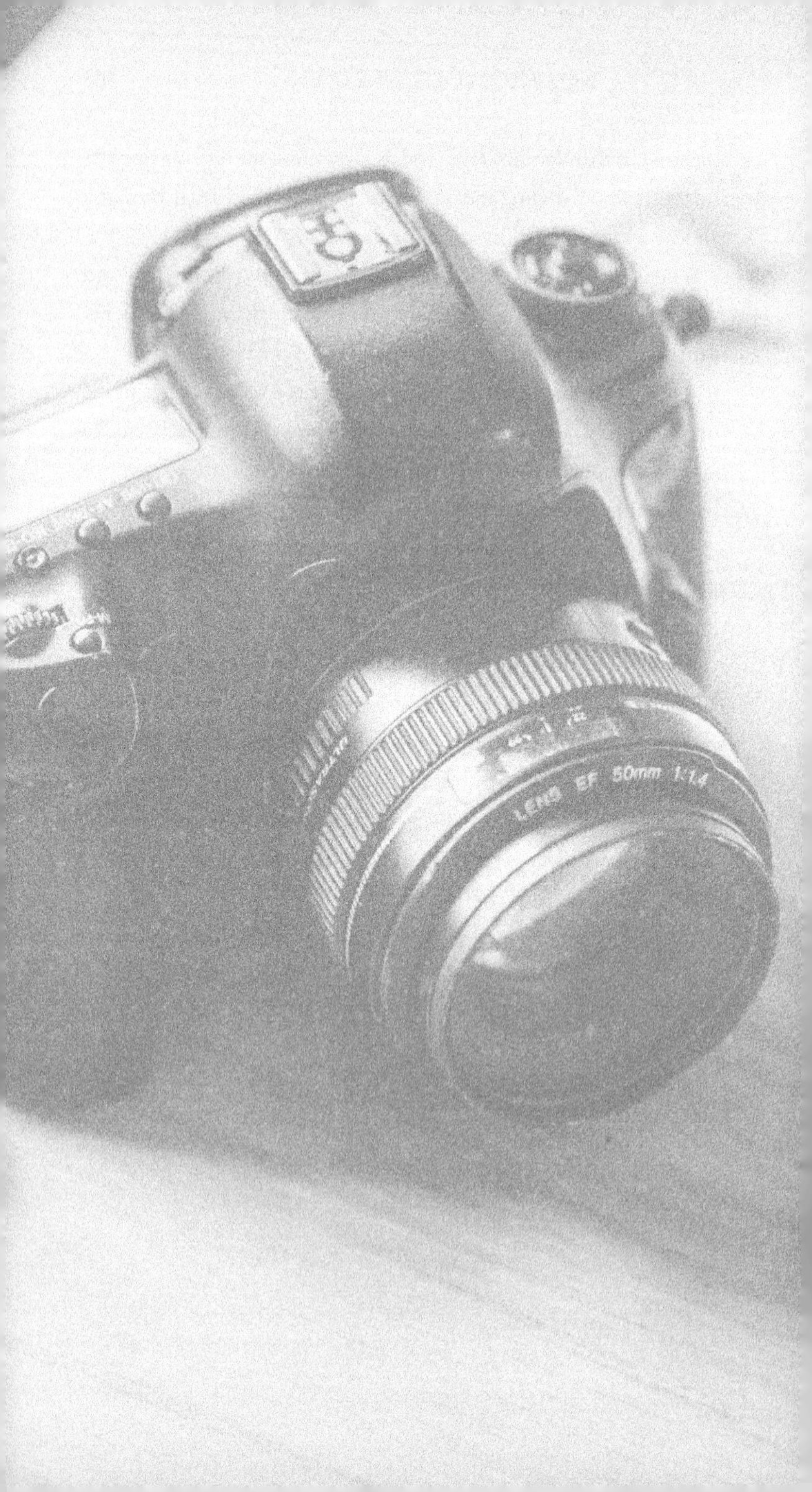
LENS EF 50mm 1:1.4

CHAPTER SIXTY-SEVEN

Poppy

Throwing on my jacket over my long sleeve and leggings, I catch my nail on the sleeve and let out an entirely too loud sigh at the pinch of pain. Also, it's cold. Even though it's almost spring, the air feels thin and like winter is going to overstay her welcome. And, I'm angry. Still upset over everything that was said between Owen and me last night. We had that one, beautiful kiss, before everything fell apart again.

Usually I am very adept at explaining how I feel and knowing exactly what I want. But for some reason, in this situation, it feels like there's no winning for anyone, and any step I take I'll lose something or someone that I love.

Turning on a teaching podcast, I push in my earbuds and lock the door before heading down the sidewalk toward the boardwalk. I usually avoid running on it in the winter because it gets so icy, but today it feels like I could use a little of that cold air to shock my system back to normal. Maybe even into making a choice about what I actually want *without* anyone else's input.

I've only made it less than a mile before I switch off the podcast and turn on some music instead. My brain just can't focus today and I feel like I need to veg out and not try to think too much right now. Once I make it to the boardwalk, I'm caught up by the way the sunrise looks over the water. The oranges mixing with the pinks and blending seamlessly into the blues of the water, cause me to stare a little longer before continuing on my way, a little more at peace.

You would miss this. And I know I would. There is nothing quite like running here. It's beautiful and feels so comfortable and homey. Around every corner is someone I know and love. I know exactly what I would get with staying here and I don't think there's anything wrong with that. Especially since Owen is here.

You love Owen. And I do. With all my heart. He has made my life here brighter and more beautiful than I had imagined it could be this year. I can't picture moving somewhere without him.

Before my imaginary pros and cons list can continue, my heart hitches at the sight of Steven coming out of one of the bakery two doors in front of where I am. He sees me before I can make any sort of unhinged maneuver to hide, which is probably for the best.

"Hey, Poppy," he calls out.

"Hi." I stop in front of him. Noticing for the first time all the bags he's carrying.

Seeing my eyes land on the many bags of bread, he quickly adds, "They're for lunch. Jennifer is hosting my family at her parents' home in Cape Cod. We're about to head out now. He nods towards a car parked across the street. I quickly recognize the dark-haired woman from that day Owen and I ran into his family while running.

"That sounds nice." I am stammering and wish I could find my voice to ask him all the questions I've had brewing now that our time together has a little perspective.

"Listen, Poppy, I—" Before he can get the words out, Jennifer is calling to him from the car and begging him to hurry up.

He starts to move towards their car, but turns back to add, "I am sorry. For how things went with us. I was an asshole and you deserved better. Owen seemed like a nice guy and I hope he knows what he has with you."

I'm shocked into silence and he continues to walk away. Before he's too far, I call out, "I hope that Jennifer is good for you too."

Turning back, he says, "She is. We are very different, but we try to see everything from each other's perspective. Try to think outside of the box when we disagree and it seems to work for us." He gives me one of his handsome smiles I used to love. "Good seeing you, Poppy."

"You too." A stunned calm washes over me. I never felt the need for further closure with him or an apology; this was unexpected. His words also gave me an idea that I am all too eager to get home and call Sally about.

I decide I can't wait and whip out my phone only to find six missed calls from Noah and even more messages. Quickly I attempt to call Noah back, but have no service. *Damnit*. I've heard Clara complaining about service all summer, but never had an issue until now.

Scanning his messages I go into a panic. The senior art show is a day away and our venue is damaged, as well as some of the students' art. The venue owner called while I was still asleep, but I assumed it was about final preparations for Monday. I try to make another call to Noah, only to find that there's still no service. *What are we going to do?*

Of all the days... at least I don't live too far from here and my phone has always worked fine there. Turning my heel, I start the jog home, breathing deeply in a dire attempt to keep the rising stress at bay.

CHAPTER SIXTY-EIGHT

Owen

Just because I'm giving her space to weigh her options before adding my feelings to the mix, doesn't mean I get to be a jerk and not apologize. The flowers in my hand are in jeopardy of freezing soon as I sit on her front steps. My dad sent a bouquet to my place when I was offered my position for next year at Honey Cove. We still have a few weeks before we need to sign the contracts, but the school likes to know who plans to return so they can start posting open positions by spring break. I should be elated, but I'm just feeling confused.

I check the time once more and it's only seven fifteen. My shower was possibly the fastest I've ever taken and I'm pretty sure I didn't miss any teeth in my haste to brush them. Running my tongue over them, I reassure myself that I did a proper job.

Oh god, I really screwed up last night if I'm sitting here checking my damn teeth.

Wrapping my scarf around my neck once more, I try to keep warm. I'm sure she's out in her warm, but fantastically tight, running pants and her fitted jacket. Her cheeks are likely bright red from the cold air and exertion. Just picturing her coming home from a run makes me want to get her a cup of coffee and curl up under a blanket with her.

My phone starts buzzing in my jeans. It can't be Poppy because she's not back yet, so I let it ring and go to voicemail. After a moment of silence, it starts back up and I automatically wonder if everyone is okay.

Carefully setting the flowers, vase and all, against her front door so they don't tip over, I stand, remove my glove with my teeth and awkwardly lift my jacket so I can grab my phone out of my front pocket. I barely read Noah's name on the screen before I swipe to answer it before it goes to voicemail, again.

"Are you alright?" I ask in lieu of a greeting.

"I'm okay, but are you with Poppy?" he sounds wide awake, which is odd for a Saturday morning at this hour.

"No, but I'm at her house," I begin.

"Did you two figure things out finally?" he asks.

"Unfortunately, we didn't, but I'm here with an apology bouquet and she's still out for a run."

Noah curses under his breath. "So, you know how the senior art show is being set up this weekend?"

"Yeah, of course. My offer to help still stands."

"Well, we might need you because a pipe burst and they can't get a hold of Poppy."

"Oh shit." My heart sinks thinking about how crushed not only she will be, but all the students. "What can I do?"

He sighs. "Unfortunately nothing right now. She's the one we need to find. Do you know when she'll be back?"

"She didn't say where she was going and she sent her message less than an hour ago saying she was going out." Depending on how she's feeling, she's sometimes only gone for fifteen minutes, but she's usually gone for an hour or two.

"Okay, we'll just have to wait."

"There has to be something we can do to help with the clean up, right?" I reach back into my pocket and pull out my keys, flipping through them to find the one she gave me to her house.

"No, the space is completely unusable and we have to find a replacement site or postpone, which is why we need Poppy since she knows the art pieces and how much floor and wall space we'll need."

"Hang on for one second," I say, putting the phone on mute and dropping it into my big coat pocket so it doesn't end up in the snow. I pick up the vase and unlock the door, entering the house, immediately missing her presence. Kicking off my boots and shutting the door so her house doesn't get cold, I grab my phone again. "Okay, I'm back. Tell me what *you* know about the art pieces this year. I've seen a couple and I wonder if we can at least have a few ideas ready for her so she doesn't feel totally overwhelmed when she sees her phone."

As he talks to me about the sculptures he has seen and helped pack up for transport, I write out a quick note for Poppy and set it next to the flowers on her kitchen counter:

I'm sorry, and I love you. Take whatever time you need to weigh your options, I'm here whenever you need to talk through anything.

Love,

Owen

Even though there's a lot more that I want to say to her, I hope this helps take some worries off her shoulders.

"...and those sculptures were supposed to go on medium-sized pillars, but the pillars were in the room with the most damage, so we won't have access to any of those."

"Do you know anything about the art itself?" I ask, feeling nervous for the students.

"It sounds like any damage was likely minimal because they were being stored in another room until tomorrow when we were supposed to set up, so we got really lucky."

"Definitely," I breathe a sigh of relief. "Be sure to tell her that right away if you're the one to deliver the news."

"Aren't you going to stay there to apologize?" he asks.

"I'm going to get coffee and muffins, she's going to be so stressed out when she hears and she'll likely run right out the door without grabbing anything to eat," I say, stepping into my boots and locking the front door from the inside on my way out.

The line is quiet for a moment.

"Noah, are you still there?"

"You're doing the right thing, Owen."

"What do you mean?"

There's another pause. "She's confused and is trying to not make the same mistakes she has in the past. And I know you haven't asked, but no, she hasn't told me anything she hasn't already said to you. But, you've made her so happy and you're doing the right thing, even if it's hard." His words stop me on the way to my car, hitting deep. "Steven just made decisions and then presented pretty ridiculous options for her to choose between. I'm quite positive she knows she's overcompensating in trying to figure out what *she* needs and wants, but there was so much she didn't see with her ex that she's rightfully terrified it might happen again. She wouldn't think this hard and this long about it, if she didn't love you."

A croaking sound comes out of me and I clear my throat and try again. "Thank you, I mean it."

"No problem, you've probably figured out that I like to butt-in every now and then."

"Well, I appreciate it more than you know."

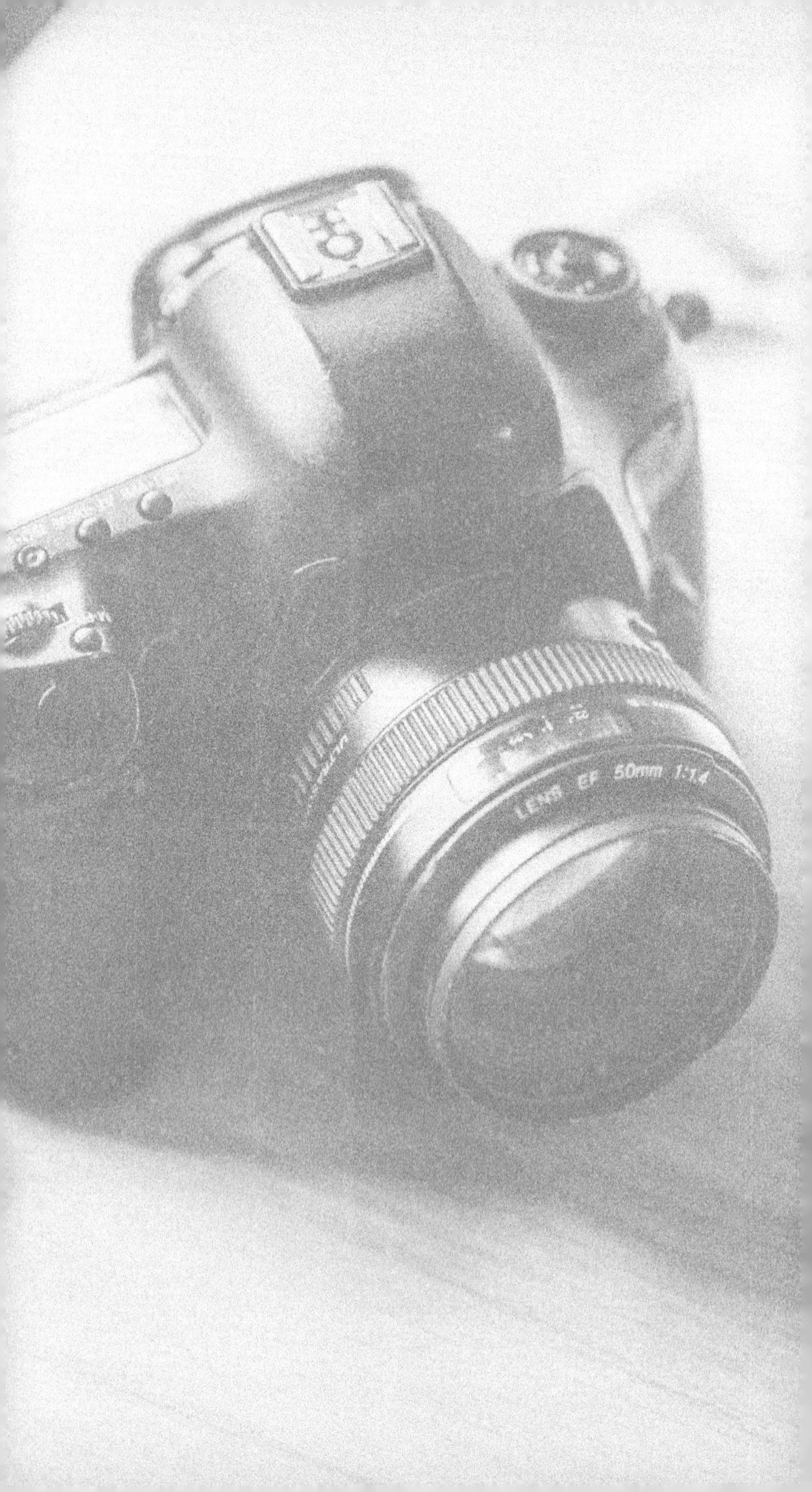
LENS EF 50mm 1:1.4

CHAPTER SIXTY-NINE

Poppy

"Noah, I'm sorry," I stammer out after he picks up. I'm breathing heavily from the faster-than-normal jog home and collapse onto my dining chair with a glass of water. Seeing Owen's sweet note and flowers melt my heart a little. *I wonder when he stopped by.* I feel a pull to want to talk to him about my plan right away, but the art show crisis is more pressing right now and I should talk to Sally first.

"It's okay. Where were you? Have you seen my messages?" He sounds flustered and slightly annoyed, but I know he's just worried for the kids.

"I was out running on the boardwalk, and I didn't have service to call back. What happened?"

"A pipe burst and we need to find a new place to host the show. The manager called and said some of the art has been damaged, so I'm thinking we head over there to figure out where things are at?"

"Oh my god, what are we going to do?" Hanging my head, I just can't imagine all these seniors and having to tell them their art is ruined. *They've worked so hard and we only have two days to figure this out.*

"Let's go see what's happening first before you let yourself go into full on panic mode, okay? Can I pick you up?" Noah may be worried, but he's always been the levelheaded one, which I appreciate. He's helped out in more than one crisis and is always a voice of reason.

"Yes, I just got home so I'll shower quickly while you drive over."

"See you soon."

After hanging up I try to lower my level of freaking out, but it's of no use. Jumping into the shower, I remember that I wanted to call Sally and dial her number as the water drips onto my bathroom tile forming little pools of water that I barely notice.

Fifteen minutes later and I feel like a new woman. A shower and my talk with Sally gave me a new sense of peace and perspective. I notice that the floor has puddles all over it though, so I grab an extra towel from the cabinet and try to soak up some of the water so I don't slip and fall. Not wanting to waste too much time, I end up throwing the towel onto the floor, pull my hair up into a bun, pin back my bangs and throw a little mascara on before grabbing an old sweatshirt and jeans to wear to the venue.

Originally, we had decided on this older building that is now available for rentals because of the historical feel and its large space. It has all the old world charm you could ask for, but apparently also all the old world pipes, which in our case was not good. I grab my bag, a snack and head towards the living room window to watch for Noah, feeling significantly more at ease with having talked with Sally. As soon as this is figured out I'll call Owen. *One problem to solve at a time.*

Looking at my phone, I think of all the students and how brokenhearted they will be if we can't figure this out. I should at least email soon so they have a heads-up. *I'll message when I know more; I don't want to worry them unnecessarily.* I hope we can figure this out quickly and that the damage isn't too bad. I know Noah said some of the art had issues, but I'm hoping he's exaggerating and things can be solved quickly. The art show is in less than forty-eight hours and I can't imagine we'd be able to find somewhere new in that amount of time.

Soon, Noah pulls up and I run out to his car. He hands me a cup of coffee before launching into his story of what happened. I gasp as he tells me what the manager of the venue shared. *This could actually be worse than I thought*, my panic comes back in full swing.

After the short drive over, we head inside and are met with a musty smell we weren't expecting. "Didn't this just happen? I was here yesterday and it was fine."

"We think it started earlier on Thursday or Friday with a small leak in the wall that was hidden before some of the other pipes fully burst last night." The manager walks towards us from the front office. "Thanks for coming over and we're so sorry."

"Where is everything?" Noah asks.

"Right over here." The manager points towards a pile of sculptures, canvases, and fabric in a heap. "I'm sorry for the mess of things, I know the kids worked hard. We were just trying to save things as quickly as we could and then didn't want to touch things and possibly ruin them more."

"Thank you," Noah and I both say in unison as we stoop down to survey the damage.

"This is bad." He runs his hand through his hair before looking over at me. "What do you want to do?"

Feeling my newfound positive attitude from earlier return, I respond, "Let's get to work." And we dive in.

CHAPTER SEVENTY

Owen

The familiar sound of the bell rings as I enter Bobbi's and it's a little busier than usual for a Saturday morning. I know I've seen the woman in line ahead of me, but I can't place her until Cicely comes out of the bathroom, busy on her phone, and joins her.

"Mom, it looks like they don't have the purple dress—" Cicely looks up and her eyes widen in surprise. "Mr. Wright?"

"Good morning," I say, greeting both Cicely and her mom, whose name I can't recall. "What are you two up to before eight on a Saturday?"

"Oh, we're driving out to a few boutiques today for prom dress shopping." Her mom turns to Clara behind the counter to place their order.

"What are you doing this early on a weekend?" Cicely always gets right to the point.

There's no way I'd tell a student I was awake early to apologize for being an ass to my girlfriend, but I give myself a split second to weigh whether it's a bad idea to tell her about the damage.

"Actually, there might be something you can help me with. I don't have that many details, just what Noah has told me, but the building the art show is scheduled to be in had a pipe burst. It sounds like the art was stored in a separate room that had a little less damage."

She looks confused at first, but then I see the moment it sinks in. "Is my piece okay? I just finished it and it took months to create."

"I'm not sure what the full process will be, but I'm positive that Ms. Edwards is going to give you all that information when she's been able to go through everything."

She turns to her mom who is paying for their order and looks like she might cry. "Is there anything I can do? Can I go check myself?"

God, I'm making a mess out of this and stressing Cicely out which isn't helping a damn thing, so I try to refocus. "Let's let them figure that piece out; this all just happened so they'll be busy keeping your art safe."

She nods, her eyes shining.

"I was hoping you might be able to help me. Again, we don't have all the details, but the space won't be usable for the show on Monday," I say quickly, not wanting to belabor the possible point of the senior art show being ruined. "But, if you can talk to me about the pieces and what they need to be displayed, I'd like to try to find a location so the show can be set up tomorrow and still open on Monday."

"What happened with the show?" her mom asks and her daughter gives her a surprisingly calm summary while I place an order for three coffees to go.

"Can we go shopping another weekend, Mom? I want to be here today to help where I can."

"Of course, honey. Once we know what we can do, then we can check with some other families. I'm sure they'll be eager to help make sure the show can open on Monday."

I smile hearing how supportive both Cicely and her mom are.

"I didn't mean to eavesdrop," Clara says, looking apologetic, "but I'd like to offer coffee and pastries for everyone setting up today and tomorrow. I'd offer the cafe to host the event, but there's no way it's big enough. Poppy already placed an order for Monday, but I'd like to help somehow."

"That's really generous of you, thanks," I say, writing my number down on an order ticket she hands me.

"Just let me know how many people will be setting up and what time."

"Absolutely, thanks, again."

Cicely is at a table, waving me over while her mom is talking to someone on the phone near the door. Setting my coffees on the table, I pull out my phone to take notes and as Cicely scrolls through her photos, showing me each time she has one of a project.

"Ugh, I don't have a picture of everyone's." Frustration laces her voice.

"What you have has already been really helpful already," I say, trying to reassure her. "Noah mentioned the pillars are unusable for some of the sculptures. Do you think tables would be okay?"

She makes a face like she took a bite of something sour. "I mean, sure? But it wouldn't display them well."

"Is there something we could use instead? Or something we can add to the tables that could help display the sculptures if we don't have another option?" I ask.

Cicely thinks for a moment and suddenly smiles. "The theater department should have hat boxes."

"Hat boxes?"

"Yes, they're round and pretty sturdy." She types furiously as she talks. "I was in a production a few years ago and they have more than we'd need. We could easily drape white fabric or even sheets over the hat boxes which could be set on a few tables spread out in whatever space we use and it would have a similar effect as a pillar."

"That's perfect," I say, sending an email out to Ms. Neeymeyer since she organizes the musicals and I know she'd be able to tell me what we might be able to use.

"Okay, so everything else is something that can hang on the wall, but there aren't a lot of places with empty wall space." She scrolls through her photos once more and shows me one of her pieces early in the process. "That's it."

"The art room?"

"No, the easels," she says, pointing to the photo. "We have a ton of easels for working on so we can stand or sit upright if we want, so there are a bunch of sizes too. The easels would make it so we wouldn't need open wall space. So now, we just need a space with some tables we can move around and room to set up the easels."

I think about Honey Cove Books, and the way Grace transforms the space for author visits, and say, "Let me make a phone call."

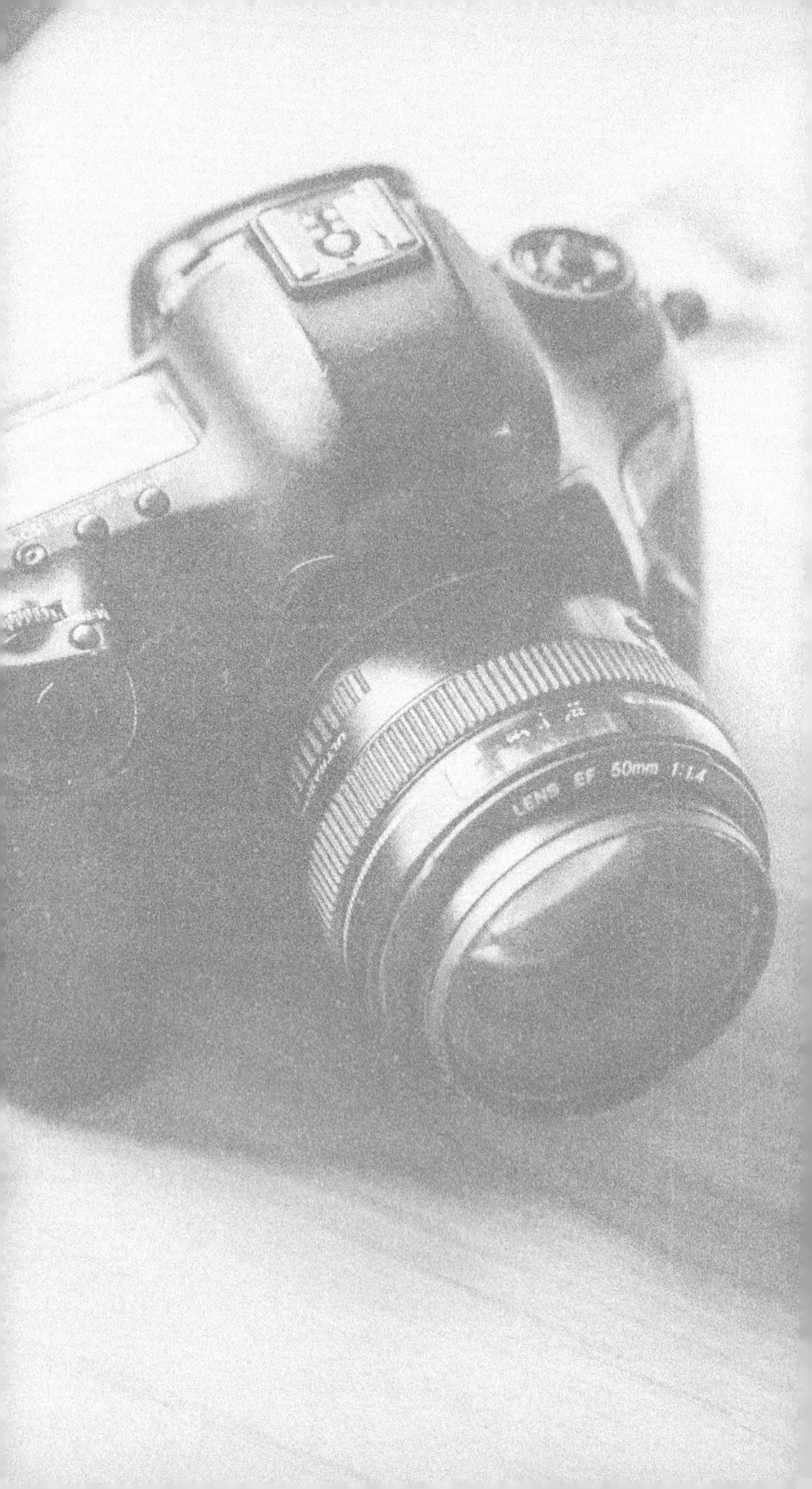
LENS EF 50mm 1:1.4

CHAPTER SEVENTY-ONE

Poppy

"What do you think of this one?" Noah holds up a badly water-damaged watercolor landscape. *Bryce will be so sad.* Looking at it, there isn't much that can be done, but I feel like we owe it to the kids to bring every piece back in the best shape that we can.

"Let's lay that one out to dry at my house. I have some fans we can use. We might be able to cut off the bad parts since they're mostly along the edges."

Noah brings the piece out to his car where we've already lugged most of the sculptures, which were thankfully not too damaged. Most were fired clay so the water didn't have too bad of an effect on them. Sighing, I look around. We've separated most of the rest into piles and may need to make a couple trips. Noah's car isn't the largest and it took us a full van to get everything here yesterday.

My eyes catch on Noah as he starts walking back towards our piles. He's been on his phone a lot which is odd for him. I wonder if he's messaging with students or maybe someone new in his life. I think he was dating someone a few towns over at some point.

There are a few pieces that are unsalvageable and I haven't decided yet how I'm going to break it to those students. One is a pastel that must have been directly under one of the leaks and where was once a beautiful self portrait is streaks of color, the rich hues now blended out to soft pinks and yellows. I remember I took photos of all the pieces a few days ago and have the idea to have the photos printed in lieu of the actual art for the show Monday.

I text my mom to see if she can swing over to Maple Springs to pick up some prints this afternoon. They know me well and won't bat an eye at my asking for a rush job, especially when they know what it's for. Grabbing a pen and pad of paper from my purse, I start to make a list of the pieces that are ruined so I can send those photos as soon as possible.

"What's next?"

"Let's still pack these." I point to the pile of unusable projects. "I'd like to still give them back to the students even if we can't use them."

He grabs another load and I know that's all that will fit. We'll have to come back after dropping everything off at my house. I don't know where I'm going to put everything or where they will dry out, but try to keep the mindset of *first things first*. I haven't even thought of a back up plan. *God.* I think we'll have to postpone. Maybe until after spring break? I know a lot of the seniors will be checked out by then. It isn't ideal, but nothing about this situation is.

"We'll be back," I call out to the manager who waves back from the office. He's also been on the phone constantly between the insurance company, plumbers, and a restoration company. He definitely has his hands full too. I make a mental note to bring him some coffee or something when we come back for the rest of the pieces.

Meeting Noah out by the car, I breathe in the cool afternoon air. The sun is staying out later now and it's nice to feel a breeze after being inside the musty building for so long. "Thank you for your help."

"Of course, I always like helping with the art show."

"Even when it's sopping wet and molding?" I laugh.

"Even then." Noah's eyes flash with something I'm not quite sure of before he hops into the car. "We're going to make a pit stop before heading back to your place."

I feel slightly annoyed, wanting to get everything drying and get back here as quickly as possible, but decide on diplomacy. "Where do we need to stop?"

"You'll see."

I narrow my eyes at him. "Noah, what are you up to?"

He shrugs at me, turning on the radio as we head down the road.

If there's one thing I've learned about him, it's that once he's decided on something, there's no changing his mind. It could be helping a student, brightening another teacher's day, or running a marathon, he sticks to what he sets his mind to. I realize quickly there will be no getting any info from him about wherever it is we're stopping, but if he believes it's important, I'll trust him. Although my stomach is in knots about what we're going to do for the art show.

My mind gets swept up in thinking of options of venues and timelines for rescheduling when I see that we've stopped. Turning to the side I see that we're at the bookstore. The same one Owen and I went to on our date. "Just itching to get a new book?"

"No, come with me." He gestures to me as he gets out of the car. I slide out and place the pieces I had on my lap back on the seat and close the door. *I'm completely and utterly confused.*

"Noah, what are we doing? We really need to figure out what we're going to do." My patience is waning and while I think I've been holding things together fairly well, that can change. *Very* quickly.

He holds the door open as I give him my most quizzical look, but turning I see what he's been hiding. The shorter bookshelves up front have been pushed back and tables are in their places. My seniors are bustling around, hanging signs and the most beautiful twinkle lights along the store walls. Grace gives me a small wave from behind the counter before nodding towards the back of the room.

"Ms. Edwards, you came!" Bryce stands right in front of me and it's all I can do to hold back the tears that have been building over the last few days. "Come and see what we've done."

CHAPTER SEVENTY-TWO

Owen

Her eyes swim with emotion when she sees what we've been up to. Poppy is led around the space, the students animatedly pointing out the spots they taped to represent where each easel could be placed.

Cicely was able to get most of the senior art students to the store within twenty minutes of Grace meeting us. They all shared a moment of panic and commiseration before dividing up tasks and away we went. A few met Ms. Neemeyer at the high school for a bundle of hat boxes and she even sent panels of black fabric from a recent production.

I stay off to the side, busy standing on a ladder to get the final batch of twinkle lights hung under Cicely's guidance.

"To the left," she says, comparing how far each section 'dips' so they're all even. "A little more."

Adjusting the lights with one hand, the other holds a nail ready to be tapped into the top of the bookshelf to hold everything in place.

"That's perfect." Both of her hands are held out in front of her, like she's about to catch something that might fall.

"Okay, one second and you can do your final inspection." Pinching the nail next to the wire, I grab the hammer from my pocket and tap it in before stepping down the ladder and gesturing to the shelves. "What do you think?"

Everything has been so tense for the students the past couple of hours that I'm not surprised to see Cicely wave a few classmates over to help sign off that everything is perfect. As they're looking from shelf to shelf, I take a peek at Poppy. Her back is to me but I can tell she's wiping her eyes as she nods at whatever they're telling her.

"They're perfect, Mr. Wright," Cicely says, drawing my attention back to their mini critique group.

"Excellent. Why don't you go show Ms. Edwards the solution for the damaged pillars you came up with?"

She grabs her friends' hands and off they run to Poppy. Noah narrowly avoids being run over by the three of them and stands next to me.

"She looked completely surprised," I say to him. "How'd you keep it a secret?"

He chuckles. "Not easily at the end, but she was distracted by everything we needed to go through."

"How bad is it?"

Blowing out a breath, he already sounds tired. "Some of the pieces are great, some might be fine once they're dry, some will have minor damage, and a few are completely beyond repair."

"Damn," I mutter under my breath.

"My sentiments exactly."

Grace comes by with two cups of coffee from Bobbi's. "I thought you two might like this after your crazy morning."

"It's not like yours has been an average Saturday at the shop," I say, noticing that Noah is a little quieter than usual.

"Thanks," he says as he accepts his coffee before clearing his throat. "This is really amazing, Grace."

She blushes and waves away the compliment. "Anyone would have done this. I'm just the first person Owen called."

"No," he says gently. "Not everyone would have turned their store upside down for a small group of students at a moment's notice."

Just then, amidst a group of art students who are pointing in our direction, Poppy's gaze finds mine. All the tension and frustration that's been slowly driving a wedge between us seems to melt away in that one look. It's not gratitude, it's just love.

For the first time since she got the call from Sally, I feel like I can fully breathe. We don't have answers right now, but something feels like it's less...hopeless.

The moment is broken by the seniors asking her a dozen questions at once. Noah and Grace continue a quiet conversation but all my focus is back on Poppy.

"You've all done..." She sniffles a little and starts again. "I can't believe what you've all been able to put together this morning. Truly." Taking a deep breath, she continues, "As you all know, when you finished your projects, I took a few photos of each one so you could add them to your digital portfolios. I've sent some of those photos to be printed so all of your pieces could be displayed at our show on Monday."

"Does that mean we lost our projects?" someone farther back in the group asks.

"I'm so sorry," Poppy says, getting choked up. "Noah and I have a batch we're going to dry out to see what we can save, but a few of the projects were completely damaged. I didn't know that I'd be seeing you all so soon so I don't have a list for the state of everyone's projects, but I can tell you which prints I had ordered to be safe while we see what we can save."

Noah declines my help to unload the damaged art at Poppy's place, but takes my keys so she can continue to focus on the students and their questions. She's calm going through the list of photos she ordered, being mindful of the anxious state the seniors are in.

A few of the book displays were piled on the counter while Grace carted batches to the back room to store during the show, so I make myself useful and load the now-empty cart.

"Thank you so much for doing this," Grace says behind me. Damn, I didn't even hear her approach.

"No problem, you've been so accommodating and I know I've said it and Noah has said it, but really, thank you."

She flusters when I mention Noah's name, but I don't pry. She gets on the far side of the cart and gives it a shove to gain momentum. "I love that I can help. Honey Cove means a lot to me and I'm happy you thought of this space, it's kind of perfect to have some community art in here. Maybe not a full show all the time, but it's giving me ideas."

When I turn around, the students are busy making adjustments to the makeshift pillars and tape marks for the easels. And Poppy is walking over to me, her eyes shining again.

"Ms. Edwards, it looks like we might have a senior art show on Monday even with the damage."

Without saying a word, she throws her arms around my neck and mine wrap around her waist, feeling calm after such a crazy morning. A quiet sigh leaves both of us as we hold one another.

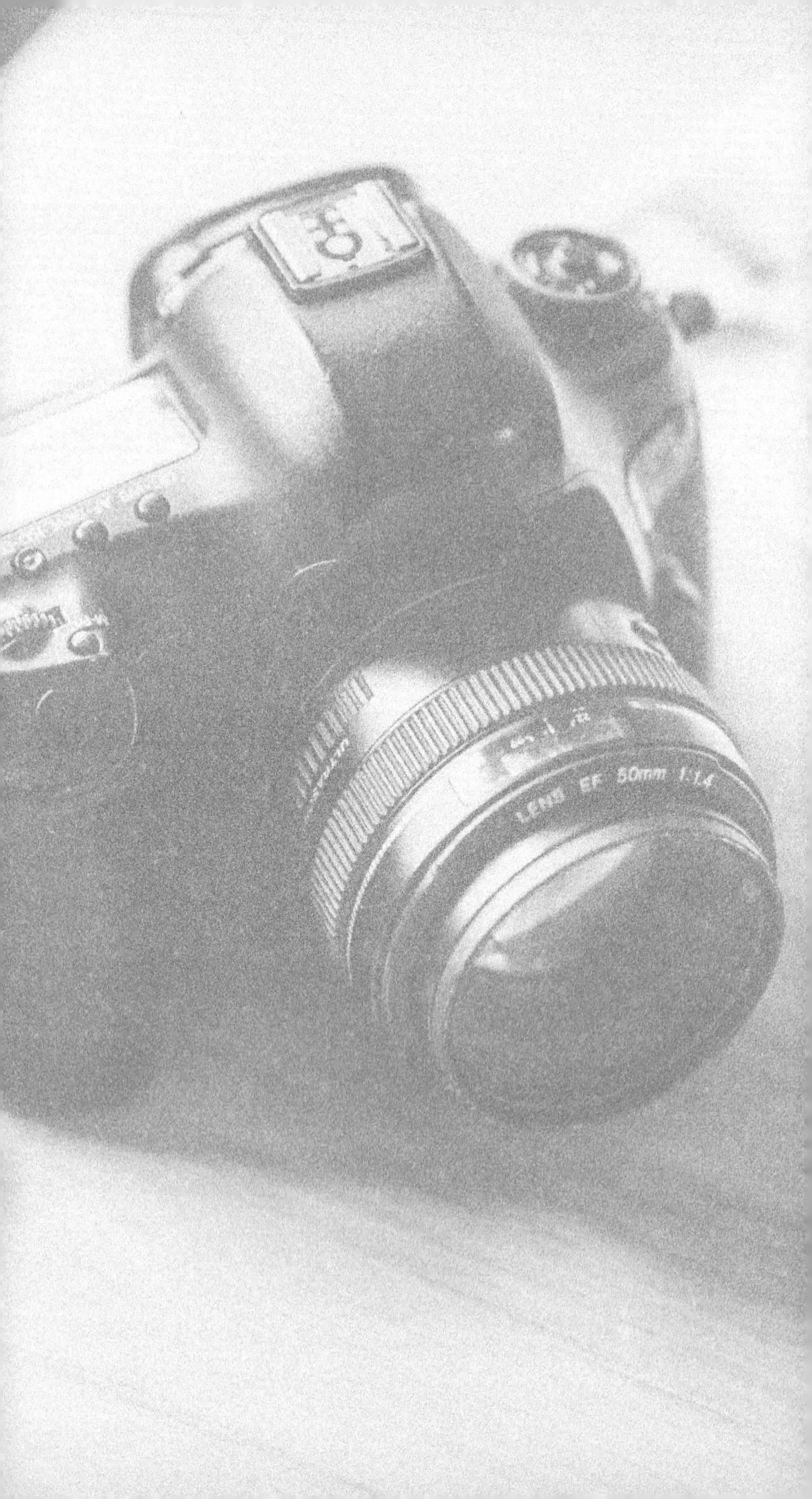
LENS EF 50mm 1:1.4

CHAPTER SEVENTY-THREE

Poppy

"Thank you so much for everything." Gesturing to the beautiful store, I see all my sweet seniors who have worked so hard coming together to make this event happen. My eyes fill with tears once more. "This means so much to me and it's a huge thing for the students. I still can't believe you did all this in less than a day."

"Of course, I'm glad they're happy but I..." Owen leans down until his breath is on my ear. "I did it for you. I'm sorry about how things ended last night."

"I'm sorry, too, but I actually need to talk to you about that." It pains me but I pull away from him. I know I'll feel better once everything is out and in the open. I know that he may still not agree with the plan I've concocted in my mind, but if I don't talk to him about it now I will lose my mind.

I pull his hand and tug him towards the back of the store where things will be a little more private. His eyes are wide and he's nervously drumming his fingers along his thigh as we walk. My heart beats a little faster too. I've been thinking through all of his possible reactions and I just don't know how this will go.

Once we're in a quiet space, he turns towards me. "First, can I say something? I know you wanted to figure this out on your own and I want to respect that, but I also don't want you to make a choice based on what you *think* I think, rather than what I do, actually, think. Does that make sense?"

I can't help but let out a small giggle. His rambling when he's nervous is quickly becoming one of my favorite things about him. "Of course."

"I want to say that it's more important for me to be with the person who feels like home to me than to live in a small town." He pauses and lowers his voice. "I love you. Even if that means living in a new town every other month, I'd choose that every time over losing you."

His admission warms my heart, he would choose me over the dream that's been driving him for years to find a job in Honey Cove. "But, what if we didn't have to choose?"

"What do you mean?" He looks at me quizzically.

"I ran into Steven this morning." *Oof, not the right way to start.*

"What does he have to do with this?" He's still holding my hands, but I can feel his body leaning away from me, suddenly on edge.

"No, sorry, this isn't about him. He said something that got me thinking and I called Sally because she said she was open to me making the job what I wanted, right?"

He nods, still unsure of where I'm going with this. *I'd be confused too.* Maybe I'm the rambling one. "I asked her if I could be there on breaks and do work remotely the other parts of the year. It would be part-time, so I can keep teaching if I want. We can live here, but travel during breaks." Pausing, I look into his eyes for confirmation, encouragement, or disagreement before tentatively adding, "Or, I could travel there by myself too."

His eyes are still a pool of uncertainty that I can't read. He smirks a little but I can't help myself from adding more. "It's like what you told me your grandma used to say. That things don't always come how we want them to, but how they're meant to. It isn't the perfect job situation for *us*, but I think this would give us both the things we want."

I end my last sentence like a question and am about to start adding more before he quiets me with his stare, lifting my chin up to look at him. I'm enveloped into his rich dark eyes that drew me to him that first night at Andi's wedding and everything else fades away. "I think that sounds absolutely amazing."

"You're okay with it, the traveling on breaks? It might mean missing some holidays here." I want to make sure he fully understands what he's signing onto before getting my hopes up.

"We can always celebrate on a different schedule with our friends and family here. We can make it work, and it will be fine because we'll be together." Brushing a strand of my hair from my face, he touches his lips lightly to my forehead.

A weight falls off my shoulders and I feel lighter than I have since first getting the call from Sally. Without thinking of where we are or *who* is around us, I throw my arms around his neck and he lifts me up into a kiss as fresh tears fall down my cheeks.

"I knew it," a voice loudly rings out behind us, shocking us out of our solitary moment together. Turning we both see Cicely standing, hands on her hips, looking at us like she just caught her parents together.

Before we can even respond, we both erupt into laughter. Cicely looks very proud of herself as she turns on her heel and walks back towards the set-up area.

"She's never going to let that go."

"No, but she's a senior and it won't matter much longer." He pulls me into him for another hug. Our bodies are tightly against one another and I look up to feel the full heat of his gaze on me before melting into another blissful kiss.

CHAPTER SEVENTY-FOUR

Owen

Finally, some time after ten, Noah leaves Poppy's house. We've gone through the art so closely and have pieces carefully propped, draped, and laying throughout her kitchen, dining room, office, and living room just to make sure they'll dry thoroughly. Not to mention the amount of fans running at their lowest speed. It looks like we'll be able to save a handful of pieces that Poppy printed photos for, which feels like a huge win.

"Did you see how often Grace blushed around Noah?" she whispers while locking her front door as he heads to his car out front.

"Is she one of his exes?" I ask, recalling Noah telling me that he felt like he was expanding his dating search farther outside of Honey Cove since things weren't working out here.

"Not that I remember from high school and I feel like he would have mentioned it since we've become close these past few years."

Wrapping her in my arms, I kiss the little crease between her eyebrows. "We can grill him on his complete dating history next weekend, after we've all recovered from this show."

She looks around her house, taking in the scene. "I can't believe it's still happening. Thank you."

Her lips brush mine and everything shifts, the kiss deepening. The tension, the wondering, the frustration, and the stress not only from today, but these last few weeks collide with the promise of our future. Together.

Running my hands down to the back of her thighs, squeezing her amazing ass on the way, I scoop her up and she hooks her ankles behind my back. Even with navigating the artwork drying everywhere, I carry her to the bedroom without my mouth leaving hers, our kisses becoming more and more intense as our need ratchets up.

Kicking her door closed simply out of habit from having Samson at my place, we're encased in darkness as I lay her down on the bed. She loosens her legs and tugs my shirt up and over my head, pulling me right back down on top of her. A gasp escapes her as my fingers trace the sensitive skin just above her jeans. Making quick work of our pants, I pull her oversized sweatshirt and bra off and hate that I can't see her.

She grabs the waistband of my underwear, trying to yank me back to her as I push up to turn on her bedside lamp.

"Come back here," she whispers.

"Patience, my Poppy," I say, turning the light onto its lowest setting. While I'm there, I rifle through her drawer for a condom, tossing that on the edge of the bed. Hot kisses trail down my side and a deep growl escapes me.

"Oh my god, that sound," she moans against my skin.

Sitting up, I look down at her, drinking in her flushed, perfect body. I take my time slipping her underwear down her long legs, letting my fingers splay over her soft skin. When I've pulled them all the way off, I slowly kiss my way up her legs until she tugs me back up to her so she can kiss me again.

"I'm the luckiest guy ever," I say, my voice husky with my own need.

"You seem to be delaying *getting* lucky," she mumbles, snaking her leg behind my back and bringing our bodies completely flush.

"I just needed to take a moment to appreciate everything I have," I say, smirking before I close the gap once more and kiss her like she's my other half.

Pulling both of her hands above her head, I take both her wrists in one hand and she lets out a long moan, grinding her hips against me. I trail my fingers down her arm, over her pebbled nipple and down her belly, leaving goosebumps in their wake. When I slide my finger through her folds, she shudders and tilts her hips to give me better access. Since she's so ready for this, I slip two fingers into her, while my thumb works her clit.

Being able to hold her without all of these worries weighing us down magnifies every connection. Each hitch of her breath, especially when I find that spot inside of her, is something that's mine. Knowing that she was able to take the time she needed to understand her wants and in that process, thinking about what could make *both* of us happy feels like we're both feeling the same need to stay together. No matter where we go, we're still "just" Poppy and Owen.

As she begins to peak, I trail kisses over to that sensitive spot just behind her ear, darting my tongue out just the way she likes it. She lets out a whimper and I nip at her earlobe before her breath catches and she whispers my name, tensing. My fingers pump faster and my thumb shifts just a little, driving her right over the edge. She bites her lip to keep from crying out as her body trembles with pleasure and she clamps down on my fingers.

When I release her wrists, her hands rake through my hair as her tongue finds mine in a slow, deep kiss. We relax into her bed, just holding each other close.

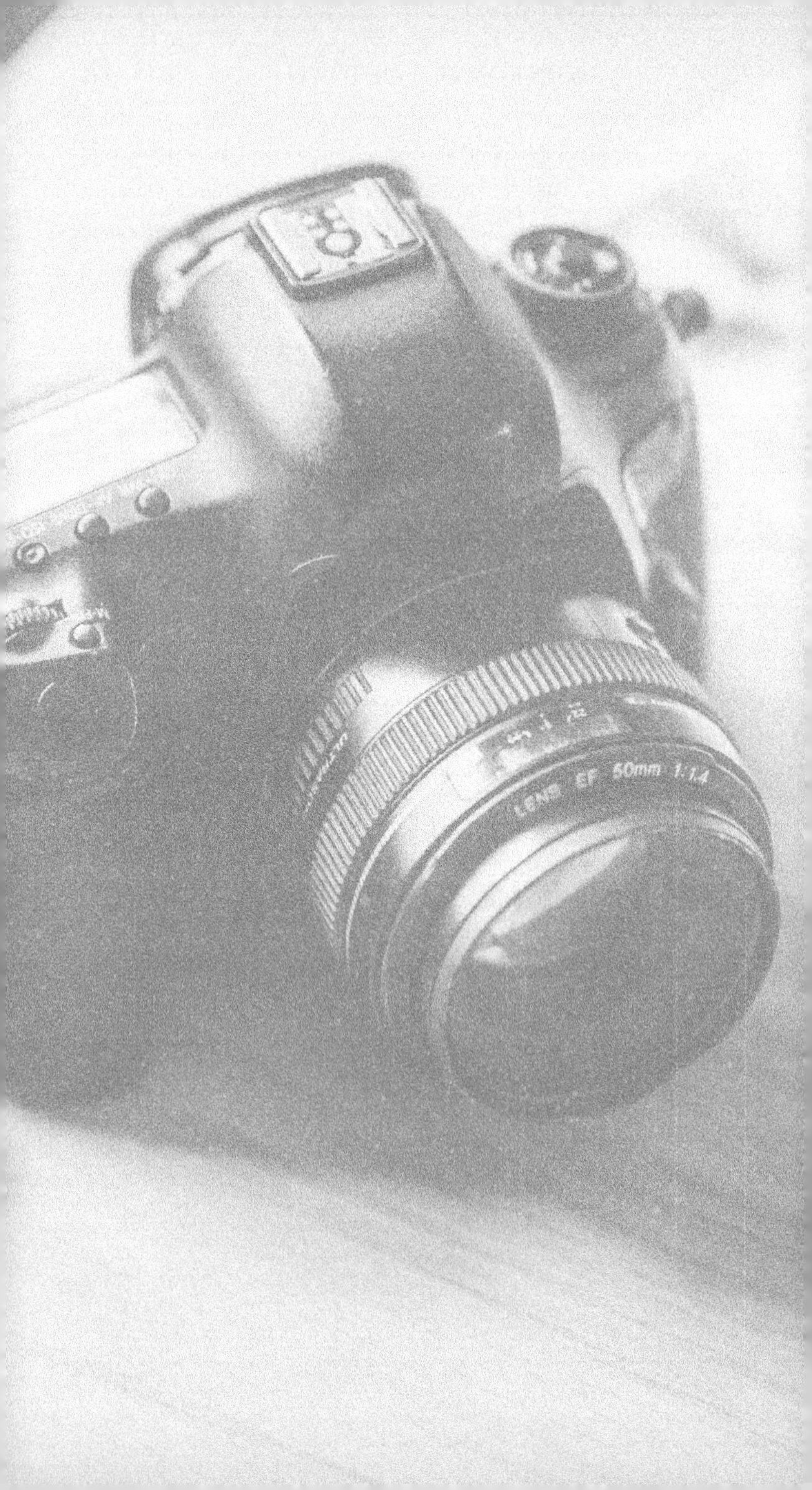
LENS EF 50mm 1:1.4

CHAPTER SEVENTY-FIVE

Poppy

"That was amazing," I whisper breathlessly against his neck. He moves to kiss down my ear and I let out a moan. *God, this man.* Turning his back to me for a second, he quickly slides the condom on before scooting next to me again.

"Come here," he says as he moves closer behind me and pulls me against him. My skin is still tingling from the first time, but feeling his hand rove up and down my body like he's memorizing every part has me thinking about another. Relishing in the warmth of his hands, I get lost in the sensation of being here with him.

His kisses move up and down my shoulder and arms, his hands reach around to cup my breasts and then run down to my thighs. His touch is intoxicating and I can barely think straight with how tightly he's holding me, everything in my body feels on fire.

Being up against him, close like this, has my heart racing. With everything going on lately, this release of tension feels like a long time coming and now we can finally just let go and know that everything that was between us is put to rest. We can talk more about the details later, but I'm so relieved to be on the same page and if anything, this has made me feel even closer to him.

I love that he let me come to my own decision and that I didn't feel pressured to put his needs first. That means a lot. While I'm trying to be patient and stay in the moment, I can't resist the feel of him and don't think I can wait much longer.

"I need you." I let the words float out into the air, leaning back and pushing my entire body against him, showing him how much I want him. Reaching back, I hook my hand around his neck, pulling him tighter against me.

"Alright, alright," he chides me and I feel his lips pull into a smile as he moves slightly lower on the bed, lifting my leg up before guiding himself inside me. I gasp at the sudden fullness of him, then moan as the sensation of him being so close overtakes me again.

He keeps his arms wrapped around me as he thrusts, reaching down to rub my clit, our hearts beating in tandem. Taking his time, we ride the waves together until we both cry out as the pleasure overtakes us. Thankfully, we're at my house and not at his, where we can be safely as loud as we want without risking anyone else overhearing. Or any cat interrupting.

Another round of kisses are peppered against my face before he moves to clean himself up and I cuddle into him. "You're amazing," he says into my hair and I wrap my arms around his waist, pulling him closer.

"You're not so bad yourself." Leaning back, I look up into his eyes before adding, "Thank you for being open to the job in Toronto. It means a lot to me that you were willing to sacrifice something you've wanted for a long time if it meant we got to be together."

"Of course. And I'm excited to meet Sally."

"You will love her, and I can't wait to show you around the city."

"It will be perfect. You'll have to teach me how to be your photography assistant for parties and weddings and things."

"You'll be the best assistant. They have an outdoor area where they have all the receptions. I may have crashed a few while I was there last time." His eyebrows raise, but he can't be *all* that surprised.

"I have two questions." He looks back at me mischievously this time. Pausing for dramatic effect before continuing. "Can we dance under the stars at every one?"

"Definitely." I pause for a second wondering what his next question is. "And..."

"Are there bees there?"

CHAPTER SEVENTY-SIX

Owen

Spring Break

"It's about an eleven hour drive, so it would make sense for us to think about it at the start of the summer."

That adorable crease is back between Poppy's eyebrows. "But then we'd only have one car in Honey Cove."

"Right," I say, turning down a quiet street in Toronto. "So we'll have one of our cars here and the other available for when we're visiting Honey Cove in the summer. When it's time to get back before meetings and back-to-school workshops begin, we'll drive the Toronto car home."

"Let's make sure you like it here enough to stay for the majority of your summer vacation before we decide."

Shrugging I say, "I already know I'm going to like it here."

"I know you say that now, but what if it's all the things you didn't love about New York City?" Doubt creeps into her voice again.

"Babe, I completely understand that you're worried I'm going to hate it here, but you keep forgetting there's one huge difference between New York and Toronto."

"The fact that one's a Canadian city?" she asks.

"Well, there's that, yes," I concede chuckling. "But Toronto has *you*. And on top of that, it has your dream job. A dream job that allows you to continue teaching and being near your family."

Reaching over the console, she gives my hand a squeeze. "A dream job that I could accept without losing you."

"Ha, like that was going to happen. I'm afraid you're stuck with me." I bring our hands up and kiss hers.

"Oh this is it just up ahead," she cries out, pointing down the street on our right.

As I pull into the driveway that will take us around to the back to park, I take in the beautiful brick building with ivy growing up one side, highlighting the historic nature of the inn. Everything about the exterior seems to be very well taken care of.

"I can see why people would book this for a wedding venue," I comment.

She nods, watching my reactions as I take it all in. "I can't wait to see what the proposals are for a permanent open-air space for receptions, dinners, and dances in the summer months."

"How does it feel being back again?" I ask, thinking about how the last time she was here, she needed to escape and heal.

A beautiful smile lights up her face. "It feels exciting and, as cheesy as it may sound, full of possibilities."

Pulling into a spot designated for staff remembers, I park our rental car just as a blonde woman comes out the entrance, waving animatedly to us.

"Sally?" I ask.

"The one and only," she says smiling. "I think you're going to love her."

How could I not love anyone who makes Poppy light up and love her dreams?

A few hours later, we are almost unpacked and have checked out the space that will be ours whenever we're here. It's larger than we expected and it's furnished comfortably.

"Samson is going to love this place," Poppy says, walking around the couch in the living room. "We might need to do something about these drapes, I could see him shredding them for some reason."

Looking at the drapes in question, I see they're sheer, which is definitely something that would be hard for my cat to resist. "I think you might be right."

"We can ask about that, since they know we'll be here with him in June," she says. Then she lets out a surprised squeak when I tug her hand, pulling her into my arms.

"I love that you're thinking about bringing Samson here."

"Who would have thought we'd be here, starting this adventure together after meeting at Andi and Brandon's wedding?"

"I don't know anyone could have predicted we'd be in Toronto, but there was something about you that drew me in from day one," I say, tucking her hair behind her ear. "Something felt right and deep inside, it's like I knew. I think Brandon and Andi saw it, too, but maybe a little bit later than I did."

"There's no way you knew at their wedding that we'd become a couple," she says, swatting my chest.

"Did I know we'd even *see* each other after the wedding? No. Hell, I was packing up my apartment to move back to New York that weekend because I had *just* been told someone else had been hired at Honey Cove." I release my hold on her and pull out my wallet. "But from that first night, I knew there was something about you, Poppy Edwards. Even if I had moved back, I would've wondered about you. You connected with something deep inside of me from the start."

I hand her a slip of paper that's clearly been folded, and refolded, over and over.

"And you've made every moment with you memorable. I couldn't be more grateful for you or imagine being able to love you more than I do already."

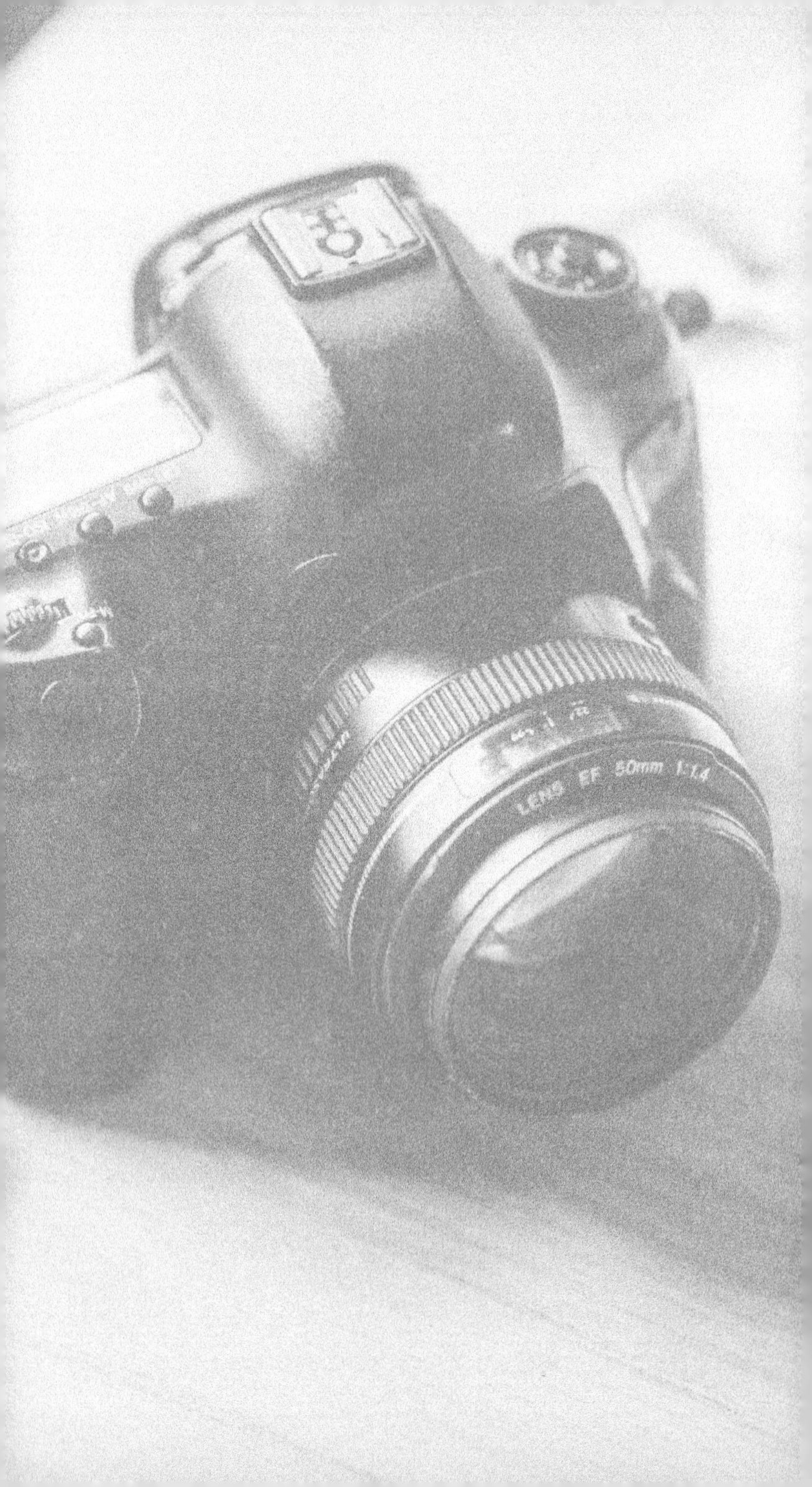
LENS EF 50mm 1:1.4

CHAPTER SEVENTY-SEVEN

Poppy

Opening up Owen's note, I see it's the letter I left him that very first morning after our impromptu rendezvous at Andi's wedding. *Thank you, Owen. You made my first night back in Honey Cove completely memorable.*

"You kept it?" My voice is barely a whisper. *I can't believe he kept it.* Who keeps a note from a one-night stand?

"Of course. Like I said, I knew there was just something about you that drew me to you. I've never felt like that before." His warm eyes smile at me, crinkling at the edges and he holds out his hand for me to grab.

"Me either, but I will say, seeing you at that first staff meeting threw me for a loop." Squeezing his wrist I wrinkle my nose at him. That did freak me out. But I quickly felt better after hearing the whole story from Noah and the other staff. Things fell into place.

"I bet you thought I was a bit of a creeper then, huh?" He nudges me with his elbow before kissing my cheek.

"Just a little. But I know the truth now."

"Oh yeah, and what is that?"

"That you're a kind, amazing man who is ridiculously good at sex and holds my heart in his very capable hands." I shake my head for an added effect before smirking at him and planting a kiss on his cheek.

He lets out a deep laugh before we move to look out our window onto the city. "I'll take it," he adds as he wraps his arms around me from behind. "The city is beautiful."

"It is." We stand in silence for a few minutes, taking in the view before he sighs and goes to unpack the rest of his bag.

"What would you like to do tonight? You don't have to work until tomorrow morning, right?" He lays his things out on the crisp linen bedspread and I sink down against the pillows and open up my planner to double check my schedule.

"Yup, today is just for settling and getting our bearings. I was thinking we could go out to my favorite restaurant down the street?"

"That sounds good. Anything else you'd like to see or get?"

"Coffee, for sure." I crawl towards him at the end of the bed, another idea popping into my head. "Also, I think we should make our first night in Toronto *completely memorable*."

acknowledgments

There are so many people that we are thankful for and who have helped us on our writing journey.

Alpha readers - you see the early, unpolished version of our stories and your feedback helps shape our plot and bring our characters to life. We're so grateful for you.

Kristen - your edits and insights were so helpful in making everything come together.

Andra - you saw a few versions of this story including proofreading it and we're so lucky to have found you.

Our families - without you none of this would be possible. You've supported our dreams so we could take our idea of two teachers falling in love and turn it into a novel we're proud of.

Thank you to everyone from the bottom of our hearts.

And to our new readers, we hope you enjoy your time in Honey Cove and are delighted you're here.

ABOUT THE
authors

Natalie Jess is a Midwest author who loves living in a place with snowy winters. She grew up reading way past her bedtime and never broke that habit - except now the books she reads, and writes, are definitely for adults.

Evy Aster is a contemporary romance author who loves to create fun, fluffy, quick reads with a little humor. When she isn't writing, you can find her sitting by a lake with some tea and her family.